DATA STRUCTURES
IN JAVA

DATA STRUCTURES
IN JAVA

Oswald Campesato

MERCURY LEARNING AND INFORMATION
Dulles, Virginia
Boston, Massachusetts
New Delhi

Publisher: David Pallai

MERCURY LEARNING AND INFORMATION
22841 Quicksilver Drive
Dulles, VA 20166
info@merclearning.com
www.merclearning.com
1-800-232-0223

O. Campesato. *Data Structures in Java.*
ISBN: 978-1-68392-955-0

The publisher recognizes and respects all marks used by companies, manufacturers, and developers as a means to distinguish their products. All brand names and product names mentioned in this book are trademarks or service marks of their respective companies. Any omission or misuse (of any kind) of service marks or trademarks, etc. is not an attempt to infringe on the property of others.

Library of Congress Control Number: 2023931653
232425321   Printed on acid-free paper in the United States of America.

Our titles are available for adoption, license, or bulk purchase by institutions, corporations, etc. For additional information, please contact the Customer Service Dept. at 800-232-0223(toll free).

*I'd like to dedicate this book to my parents
– may this bring joy and happiness into their lives.*

CONTENTS

PREFACE

WHAT IS THE PRIMARY VALUE PROPOSITION FOR THIS BOOK?

This book contains a fast-paced introduction to as much relevant information about data structures in `Java` as possible that can be reasonably included in a book of this size.

THE TARGET AUDIENCE

This book is intended primarily for people who have some exposure to Java and are interested in learning about data structures. This book is also intended to reach an international audience of readers with highly diverse backgrounds in various age groups. While many readers know how to read English, their native spoken language is not English (which could be their second, third, or even fourth language). Consequently, this book uses standard English rather than colloquial expressions that might be confusing to those readers. As such, this book endeavors to provide a comfortable and meaningful learning experience for the intended readers.

WHAT WILL I LEARN FROM THIS BOOK?

The first chapter contains a quick introduction to Java, along with some Java code samples to check for leap years, find divisors of a number, and working with arrays of strings. The second chapter introduces recursion and contains code samples to check if a positive number is prime, to find the prime divisors of a positive integer, to calculate the GCD (greatest common divisor) and LCM (lowest common multiple) of a pair of positive integers.

The third chapter contains Java code samples involving strings and arrays, such as finding binary substrings of a number, checking if strings contain unique characters, counting bits in a range of numbers, and how to compute XOR without using the XOR function.

Chapters 4 through 6 contain Java code samples involving search algorithms, concepts in linked lists, and tasks involving linked lists. Finally, Chapter 7 discusses data structures called queues and stacks, along with some Java code samples.

DO I NEED TO LEARN THE THEORY PORTIONS OF THIS BOOK?

Once again, the answer depends on the extent to which you plan to work with data structures in Java. In general, you will probably need to learn many (most?) of the topics that you encounter in this book if you are plan to advance beyond a beginner-level developer in application development in Java.

GETTING THE MOST FROM THIS BOOK

Some programmers learn well from prose, others learn well from sample code (and lots of it), which means that there's no single style that can be used for everyone.

Moreover, some programmers want to run the code first, see what it does, and then return to the code to delve into the details (and others use the opposite approach).

Consequently, there are various types of code samples in this book: some are short, some are long, and other code samples "build" from earlier code samples.

WHAT DO I NEED TO KNOW FOR THIS BOOK?

A basic knowledge of Java is the most helpful skill, and some exposure to recursion and data structures is obviously helpful. Knowledge of other programming languages can also be helpful because of the exposure to programming concepts and constructs. The less technical knowledge that you have, the more diligence will be required in order to understand the various topics that are covered.

If you want to be sure that you can grasp the material in this book, glance through some of the code samples to get an idea of how much is familiar to you and how much is new for you.

DON'T THE COMPANION FILES OBVIATE THE NEED FOR THIS BOOK?

The companion files contain all the code samples to save you time and effort from the error-prone process of manually typing code into a text file. In addition, there are situations during which you might not have easy access to the companion files. Furthermore, the code samples in the book provide explanations that are not available on the companion files.

DOES THIS BOOK CONTAIN PRODUCTION-LEVEL CODE SAMPLES?

The primary purpose of the code samples in this book is to show you how to use Java in order to solve a variety of programming tasks. Clarity has higher priority than writing more compact code that is more difficult to understand (and possibly more prone to bugs). If you decide to use any of the code in this book in a production environment, you ought to subject that code to the same rigorous analysis as the other parts of your code base.

Another detail to keep in mind is that many code samples in this book contain "commented out" code snippets (often `println()` statements) that were used during the development of the code samples. Those code snippets are intentionally included so that you can uncomment any of those code snippets if you want to see the execution path of the code samples.

WHAT ARE THE NONTECHNICAL PREREQUISITES FOR THIS BOOK?

Although the answer to this question is marore difficult to quantify, it's especially important to have strong desire to learn about data structures, along with the motivation and discipline to read and understand the code samples.

HOW DO I SET UP A COMMAND SHELL?

If you are a Mac user, there are three ways to do so. The first method is to use `Finder` to navigate to `Applications > Utilities` and then double click on the `Utilities` application. Next, if you already have a command shell available, you can launch a new command shell by typing the following command:

```
open /Applications/Utilities/Terminal.app
```

A second method for Mac users is to open a new command shell on a MacBook from a command shell that is already visible simply by clicking `command+n` in that command shell, and your Mac will launch another command shell.

If you are a PC user, you can install Cygwin (open source *https://cygwin.com/*) that simulates bash commands, or use another toolkit such as MKS (a commercial product). Please read the online documentation that describes the download and installation process. Note that custom aliases are not automatically set if they are defined in a file other than the main start-up file (such as .bash_login).

COMPANION FILES

All the code samples and figures in this book may be obtained by writing to the publisher at *info@merclearning.com*.

WHAT ARE THE "NEXT STEPS" AFTER FINISHING THIS BOOK?

The answer to this question varies widely, mainly because the answer depends heavily on your objectives. One possibility involves learning about more complex data structures and implementing them in Java. Another option is to prepare for job interviews for careers involving Java.

CHAPTER 1

INTRODUCTION TO JAVA

This fast-paced chapter introduces you to an assortment of topics in Java. In many cases explanations are succinct, especially when the purpose of the code is intuitive.

The first section of this chapter contains information about downloading Java onto your machine. You will also learn about Java data types and operators, as well as their precedence.

The second section shows you how to create, compile, and launch a Java class from the command line. You will learn how to create a "Hello World" code sample that will be extended in Chapter 2 to help you understand constructors in Java.

The third section discusses numbers, random numbers, and trigonometric functions in Java. The fourth section briefly covers Java characters and strings, and the significance of the new operator. You will learn how to determine if two strings are equal, and you will learn some other useful string-related functions in Java.

A VERY BRIEF INTRODUCTION TO JAVA

Java is an object-oriented programming language that enables you to run your code on many different hardware platforms, including desktops, mobile devices, and the Raspberry PI. You need to install a platform-specific Java distribution for each platform where you intend to launch Java code (see the next section for details).

The following link contains a diagram of the Java 2023 road map as well as a layout of Java features:

https://medium.com/javarevisited/the-java-programmer-roadmap-f9db163ef2c2

If you want to learn about the new features that were introduced in different Java releases, navigate to the following website:

https://www.javatpoint.com/history-of-java

Downloading a Java Release (Short Version)

In view of the many Java releases that are available, how do you decide which version will be best for you? The answer to this question probably involves one or more of the following:

- the version of Java that your company uses
- the latest LTS (long term support)
- the version of Java that you prefer
- the latest version of Java
- the features of Java that you need

One other point to keep in mind is that you can also download multiple versions of Java onto your machine if you want to address all the points in the preceding bullet list.

After you have made a determination regarding the version(s) of Java that will work best for you, navigate to the following website and then download the Java distribution for your machine:

https://docs.oracle.com/javase/10/install/toc.htm

SELECTING A VERSION OF JAVA (DETAILED VERSION)

Java 17 is available as this book goes to print, and Java 18 was released in March 2022. Older versions of Java had release cycles that sometimes involves three or more years, whereas newer versions of Java will be released every six months. At the same time, newer releases will have a much more limited set of updates.

Java 8 and Java 11

Java 8 and Java 11 previously had LTS (long-term support) status and currently Java 17 has LTS status. Due to various factors, some larger companies are still working with Java 8, which was one of the most significant releases in the history of Java. If you are interested, the Oracle website that contains a list of the features of Java 8. In fact, almost all the features in Java 8 will work correctly in all subsequent releases, up to and including Java 17.

However, Java 8 and Java 11 have been deprecated, and currently Java 17 has LTS status. So, which version of Java is recommended? The answer depends on your requirements. If you are unencumbered with maintaining or developing code for older Java versions, then it's probably safe to work with Java 17. If you don't have a choice, then consider working with Java 13, Java 11, or Java 8 (in this order).

Navigate to the following URL for information regarding earlier versions of Java and release dates for future versions of Java:

https://www.oracle.com/java/technologies/java-se-support-roadmap.html

Java Version Numbers

Up until Java 8, the numbering sequence had the form 1.x. Hence, Java 7 was also called Java 1.7, and Java 8 was called Java 8. However, this older naming convention has been dropped starting from `Java` 9. For example, if you type the command `java -version` and you have `Java` 13 installed on your machine, you will see something similar to the following output:

```
java 13.0.1 2019-10-15
Java(TM) SE Runtime Environment (build 13.0.1+9)
Java HotSpot(TM) 64-Bit Server VM (build 13.0.1+9, mixed mode, sharing)
```

Aim for a solid grasp of `Java` 13, and then increase your knowledge by learning about the new features that are available in versions after `Java` 13.

JRE Versus a JDK

A `JRE` (Java runtime environment) enables you to launch `Java` code, which means that a `Java` provides the `java` command-line tool. If you are on a `Unix/Linux` type of machine, type the following command:

```
$ which java
```

The preceding command displays the following type of output:

```
$ /usr/bin/java
```

However, a `JDK` (Java development kit) enables you to compile and launch `Java` code. Although the `JRE` and `JDK` were available as separate downloads until `Java` 8, they have been merged: that is, starting from `Java` 9, the `Java` download is the `JDK` with the `JRE` included.

Java Distributions

There are various sites offering the several `Java JDK`: the `OpenJDK` project, the `OracleJDK`, and `AdoptOpenJDK`. The `OpenJDK` project is the only project site that contains the `Java` source code.

`Oracle` provides `OpenJDK`, which is free to use for your `Java` applications. Updates for older versions are not supported: for example, as soon as `Java` 13 was available, updates to `Java` 12 were discontinued. `Oracle` also provides `OracleJDK`, which is free to use only during development: if you deploy your code to a production environment, you must pay a fee to `Oracle` (which will provide you with additional support).

Starting from 2017, you can also use `AdoptOpenJDK`, which was developed by various developers and vendors, and is freely available (just like `OpenJDK`).

JAVA IDES

Many people prefer to work in an IDE, and there are very good IDEs available for many programming languages. For example, if you plan to develop `Android` applications, it's worthwhile to do so in `Android Studio`, which is an alternative for people who are unfamiliar with the command line.

If you want to write `Java` code in an IDE (integrated development environment), there are various IDEs that support `Java`, such as NetBeans and Eclipse. However, this book focuses on working with `Java` from the command line, and you can create `Java` classes with a text editor of your choice (or if you prefer, from an IDE). Developing `Java` code from the command line involves simple manual steps, such as updating the `CLASSPATH` environment variable to include `JAR` files and sometimes also including compiled `Java` class files.

This chapter also contains a brief section that shows you how to create a simple `JAR` file that contains compiled `Java` code, and after adding this `JAR` file to the `CLASSPATH` variable, you will see how to invoke your custom `Java` code in your custom `JAR` file. The key point to keep in mind is that the `Java` code samples in this book are short (and often simple) enough that you don't need an IDE.

If you want to write `Java` code in an IDE, there are several IDEs that support `Java`, and the following link contains 10 of them:

https://www.educative.io/blog/best-java-ides-2021

However, the `Java` code samples in this chapter are launched from the command line, and the source code is along with a text editor of your choice for creating the `Java` classes. Working from the command line does involve some additional effort, such as manually updating the `CLASSPATH` environment variable to include `JAR` (`Java` archive) files and compiled `Java` class files.

DATA TYPES, OPERATORS, AND THEIR PRECEDENCE

`Java` supports the usual set of primitive types that are available in many other compiled languages, along with object-based counterparts. For example, the primitive types `int`, `double`, and `float` have the class-based counterparts `Integer`, `Double`, and `Float`, respectively.

Some data structures, such as hash tables, do not support primitive data types, which is why class-based counterparts are necessary. For instance, if you need a hash table to maintain a set of integers, you need to create an `Integer`-based object containing each integer and then add that object to the hash table. You then retrieve a specific `Integer`-based value object and extract its underlying `int` value. This approach obviously involves more code than simply storing and retrieving `int` values in a hash table.

Regarding primitive types: `Java` provides eight primitive data types that are keywords in the language:

- byte: 8-bit signed two's complement integer
- short: 16-bit signed two's complement integer
- int: 32-bit signed two's complement integer
- long: 64-bit signed two's complement integer
- float: single-precision 32-bit IEEE 754 floating point
- boolean: either true or false
- char: single 16-bit Unicode character

In most cases, the code samples involving arithmetic calculations in this book use integers and floating point numbers.

Java Comments

Java supports one-line comments as well as multiline comments, both of which are shown here:

```
// this is a one-line comment
/* this is a multi-line comment

that uses a C-style syntax

// and can include the one-line comment style
*/
```

However, Java does not support nested comments (and neither does C/C++), so the following is an error:

```
/* start of first comment /* start of second comment */ end of first */
```

Based on the earlier examples, the following syntax *is* correct for a comment:

```
/* start of first comment // start of second comment end of first */
```

Java Operators

Java supports the usual set of arithmetic operators, along with the standard precedence (exponentiation has higher priority than multiplication * and division /, both of which have higher priority than addition + and subtraction –). In addition, Java supports the following operators:

- arithmetic operators: +, –, °, /, %, ++, and ––
- assignment operators: =, +=, -=, °=, /=, %=, <<=, >>=, &=, ^=, and !=
- bitwise operators: &, |, ^, and ~
- boolean operations: and, or, not, and xor
- logical operators: &&, ||, and !
- Relational operators: ==, !=, >, <, >=, and <=

Java also supports the ternary operator "?" and the operator instanceOf (to check if a variable is an instance of a particular class).

CREATING AND COMPILING JAVA CLASSES

Let's start with the simplest possible Java class that does nothing other than show you the basic structure of a Java class. Listing 1.1 displays the contents of MyClass.java that defines the Java class MyClass.

LISTING 1.1: MyClass.java

```
public class MyClass
{
}
```

The first point to notice is that the name of the file in Listing 1.11 is the same as the Java class. Listing 1.1 defines the Java class MyClass that is qualified by the keywords public and class. You can have more than one class in a Java file but only one of them can be public, and that public class must match the name of the file.

Open a command shell, navigate to the directory that contains MyClass.java, and compile MyClass.java from the command line with the javac executable:

```
javac MyClass.java
```

The javac executable creates a file called MyClass.class that contains Java bytecode. Launch the Java bytecode with the Java executable (do not include any extension):

```
java MyClass
```

Note that you do not specify the suffix .java or .class when you launch the Java bytecode. The output from the preceding command is here:

```
Exception in thread "main" java.lang.NoSuchMethodError: main
```

NOTE *The name of a file with Java source code must match the public Java class in that file. For example, the file MyClass.java must define a Java class called MyClass.*

Listing 1.2 contains a main method that serves as the initial "entry point" for launching a Java class from the command line, which resolves the error that occurred in Listing 1.1.

LISTING 1.2: MyClass.java

```
public class MyClass
{
    public static void main(String[] args){}
}
```

Listing 1.2 contains the main() function whose return type is void because it returns nothing. The main() function is also static, which ensures that it will be available when we launch the Java class from the command line. Compile the code:

```
javac MyClass.java
```

Launch the class from the command line:

```
java MyClass
```

You have now successfully created, compiled, and launched a Java class called MyClass that still does nothing other than compile successfully. The next step involves displaying a text string in a Java class, which is discussed in the next section.

"HELLO WORLD" AND WORKING WITH NUMBERS

Listing 1.3 displays the contents of HelloWorld1.java that prints the string "Hello World" from a Java class.

LISTING 1.3: HelloWorld1.java

```
public class HelloWorld1
{
   public static void main (String args[])
   {
      System.out.println("Hello World");
   }
}
```

The code in Listing 1.3 is straightforward: the `main()` function contains a single `print` statement that prints the string "`Hello World`". Open a command shell to compile and launch the `Java` code in Listing 1.3:

```
javac HelloWorld1.java
```

Launch the compiled code by typing the following command:

```
java HelloWorld1
```

The output from the preceding command is here:

```
Hello World
```

The companion files contains additional code samples for this chapter that illustrate how to work with numbers, random numbers, trigonometric functions, and bit-wise operators in Java:

- Numbers.java
- RandomNumbers.java
- MathFunctions.java
- TrigFunctions.java
- Bitwise.java

Let's look at some (slightly) more interesting examples of working with numbers in `Java`.

THE JAVA STRING CLASS

A `Java` variable of type `char` is a single character, which you can define via the `char` keyword like this:

```
char ch1 = 'Z';
```

A `Java` variable of type `String` is an *object* that comprises a sequence of `char` values. As you will see later, `Java` supports `ASCII`, `UTF8`, and `Unicode` characters. The `java.lang. String` class implements the `Java` interfaces (discussed later) `Serializable`, `Comparable`, and `CharSequence`.

The `Serializable` interface does not contain methods: it's essentially a "marker" (interface). The `CharSequence` interface is for sequences of characters. In addition to the `Java` `String` class, the `Java` `StringBuffer` class and the `Java` `StringBuilder` class implement the `CharSequence` interface (more details later).

Keep in mind the following point: Every Java String is immutable, and in order to modify a Java string (such as append or delete characters), Java creates a new instance "under the hood" for us. As a result, string-related operations are less memory efficient; however, Java provides the StringBuffer and StringBuilder classes for mutable Java strings (also discussed later).

An array of characters is effectively the same as a Java String, as shown here:

```
char[] chars = {'h','e','l','l','o'};
String str1 = new String(chars);
String str2 = "hello";
```

You can access a character in a string with the charAt() method, as shown here:

```
char ch = str1.charAt(1);
```

The preceding code snippet assigns the letter "e" to the character variable ch. You can assign a single quote mark to a variable ch2 with this code snippet:

```
char ch2 = '\'';
```

Listing 1.4 displays the contents of CharsStrings.java that shows you how to define characters, arrays, and strings in Java.

LISTING 1.4: CharsStrings.java

```
public class CharsStrings
{
    public CharsStrings(){}

    public static void main (String args[])
    {
        char ch1 = 'Z';
        char ch2 = '\'';

        char[] chars = {'h','e','l','l','o'};
        String str1 = new String(chars);
        String str2 = "hello";
        String str3 = new String(chars);
        String str4 = Character.toString(ch2);

        System.out.println("ch1:    "+ch1);
        System.out.println("ch2:    "+ch2);
        System.out.println("chars:  "+chars);

        System.out.println("str1:   "+str1);
        System.out.println("str2:   "+str2);
        System.out.println("str3:   "+str3);
        System.out.println("str4:   "+str4);
    }
}
```

Listing 1.4 contains a main() method that initializes the character variable ch2, the character string variable chars, and then the string variables str1 through str4. The remaining portion of the main() method simply prints the values of all these variables. Launch the code in Listing 1.4 and you will see the following output:

```
ch1:    Z
ch2:    '
chars:  [C@5451c3a8
str1:   hello
str2:   hello
str3:   hello
str4:   '
```

The output of the chars variable is probably different from what you expected. You can use a loop to display the characters in the chars variable. Although loops are discussed in Chapter 3, here's a quick preview of a loop that displays the contents of the chars variable:

```
System.out.print("chars: ");
for(char ch : chars)
{
    System.out.print(ch);
}
System.out.println();
```

The output from the preceding loop is here:

```
chars: hello
```

Java Strings With Metacharacters

Java treats metacharacters in a string variable in the same manner as any other alphanumeric character. Thus, you don't need to escape metacharacters in Java strings, whereas it's necessary to do so when you define a char variable (see the ch2 variable in the preceding code sample).

You can concatenate two Java strings via the "+" operator, as shown here:

```
String first = "John";
String last  = "Smith";
String full  = first + " " + last;
```

Java treats the following code snippet in a slightly different way:

```
String first = "John";
String last  = "Smith";
first = first + " " + last;
```

The variables first and last are initialized with string values, and then a new block of memory is allocated that is large enough to hold the contents of the variable first, the blank space, and the contents of the variable second. These three quantities are copied into the new block of memory, which is then referenced by the variable full.

Listing 1.5 displays the contents of Strings.java that initializes and then prints several strings.

LISTING 1.5: MyStrings.java

```
public class Strings
{
    public static void main (String args[])
    {
        String str1 = "John", str2 = "Sally";
        String str3 = "*?)",   str4 = "+.@";
        String str5 = "\n\n",  str6 = "\t";

        System.out.println("str1: "+str1+" str2: "+str2);
        System.out.println("str3: "+str3+" str4: "+str4);
        System.out.println("str5: "+str5+" str6: "+str6);
    }
}
```

Listing 1.5 defines the Java class MyStrings and a main() function that initializes the strings str1 through str6 with names, metacharacters, and whitespaces. The three println() statements display their values, as shown here:

```
str1: John str2: Sally
str3: *?) str4: +.@
str5:

str6:
```

There is no visible difference between a space and a tab character in the preceding output. However, redirect the output to a file called out1 (or some other convenient name), open the file in the vi editor, issue the setting ": set list", and you will see the following output:

```
str1: John str2: Sally$
str1: John str2: Sally$
str3: *?) str4: +.@$
str5: $
$
  str6: ^I$
```

The $ symbol indicates the end of a line in the preceding output block. Notice that the last line displays ^I$, which indicates the presence of the tab character that is the value of the str6 variable in Listing 1.5.

THE JAVA NEW OPERATOR

The previous section contains several examples of directly assigning a string in Java. Another way to do so involves the new operator, which superficially looks the same, but it has an important distinction. When you initialize two variables with the same string, in the manner shown in Listing 1.6, they occupy the same memory location. When you use the new operator, the two variables will occupy different memory locations.

Listing 1.6 displays the contents of ShowPeople.java that uses the new operator to initialize two strings and then print their values.

LISTING 1.6: ShowPeople.java

```java
public class ShowPeople
{
    // cannot be initialized in main()
    String str5, str6;

    public ShowPeople(){}

    public static void main (String args[])
    {
        String str1, str2, str3, str4;

        // str1 and str2 occupy different memory locations
        str1 = new String("My name is John Smith");
        str2 = new String("My name is John Smith");

        // str3 and str4 occupy the same memory location
        str3 = "My name is Jane Andrews";
        str4 = "My name is Jane Andrews";

        System.out.println(str1);
        System.out.println(str2);

        System.out.println(str3);
        System.out.println(str4);


        // You must first declare both as "String":
      //str5 = new String("another string");
      //str6 = new String("yet another string");
    }
}
```

Listing 1.6 contains a `main()` routine that defines and initializes the string variables `str1` through `str4` and then prints their contents. The output from Listing 1.6 is here:

```
My name is John Smith
My name is John Smith
My name is Jane Andrews
My name is Jane Andrews
```

The code in Listing 1.6 straightforward, but it contains hard-coded values and therefore has no reusability. For example, you might decide to print all the names that are defined in arrays containing the names people. Perhaps you want to print names that are randomly selected from those arrays. You might even want to get a person's first name and last name from the command line and then print the person's name. Later in this chapter you will learn how to work with arrays of strings using various loop constructs, and after that you will learn how to define "accessors" and mutators for "getting" and "setting" values of variables.

The next section provides more details regarding the difference between "==" and the `equals()` method in the Java `String` class.

EQUALITY OF STRINGS

Unlike other languages, the "==" operator does not determine whether or not two strings are identical: this operator only determines if two variables are referencing the same *memory* location. The equals() method will compare the *content* of two strings whereas == operator matches the *object* or reference of the strings.

Listing 1.7 displays the contents of EqualStrings.java that illustrates how to compare two strings and determine if they have the same value or the same reference (or both).

LISTING 1.7: EqualStrings.java

```java
import java.io.IOException;

public class EqualStrings
{
    public static void main(String[] args) throws IOException
    {
        String str1 = "Pizza";
        String str2 = "Pizza";

        if (str1.equals(str2))
        {
            System.out.println("str1 and str2: equal values");
        }

        if (str1 == str2)
        {
            System.out.println("str1 and str2: equal references");
        }

        System.out.println("");

        String str3 = "Pasta";
        String str4 = new String("Pasta");

        if (str3.equals(str4))
        {
            System.out.println("str3 and str4: equal values");
        }
        else
        {
            System.out.println("str3 and str4: unequal values");
        }

        if (str3 == str4)
        {
            System.out.println("str3 and str4: equal references");
        }
        else
        {
            System.out.println("str3 and str4: unequal references");
        }
    }
}
```

Listing 1.7 defines the `Java` class `EqualStrings` and a `main()` function that defines the string variables `str1`, `str2`, `str3`, and `str4`. Launch the code in Listing 1.7 and you will see the following output:

```
str1 and str2: equal values
str1 and str2: equal references

str3 and str4: equal values
str3 and str4: unequal references
```

Remember, when you create a string literal, the JVM (Java virtual machine) checks for the presence of that string in something called the "string constant pool." If that string exists in the pool, then `Java` simply returns a reference to the pooled instance; otherwise, a new string instance is created (and it's also placed in the pool).

In order to determine whether or not two strings are identical in `Java`, use the `compareTo(str)` method, an example of which is discussed in the next section.

Comparing Strings

Listing 1.8 displays the contents of `CompareStrings.java` that illustrates how to compare two strings and determine if they have the same value or the same reference (or both).

LISTING 1.8: CompareStrings.java

```java
public class CompareStrings
{
    public CompareStrings(){}

    public static void main (String args[])
    {
        String line1 = "This is a simple sentence.";
        String line2 = "this is a simple sentence.";

        System.out.println("line1: "+line1);
        System.out.println("line2: "+line2);
        System.out.println("");

        if (line1.equalsIgnoreCase(line2)) {
          System.out.println(
            "line1 and line2 are case-insensitive equal");
        } else {
          System.out.println(
            "line1 and line2 are case-insensitive different");
        }

        if (line1.toLowerCase().equals(line1)) {
          System.out.println("line1 is all lowercase");
        } else {
          System.out.println("line1 is mixed case");
        }
    }
}
```

Listing 1.8 defines the `Java` class `CompareStrings` and a `main()` method that that defines the string variables `line1` and `line2`. Launch the code in Listing 1.8 and you will see the following output:

```
line1: This is a simple sentence.
line2: this is a simple sentence.

line1 and line2 are case-insensitive same
line1 is mixed case
```

SEARCHING FOR A SUBSTRING IN JAVA

Listing 1.9 displays the contents of `SearchString.java` that illustrates how to use the `indexOf()` method to determine whether or not a string is a substring of another string. Note that this code sample involves an `if` statement, which is discussed in more detail in the final code sample of this chapter.

LISTING 1.9: SearchString.java

```java
public class SearchString
{
    public SearchString(){}

    public static void main (String args[])
    {
        int index;
        String str1 = "zz", str2 = "Pizza";

        index = str2.indexOf(str1);
        if(index < 0)
        {
            System.out.println(str1+" is not a substring of "+str2);
        }
        else
        {
            System.out.println(str1+" is a substring of "+str2);
        }
    }
}
```

Listing 1.9 contains a main() method that initializes the string variables `str1` and `str2`, and then initializes the string variable `index` with the index position of the string `str1` in the string `str2`. If the result is negative then `str1` is not a substring of `str2`, and a message is printed. If `str1` *is* a substring of `str2`, then a corresponding message is displayed. Launch the code in Listing 1.9 and you will see the following output:

```
zz is a substring of Pizza
```

USEFUL STRING METHODS IN JAVA

The `Java` `String` class supports a plethora of useful and intuitively named methods for string-related operations, including: `compare()`, `compareTo()`, `concat()`, `equals()`, `intern()`, `length()`, `replace()`, `split()`, and `substring()`.

The Java String class has some very useful methods for managing strings, some of which are listed here (and one of which you have seen already):

- substring(idx1, idx2): the substring from index idx1 to idx2
- compareTo(str): compare a string to a given string
- indexOfStr(str): find the index of a string in another string
- lastIndexOfStr(str): find the index of the last occurrence of a string in another string

Listing 1.9 displays the contents of CapitalizeFirstAll.java that illustrates how to use the substring() method in order to capitalize the first letter of each word in a string, how to convert the string to all lowercase letters, and how to convert the string to all uppercase letters. Note that this example uses a loop, but the code execution in this code sample ought to be straightforward.

LISTING 1.9: CapitalizeFirstAll.java

```
public class BooleanExamples
{
    public CapitalizeFirstAll(){}

    public static void main (String args[])
    {
        String line1 = "this is a SIMPLE sentence.";
        String[] words = line1.split(" ");
        String line2 = "", first = "";

        for(String word: words)
        {
            first = word.substring(0,1).toUpperCase()+word.substring(1);
            line2 = line2 + first + " ";
        }

        System.out.println("line1: "+line1);
        System.out.println("line2: "+line2);

        String upper = line1.toUpperCase();
        String lower = line1.toLowerCase();

        System.out.println("Lower: "+lower);
        System.out.println("Upper: "+upper);
    }
}
```

Listing 1.9 defines the Java class CapitalizeAllFirst and a main() method that initializes the String variable line1 with a text string. The next portion of the main() method splits ("tokenizes") the contents of line1 into an array of words via the split() method.

Next, a loop iterates through each word in the words array, and sets the variable first equal to the uppercase version of the first letter of the current word, concatenated with the remaining letters of the current word, as shown here;

```
first = word.substring(0,1).toUpperCase()+word.substring(1);
```

The loop also concatenates `first` and a blank space to the string `line2`, which will consists of the words from the variable `line`, with the first letter in each word in uppercase.

The final portion of the `main()` function display the contents of the modified sentence, along with a lowercase version of the sentence, followed by an uppercase version of the original sentence. Launch the code in Listing 1.9 and you will see the following output:

```
line1: this is a SIMPLE sentence.
line2: This Is A SIMPLE Sentence.
Lower: this is a simple sentence.
Upper: THIS IS A SIMPLE SENTENCE.
```

Parsing Strings in Java

`Java` supports command-line arguments, which enables you to launch programs from the command line with different command line values. Compare `Java` strings with the `equals()` method to determine whether or not the values are the same. Although some languages compare strings via "==", in Java the "==" only compares the two references (not the values) of two strings.

Use the `parseInt()` method to (attempt to) convert a string to an integer:

```
int num = Integer.parseInt("1234");
```

Use the `substring()` method to split a string with white space characters:

```
String[] strArray = aString.split("\\s+");
```

The regular expression \s+ matches one or more occurrences of various white space characters, including " ", "\t", "\r", and "\n".

The following code snippet reverses a `Java` string via the `StringBuilder` class:

```
String rev = new StringBuilder(original).reverse().toString();
```

The companion disc contains `OverrideToString.java` and shows you how to override the default toString() method in Java.

Thus far you have seen various examples of working with strings in Java. For more information, navigate to this URL:

https://docs.oracle.com/javase/7/docs/api/java/lang/String.html

CONDITIONAL LOGIC IN JAVA

Conditional logic enables you to make decisions based on a condition. The simplest type involves a simple "if" statement but can also use if-else as well as if-else-if statements. Another Java construct is the switch statement, which also involves conditional logic, and some tasks are handled more easily with a switch statement instead of multiple if-else statements.

Listing 1.10 displays the contents of `Conditional1.java` that divides two numbers by small integers and uses the integer-valued remainder to print various messages.

LISTING 1.10: Conditional1.java

```java
public class Conditional1
{
    int x = 12, y = 15;

    public Conditional1() {}

    public void IfElseLogic()
    {
        if(x % 2 == 0) {
            System.out.println("x is even: "+x);
        } else {
            System.out.println("x is odd: "+x);
        }

        if(x % 2 == 0) {
            if(x % 4 == 0) {
                System.out.println("x is divisible by 4: "+x);
            }
        }

        if(y % 3 == 0 && y % 5 == 0) {
            System.out.println("y is divisible by 3 and 5: "+y);
        } else if(y % 3 == 0) {
            System.out.println("y is divisible only by 3: "+y);
        } else if(y % 5 == 0) {
            System.out.println("y is divisible only by 5: "+y);
        } else {
            System.out.println("y is not divisible by 3 or 5: "+y);
        }
    }

    public static void main(String args[])
    {
        Conditional1 c1 = new Conditional1();
        c1.IfElseLogic();
    }
}
```

Listing 1.10 defines the Java class `Conditional1` and the public method `IfElseLogic` that performs modulo arithmetic on the integer variables x and y that are initialized with the values of 12 and 15, respectively.

If x % 2 equals 0, then x is even; if x % 4 equals 0, then x is a multiple of 4; if y % 3 equals 0, then y is a multiple of 3. Listing 1.10 contains some if–else code blocks and also a nested block of conditional logic, and you perform a visual calculation in order to compare your results with the generated output.

Launch the code in Listing 1.10 and you will see the following output:

```
x is even: 12
x is divisible by 4: 12
y is divisible by 3 and 5: 15
```

You can create much more complex Boolean expressions involving multiple combinations of "and", "or", and "not" (this involves "!="). Use the code in Listing 1.1 as a baseline and then add your own variations.

The companion files contains BooleanExamples.java that shows you various types of Boolean expressions in Java.

DETERMINING LEAP YEARS

Listing 1.11 displays the contents of LeapYear.java that determines whether or not a given year is a leap year. In case you have forgotten, a leap year must be a multiple of 4. However, if a given year is a century that is not a multiple of 400, then that year is not a leap year. Hence, 2000 is a leap year, whereas 1700, 1800, and 1900 are not leap years.

This code sample is a nice example of using nested conditional statements. Try to write your own pseudo code and compare it with the contents of Listing 1.11.

LISTING 1.11: LeapYear.java

```java
public class LeapYear
{
    public LeapYear() {}

    // leap years are multiples of 4 except for
    // centuries that are also multiples of 400
    public void checkYear(int year)
    {
        if( year % 4 == 0)
        {
            if( year % 100 == 0)
            {
                if(year % 400 != 0)
                {
                    System.out.println(year + " is a leap year");
                }
                else
                {
                    System.out.println(year + " is not a leap year");
                }
            }
            else
            {
                System.out.println(year + " is a leap year");
            }
        }
        else
        {
            System.out.println(year + " is not a leap year");
        }
    }

    public static void main(String args[])
    {
        LeapYear ly = new LeapYear();
```

```
    int[] years = {1234, 1900, 2000, 2020, 3000, 5588};

    for (int year : years)
    {
        ly.checkYear(year);
    }
  }
}
```

Listing 1.11 defines the class LeapYear that contains the method checkYear that determines whether or not a given year is a leap year. If you look at the comment block near the beginning of Listing 1.11, you will see that the method checkYear implements the same conditional logic. Launch the code in Listing 1.11 and you will see the following output:

```
1234 is not a leap year
1900 is a leap year
2000 is not a leap year
2020 is a leap year
3000 is not a leap year
5588 is a leap year
```

FINDING THE DIVISORS OF A NUMBER

Listing 1.12 contains a `while` loop, conditional logic, and the % (modulus) operator in order to find the prime factors of any integer greater than 1.

LISTING 1.12: Divisors1.java

```
public class Divisors1
{
    public Divisors1() {}

    public void divisors(int num)
    {
        int div = 2;

        System.out.println("Number: "+num);

        while(num > 1)
        {
            if(num % div == 0)
            {
                System.out.println("divisor: "+div);
                num /= div;
            }
            else
            {
                ++div;
            }
        }
    }
}
```

```
public static void main(String args[])
{
    Divisors1 d1 = new Divisors1();
    d1.divisors(12);
}
}
```

Listing 1.12 defines the Java class Divisors1 that contains the method divisors that determines the divisors of a positive integer num. The divisors method contains a while loop that iterates while num is greater than 1.

During each iteration, if num is evenly divisible by div, then the value of div is displayed, and then num is reduced by dividing it by the value of div. If num is not evenly divisible by div, then div is incremented by 1. The output from Listing 1.8 is here:

```
Number: 12
divisor: 2
divisor: 2
divisor: 3
```

CHECKING FOR PALINDROMES

In case you've forgotten, a palindrome is a sequence of digits or characters that are identical when you read them on both directions (i.e., from left to right and from right to left).

For example, the string BoB is a palindrome, but Bob is not a palindrome. Similarly, the number 12321 is a palindrome but 1232 is not a palindrome.

Listing 1.13 displays the contents of Palindromes1.java that checks if a given string or number is a palindrome.

LISTING 1.13: Palindromes1.java

```
public class Palindromes1
{
  public Palindromes1() {}

  public void calculate(String str)
  {
      int result = 0;
      int len = str.length();

      for(int i=0; i<len/2; i++)
      {
          if(str.charAt(i) != str.charAt(len-i-1))
          {
              result = 1;
              break;
          }
      }

      if(result == 0)
      {
          System.out.println(str + ": is a palindrome");
      }
      else
```

```
        {
            System.out.println(str + ": is not a palindrome");
        }
    }

    public static void main(String args[])
    {
        String[] names = {"Dave", "BoB", "radar", "rotor"};
        int[] numbers = {1234, 767, 1234321, -101};

        Palindromes1 pal1 = new Palindromes1();

        for (String name : names)
        {
            pal1.calculate(name);
        }

        for (int num : numbers)
        {
            pal1.calculate(Integer.toString(num));
        }
    }
}
```

Listing 1.13 defines the Java class Palindromes1 that contain the method calculate to deter-mine whether or not a string is a palindrome. The main() method defines the array names that contains a set of strings and the array numbers that contains a set of numbers.

Next, the main() method instantiates the Palindromes1 class and then invokes the calculate() method with each string in the names array. Similarly, the calculate() method is invoked with each number in the numbers array by converting the numeric values to string by means of the Integer.toString() method. Launch the code in Listing 1.13 and you will see the following output:

```
Dave: is not a palindrome
BoB: is a palindrome
radar: is a palindrome
rotor: is a palindrome
1234: is not a palindrome
767: is a palindrome
1234321: is a palindrome
-101: is not a palindrome
```

The next section in this chapter shows you how to combine Java while loops with conditional logic (if-else statements) in Java code.

WORKING WITH ARRAYS OF STRINGS

This section shows you how to print the names of people from the main() routine, where the first names and last names are stored in arrays.

Listing 1.14 displays the contents of PersonArray.java that contains two private String variables for keeping track of a person's first name and last name, along with methods that enable you to access the first name and last name of any person.

LISTING 1.14: PersonArray.java

```java
public class PersonArray
{
    private String[] firstNames = {"Jane","John","Bob"};
    private String[] lastNames  = {"Smith","Jones","Stone"};

    public void displayNames()
    {
        for(int i=0; i<firstNames.length; i++)
        {
            System.out.println("My name is "+
                                firstNames[i]+" "+
                                lastNames[i]);
        }
    }

    public static void main (String args[])
    {
        PersonArray pa = new PersonArray();
        pa.displayNames();
    }
}
```

Listing 1.14 defines the Java class PersonArray that contains the method displayNames whose for loop iterates through the string arrays firstNames and lastNames. The loop variable i is used as an index into these arrays to print a person's first name and last name, as shown here:

```java
System.out.println("My name is "+
                    firstNames[i]+" "+
                    lastNames[i]);
```

Launch the code in Listing 1.14 and you will see the following output:

```
My name is John Smith
My name is Jane Andrews
```

WORKING WITH THE STRINGBUILDER CLASS

Recall that the Java String class creates an immutable sequence of characters, which can involve a significant amount of memory for many large strings. On the other hand, the Java StringBuilder class is an alternative to the String class that supports a mutable sequence of characters.

The StringBuilder class has a number of useful methods, each of which has return type StringBuilder, as shown here:

- capacity()
- charAt()
- delete()
- codePointAt()
- codePointBefore()

- codePointCount()
- deleteCharAt()
- ensureCapacity()
- getChars()
- length()
- replace()
- reverse()
- setCharAt()
- setLength()
- subSequence()

Listing 1.15 displays the contents of `PersonRandom.java` that uses a randomly generated index into an array of names in order to print a person's first name and last name.

LISTING 1.15: PersonRandom.java

```
public class PersonRandom
{
    private String[] firstNames = {"Jane", "John", "Bob"};
    private String[] lastNames  = {"Smith", "Jones", "Stone"};

    public void displayNames()
    {
        String fname, lname;
        int index, loopCount=6, maxRange=20;
        int pCount = firstNames.length;

        for(int i=0; i<loopCount; i++)
        {
            index = (int)(maxRange*Math.random());
            index = index % pCount;

            fname = firstNames[index];
            lname = lastNames[index];

            System.out.println("My name is "+
                               fname+" "+lname);
        }
    }

    public static void main (String args[])
    {
        PersonRandom pa = new PersonRandom();
        pa.displayNames();
    }
}
```

Listing 1.15 is very similar to the code in Listing 1.14: the important difference is that a name is chosen by means of a randomly generated number, as shown here:

```
index = (int)(maxRange*Math.random());
```

Launch the code in Listing 1.15 and you will see the following output:

```
My name is Jane Smith
My name is John Jones
My name is Jane Smith
My name is Jane Smith
My name is Bob Stone
My name is John Jones
```

Notice that there are six output lines even though there are only three people. This is possible because the randomly generated number is always between 0 and 2, which means that we can generate hundreds of lines of output. Of course, there will be many duplicate output lines because there are only three distinct people.

STATIC METHODS IN JAVA

Static variables are declared in the same manner as instance variables, but with the static keyword. If you declare a method as static, that method can only update static variables; however, static variables can be updated in nonstatic methods. A key point about static methods is that you can reference a static method without instantiating an object; on the other hand, nonstatic methods are only available through an instance of a class. Keep in mind the following points about static methods:

- They can call only other static methods
- They can only access static data
- The same method in all class instances
- They do not have a 'this' reference

Listing 1.16 displays the contents of StaticMethod.java that illustrates how to define and then invoke a static method in a Java class.

LISTING 1.16: StaticMethod.java

```java
public class StaticMethod
{
   public void display1()
   {
      System.out.println("Inside display1");
   }

   public static void display2()
   {
      System.out.println("Inside display2");
   }

   public static void main (String args[])
   {
      System.out.println("Inside main()");
      // cannot invoke non-static method:
   //StaticMethod.display1();
```

```
        // this works correctly:
        StaticMethod.display2();


        // this works correctly:
        StaticMethod sm = new StaticMethod();
        sm.display1();
    }
}
```

Listing 1.16 defines the Java class StaticMethod and a non-static method display1() as well as a static method display2(). The main() method invokes the display2() method without an instance of the StaticMethod class. Next, the main() method initializes the variable sm as an instance of the StaticMethod class, after which sm invokes the method display1() that is not a static method.

Other Static Types in Java

As you saw in the previous section, a static method in a Java class can be invoked without instantiating an object. In addition, you can define a static Java class containing static methods, each of which can be invoked without instantiating an instance of the Java class.

A *static block* (also called a static initialization block) is a set of instructions that is invoked once when a Java class is loaded into memory. A static block is used for initialization before object construction, as shown here:

```
class MyClass
{
    static int x;
    int y;

    static {
        x = 123;
        System.out.println("static block executed");
    }

    // other methods ...
}
```

The code shown in bold in the preceding code block is executed before (any) constructor is executed.

SUMMARY

This chapter introduced you to some Java features, such as some of its supported data types, operators, and the precedence of Java operators. You also learned how to instantiate objects that are instances of Java classes and how to perform arithmetic operations in a main() method.

You also received an overview of Java characters and strings, and the significance of the new operator. Finally, you learned how to determine if two strings are equal, as well as some other useful string-related function in Java.

CHAPTER 2

RECURSION AND COMBINATORICS

This chapter introduces you to the concept of recursion, along with various `Java` code samples, and then an introduction to concepts in combinatorics such as combination and permutations of objects.

The first part of this chapter discusses recursion, which is the most significant portion of the chapter. The code samples include finding the sum of an arithmetic series (e.g., the numbers from 1 to n), calculating the sum of a geometric series, calculating factorial values, and calculating Fibonacci numbers. Except for the iterative solution to Fibonacci numbers, these code samples do not involve data structures. However, the examples provide a foundation for working with recursion.

If you are new to recursion or if you tend to struggle with algorithms that involve recursion, here is a suggestion: *find some basic tasks that have iterative solutions and solve those tasks via recursive solutions.* The effort involved in finding recursive solutions will provide some useful practice and assist you in becoming more comfortable with recursion.

The second part of this chapter discusses concepts in combinatorics, such as permutations and combinations. Note that a thorough coverage of combinatorics can fill an entire undergraduate course in mathematics, whereas this chapter contains only some rudimentary concepts.

If you are new to recursion, some of this material might be slightly daunting, but don't be alarmed. Usually, several iterations of reading the material and code samples will lead to a better understanding of recursion.

Alternatively, you can also skip the material in this chapter until you encounter code samples later in this chapter that involve recursion. Chapter 3 contains a code sample for binary search that uses recursion, and another code sample that uses an iterative approach, so you can skip the recursion-based example for now. However, if you plan to learn about trees, then you definitely need to learn about recursion, which is the basis for all the code samples in Chapter 5 that perform various tree-related examples.

WHAT IS RECURSION?

Recursion-based algorithms can provide very elegant solutions to tasks that would be difficult to implement via iterative algorithms. For some tasks, such as calculating factorial values, the recursive solution and the iterative solution have comparable code complexity.

As a simple example, suppose that we want to add the integers from 1 to n (inclusive), and let n = 10 so that we have a concrete example. If we denote s as the partial sum of successively adding consecutive integers, then we have the following:

```
S = 1
S = S + 2
S = S + 3
. . .
S = S + 10
```

If we denote s(n) as the sum of the first n positive integers, then we have the following relationship:

```
S(1) = 1
S(n) = S(n-1) + n for n > 1
```

With the preceding observations in mind, the next section contains code samples for calculating the sum of the first n positive integers using an iterative approach and then with recursion.

ARITHMETIC SERIES

This section shows you how to calculate the sum of a set of positive integers, such as the numbers from 1 to n inclusive. The first algorithm uses an iterative approach and the second algorithm uses recursion.

Before delving into the code samples, there is a simple way to calculate the closed form sum of the integers from 1 to n inclusive, which we will denote as s. Then there are two ways to calculate S, as shown here:

```
S = 1 + 2     + 3     + . . . + (n-1) + n
S = n + (n-1) + (n-2) + . . . + 2     + 1
```

There are n columns, and each column has the sum equal to (n+1), and therefore the sum of the right side of the equals sign is n*(n+1). Since the left side of the equals sign has the sum 2*S, we have the following result:

```
2*S = n*(n+1)
```

Divide both sides by 2 and the result is the well-known formula for the arithmetic sum of the first n positive integers:

```
S = n*(n+1)/2
```

Incidentally, the preceding formula was derived by a young student who was bored with performing the calculation manually: that student was Karl F. Gauss (when he was in third grade).

Calculating Arithmetic Series (Iterative)

Listing 2.1 displays the contents of the ArithSum.java that illustrates how to calculate the sum of the numbers from 1 to n inclusive using an iterative approach.

LISTING 2.1: ArithSum.java

```
public class ArithSum
{
    public static int calcsum(int num)
    {
        int sum = 0;
        for(int i=1; i<num+1; i++)
        {
            sum += i;
        }

        return sum;
    }

    public static void main(String[] args)
    {
        int sum = 0, max = 20;

        for(int j=2; j<max+1; j++)
        {
            sum = calcsum(j);
            System.out.println("Sum from 1 to "+j+" = "+sum);
        }
    }
}
```

Listing 2.1 starts with a static method calcsum() that contains a loop to iterate through the numbers from 1 to num+1 inclusive, where num is the value of the parameter to this function. During each iteration, the variable sum (which was initialized to 0) is incremented by the value of the loop variable, and the final sum is returned.

The next portion of Listing 2.1 defines the main() method that initializes the scalar variables sum to 0 and max to 20, followed by a loop that iterates from 2 to max+1. During each iteration, the calcsum() method is invoked with the current value of the loop variable, and the returned value is printed. Launch the code in Listing 2.1 and you will see the following output:

```
sum from 1 to 2 = 3
sum from 1 to 3 = 6
sum from 1 to 4 = 10
sum from 1 to 5 = 15
sum from 1 to 6 = 21
sum from 1 to 7 = 28
sum from 1 to 8 = 36
sum from 1 to 9 = 45
sum from 1 to 10 = 55
sum from 1 to 11 = 66
```

```
sum from 1 to 12 = 78
sum from 1 to 13 = 91
sum from 1 to 14 = 105
sum from 1 to 15 = 120
sum from 1 to 16 = 136
sum from 1 to 17 = 153
sum from 1 to 18 = 171
sum from 1 to 19 = 190
sum from 1 to 20 = 210
```

Calculating Arithmetic Series (Recursive)

Listing 2.2 displays the contents of the ArithSumRecursive.py that illustrates how to calculate the sum of the numbers from 1 to n inclusive using an iterative approach.

LISTING 2.2: ArithSumRecursive.java

```java
public class ArithSumRecursive
{
    public static int calcsum(int num)
    {
        if(num == 0)
        {
            return num;
        }
        else
        {
            return num + calcsum(num-1);
        }
    }

    public static void main(String[] args)
    {
        int sum = 0, max = 20;

        for(int j=2; j<max+1; j++)
        {
            sum = calcsum(j);
            System.out.println("Sum from 1 to "+j+" = "+sum);
        }
    }
}
```

Listing 2.2 starts with a static method calcsum() that returns the value num if num equals 0, and otherwise recursively invokes the calcsum() method with the value num−1. The sum of the value of num and the result of this invocation is returned.

The next portion of Listing 2.1 defines the main() method that initializes the scalar variables sum to 0 and max to 20, followed by a loop that iterates from 2 to max+1. During each iteration, the calcsum() method is invoked with the current value of the loop variable, and the returned value is printed.

Calculating Partial Arithmetic Series

Listing 2.3 displays the contents of the arith_partial_sum.py that illustrates how to calculate the sum of the numbers from m to n inclusive, where m and n are two positive integers such that m <= n, using an iterative approach.

LISTING 2.3: ArithPartialSum.java

```java
public class ArithPartialSum
{
    public static int calcPartialSum(int m, int n)
    {
        if(n > m)
        {
            return 0;
        }
        else
        {
            return m*(m+1)/2 - (n-1)*(n)/2;
            //return m*(m+1)/2 - n*(n+1)/2;
        }
    }

    public static void main(String[] args)
    {
        int sum = 0, max = 8;

        for(int i=2; i<=max; i++)
        {
            for(int j=i+1; j<=max; j++)
            {
                sum = calcPartialSum(j,i);
                System.out.println("Sum from "+i+" to "+j+" = "+sum);
            }
        }
    }
}
```

Listing 2.3 starts with a static method calcPartialSum() that contains conditional logic to return 0 if n >= m, and otherwise return the arithmetic expression that is displayed in the "else" clause.

The next portion of Listing 2.3 defines the main() method that initializes the scalar variables sum to 0 and max to 8, followed by an outer loop that iterates from 2 to max+1. During each iteration, an inner loop iterates from i+1 to max−1, where I is the loop variable of the outer loop. The inner loop involves the calcPartialSum() method with the parameters j and ii (j is the index of the inner loop) and then prints the return value. Launch the code in Listing 2.1 and you will see the following output:

```
Sum from 2 to 3 = 5
Sum from 2 to 4 = 9
Sum from 2 to 5 = 14
```

```
Sum from 2 to 6 = 20
Sum from 2 to 7 = 27
Sum from 2 to 8 = 35
Sum from 3 to 4 = 7
Sum from 3 to 5 = 12
Sum from 3 to 6 = 18
Sum from 3 to 7 = 25
Sum from 3 to 8 = 33
Sum from 4 to 5 = 9
Sum from 4 to 6 = 15
Sum from 4 to 7 = 22
Sum from 4 to 8 = 30
Sum from 5 to 6 = 11
Sum from 5 to 7 = 18
Sum from 5 to 8 = 26
Sum from 6 to 7 = 13
Sum from 6 to 8 = 21
Sum from 7 to 8 = 15
```

GEOMETRIC SERIES

This section shows you how to calculate the geometric series of a set of positive integers, such as the numbers from 1 to n inclusive. The first algorithm uses an iterative approach and the second algorithm uses recursion.

Before delving into the code samples, there is a simple way to calculate the closed form sum of the geometric series of integers from 1 to n inclusive, where r is the ratio of consecutive terms in the geometric series. Let S denote the sum, which can be expressed as follows:

```
S   = 1+ r + r^2 + r^3 + . . . + r^(n-1) + r^n
r*S =     r + r^2 + r^3 + . . . + r^(n-1) + r^n + r^(n+1)
```

Subtract each term in the second row above from the corresponding term in the first row, and we have the following result:

```
S - r*S = 1 - r^(n+1)
```

Factor S from both terms on the left side of the preceding equation and we get the following result:

```
S*(1 - r) = 1 - r^(n+1)
```

Divide both sides of the preceding equation by the term (1-r) to get the formula for the sum of the geometric series of the first n positive integers:

```
S = [1 - r^(n+1)]/(1-r)
```

Notice that if r = 1 then the preceding equation returns an infinite value.

Calculating a Geometric Series (Iterative)

Listing 2.4 displays the contents of the GeometricSum.py that illustrates how to calculate the sum of the numbers from 1 to n inclusive using an iterative approach.

LISTING 2.4: GeometricSum.java

```java
public class GeometricSum
{
   public static int geomsum(int num, int ratio)
   {
      int partial = 0;
      int power   = 1;
      int sum     = 0;

      for(int i=1; i<num+1; i++)
      {
         partial += power;
         power *= ratio;
         sum += i;
      }

      return partial;
   }

   public static void main(String[] args)
   {
      int ratio = 2, max = 10, prod = 0;

      for(int j=2; j<max+1; j++)
      {
         prod = geomsum(j, ratio);
         System.out.println("Geometric sum for ratio = "+ratio+" from 1
to "+j+" = "+prod);
      }
   }
}
```

Listing 2.4 starts with a static method geomsum() that initializes three integer-valued scalar variables. The next portion of code is a loop that iterates through the numbers from 1 to num+1 inclusive, where num is the value of the parameter to this function. During each iteration, the three scalar variables are updated in order to keep track of the partial geometric sum of numbers. After the loop has completed the value of partial is returned.

The next portion of Listing 2.4 defines the main() method that initializes the scalar variables ratio, max, and prod to 2, 10, and 0, respectively. Next, a loop iterates from 2 to max+1. During each iteration, the geomsum() method is invoked with the current value of the loop variable j and the value of ratio. In addition, the variable prod is initialized with the return value from geomsum() and that value is printed. Launch the code in Listing 2.4 and you will see the following output:

```
geometric sum for ratio= 2 from 1 to 2 = 3
geometric sum for ratio= 2 from 1 to 3 = 7
geometric sum for ratio= 2 from 1 to 4 = 15
geometric sum for ratio= 2 from 1 to 5 = 31
geometric sum for ratio= 2 from 1 to 6 = 63
geometric sum for ratio= 2 from 1 to 7 = 127
```

```
geometric sum for ratio= 2 from 1 to 8 = 255
geometric sum for ratio= 2 from 1 to 9 = 511
geometric sum for ratio= 2 from 1 to 10 = 1023
```

Calculating Geometric Series (Recursive)

Listing 2.5 displays the contents of the GeomSumRecursive.java that illustrates how to calculate the sum of the geometric series of the numbers from 1 to n inclusive using recursion. Note that the following code sample uses tail recursion.

LISTING 2.5: GeoSumRecursive.java

```java
public class GeoSumRecursive
{
    public static int geomsum(int num, int ratio, int term, int sum)
    {
        if(num == 1)
        {
            return sum;
        }
        else
        {
            term *= ratio;;
            sum  += term;;
            return geomsum(num-1,ratio,term,sum);
        }
    }

    public static void main(String[] args)
    {
        int max = 10, ratio = 2, sum = 1, term = 1, prod = 0;

        for(int j=2; j<max+1; j++)
        {
            prod = geomsum(j, ratio, term, sum);
            System.out.println("Geometric sum for ratio = "+ratio+" from 1
to "+j+" = "+prod);
        }
    }
}
```

Listing 2.5 starts with a static method geomsum() that contains conditional logic to return 0 if num equals 1, and otherwise update the variables term and sum and then return the result of invoking geomsum() with the updated values.

The next portion of Listing 2.5 defines the main() method that initializes the scalar variables max, ratio, sum, term, and prod to 10, 2, 1, 1, and 0, respectively. Next, a loop iterates from 2 to max+1, and during each iteration, the geomsum() method is invoked with the parameters j, ratio, term, and sum. The result of this invocation is assigned to the variable prod, which is then printed. Launch the code in Listing 2.1 and you will see the following output:

```
Geometric sum for ratio = 2 from 1 to 2 = 3
Geometric sum for ratio = 2 from 1 to 3 = 7
Geometric sum for ratio = 2 from 1 to 4 = 15
```

```
Geometric sum for ratio = 2 from 1 to 5 = 31
Geometric sum for ratio = 2 from 1 to 6 = 63
Geometric sum for ratio = 2 from 1 to 7 = 127
Geometric sum for ratio = 2 from 1 to 8 = 255
Geometric sum for ratio = 2 from 1 to 9 = 511
Geometric sum for ratio = 2 from 1 to 10 = 1023
```

FACTORIAL VALUES

This section contains three code samples for calculating factorial values: the first code sample uses a loop and the other two code samples use recursion.

As a reminder, the *factorial* value of a positive integer n is the product of all the numbers from 1 to n (inclusive). Hence, we have the following values:

```
Factorial(2)  = 2*1 = 2
Factorial(3)  = 3*2*1 = 6
Factorial(4)  = 4*3*2*1 = 24
Factorial(5)  = 5*4*3*2*1 = 120
Factorial(6)  = 6*5*4*3*2*1 = 720
Factorial(7)  = 7*6*5*4*3*2*1 = 5040
```

If you look at the preceding list of calculations, you can see some interesting relationships among factorial numbers:

```
Factorial(3) = 3 * Factorial(2)
Factorial(4) = 4 * Factorial(3)
Factorial(5) = 5 * Factorial(4)
Factorial(6) = 6 * Factorial(5)
Factorial(7) = 7 * Factorial(6)
```

Based on the preceding observations, it's reasonably intuitive to infer the following relationship for factorial numbers:

```
Factorial(1) = 1
Factorial(n) = n * Factorial(n-1) for n > 1
```

The next section uses the preceding formula in order to calculate the factorial value of various numbers.

Calculating Factorial Values (Iterative)

Listing 2.6 displays the contents of the Factorial1.py that illustrates how to calculate factorial numbers using an iterative approach.

LISTING 2.6: Factorial1.py

```
public class Factorial1
{
    public static int factorial(int num)
    {
        int prod = 1;
        for(int i=1; i<num+1; i++)
```

```
        {
            prod *= i;
        }

        return prod;
    }

    public static void main(String[] args)
    {
        int prod= 0, max = 15;

        for(int j=1; j<=max; j++)
        {
            prod = factorial(j);
            System.out.println("Factorial "+j+" = "+prod);
        }
    }
}
```

Listing 2.6 starts with a static method factorial() that contains a loop to iterate through the numbers from 1 to n inclusive, where n is the value of the parameter to this function. During each iteration, the variable prod (which was initialized to 1) is multiplied by the value of the loop variable i, and the final product is returned.

The next portion of Listing 2.1 defines the main() method that initializes the scalar variables prod to 0 and max to 15, followed by a loop that iterates from 1 to max inclusive. During each iteration, the factorial() method is invoked with the current value of the loop variable j, and the returned value is assigned to the variable prod and then printed. Launch the code in Listing 2.6 and you will see the following output:

```
factorial 0 = 1
factorial 1 = 1
factorial 2 = 1
factorial 3 = 2
factorial 4 = 6
factorial 5 = 24
factorial 6 = 120
factorial 7 = 720
factorial 8 = 5040
factorial 9 = 40320
factorial 10 = 362880
factorial 11 = 3628800
factorial 12 = 39916800
factorial 13 = 479001600
factorial 14 = 6227020800
factorial 15 = 87178291200
factorial 16 = 1307674368000
factorial 17 = 20922789888000
factorial 18 = 355687428096000
factorial 19 = 6402373705728000
```

Calculating Factorial Values (Recursive)

Listing 2.7 displays the contents of the Factorial2.py that illustrates how to calculate factorial values using recursion.

LISTING 2.7: Factorial2.py

```
public class Factorial2
{
    public static int factorial(int num)
    {
        if(num <= 1)
        {
            return 1;
        }
        else
        {
            return num * factorial(num-1);
        }
    }

    public static void main(String[] args)
    {
        int prod= 0, max = 15;

        for(int j=1; j<=max; j++)
        {
            prod = factorial(j);
            System.out.println("Factorial "+j+" = "+prod);
        }
    }
}
```

Listing 2.7 starts with a static method `factorial()` that contains conditional logic to return 1 if num is at most 1, and otherwise return the product of num and result of invoking `factorial()` with the value num−1.

The next portion of Listing 2.7 defines the `main()` method that initializes the scalar variables prod and max to 0 and 15, respectively. Next, a loop iterates from 1 to max inclusive, and during each iteration, the `factorial()` method is invoked with the loop variable j. The result of this invocation is assigned to the variable prod, which is then printed. Launch the code in Listing 2.7 and you will see the same output as the preceding example.

Calculating Factorial Values (Tail Recursion)

Listing 2.8 displays the contents of the `Factorial3.py` that illustrates how to calculate factorial values using tail recursion.

LISTING 2.8: Factorial3.py

```
public class Factorial3
{
    public static int factorial(int num, int prod)
    {
        if(num <= 1)
        {
            return prod;
        }
        else
        {
```

```
            return factorial(num-1, num*prod);
        }
    }

    public static void main(String[] args)
    {
        int prod= 0, max = 15;

        for(int j=1; j<=max; j++)
        {
            prod = factorial(j, 1);
            System.out.println("Factorial "+j+" = "+prod);
        }
    }
}
```

Listing 2.8 starts with a static method `factorial()` that contains conditional logic to return prod if num is at most 1, and otherwise return the product of num and result of invoking `facto-rial()` with the value n−1 and n*prod.

The next portion of Listing 2.8 defines the `main()` method that initializes the scalar variables prod and max to 0 and 15, respectively. Next, a loop iterates from 1 to max inclusive, and during each iteration, the `factorial()` method is invoked with the loop variable j and the number 1. The result of this invocation is assigned to the variable prod, which is then printed. Launch the code in Listing 2.8 and you will see the same output as the preceding example.

FIBONACCI NUMBERS

Fibonacci numbers have some real-life counterparts, such as the pattern of sunflower seeds and the locations where tree branches form. Here is the definition of the Fibonacci sequence:

```
Fib(0) = 0
Fib(1) = 1
Fib(n) = Fib(n-1)+Fib(n-2) for n >= 2
```

Note that it's possible to specify different "seed" values for `Fib(0)` and `Fib(1)`, but the values 0 and 1 are the most commonly used values.

Calculating Fibonacci Numbers (Recursive)

Listing 2.9 displays the contents of the `Fibonacci1.py` that illustrates how to calculate Fibonacci numbers using recursion.

LISTING 2.9: Fibonacci1.py

```
public class Fibonacci1
{
    // very inefficient:
    public static int fibonacci(int num)
    {
        if(num <= 1)
        {
            return num;
```

```
        }
        else
        {
            return fibonacci(num-2) + fibonacci(num-1);
        }
    }

    public static void main(String[] args)
    {
        int fib = 0, max = 20;

        for(int j=0; j<=max; j++)
        {
            fib = fibonacci(j);
            System.out.println("Fibonacci of "+j+" = "+fib);
        }
    }
}
```

Listing 2.9 starts with a static method fibonacci() that contains conditional logic to return num if num is at most 1, and otherwise return the sum of fibonacci(num–2) and fibonacci(n–1).

The next portion of Listing 2.9 defines the main() method that initializes the scalar variables fib and max to 0 and 20, respectively. Next, a loop iterates from 1 to max inclusive, and during each iteration, the fibonacci() method is invoked with the loop variable j. The result of this invocation is assigned to the variable fib, which is then printed. Launch the code in Listing 2.8 and you will see the following output:

```
fibonacci 0 = 0
fibonacci 1 = 1
fibonacci 2 = 1
fibonacci 3 = 2
fibonacci 4 = 3
fibonacci 5 = 5
fibonacci 6 = 8
fibonacci 7 = 13
fibonacci 8 = 21
fibonacci 9 = 34
fibonacci 10 = 55
fibonacci 11 = 89
fibonacci 12 = 144
fibonacci 13 = 233
fibonacci 14 = 377
fibonacci 15 = 610
fibonacci 16 = 987
fibonacci 17 = 1597
fibonacci 18 = 2584
fibonacci 19 = 4181
```

Calculating Fibonacci Numbers (Iterative)

Listing 2.10 displays the contents of the Fibonacci2.py that illustrates how to calculate Fibonacci numbers using an iterative approach.

LISTING 2.10: Fibonacci2.py

```
public class Fibonacci2
{
    public static void main(String[] args)
    {
        int max = 21;
        int arr1[] = new int[max];
        arr1[0] = 0;
        arr1= 1;

        for(int j=2; j<max; j++)
        {
            arr1[j] = arr1[j-1] + arr1[j-2];
            System.out.println("Fibonacci of "+j+" = "+arr1[j]);
        }
    }
}
```

Listing 2.10 defines the main() method that initializes the scalar variable max and the integer array arr1 that is initialized with max number of entries. Notice that the first two entries are assigned 0 and 1: you can also use different initial values. Next, a loop iterates from 2 to max, and during each iteration, the jth element of arr1 is initialized with the sum of arr1[j–1] and arr1[j–2]. The next code snippet prints the contents of arr1[j]. As you can see, no recursion is used in this code sample. Launch the code in Listing 2.10 and you will see the same output as Listing 2.x in the previous example.

TASK: REVERSE A STRING VIA RECURSION

Listing 2.12 displays the contents of the Java file Reverse.java that illustrates how to use recursion in order to reverse a string.

LISTING 2.12: Reverse.java

```
public class Reverse
{
    public static String reverser(String str)
    {
        int strLen = str.length();
        if(strLen == 1) {
            return str;
        }

        String lastPart  = str.substring(strLen-1,strLen);
        String firstPart = str.substring(0,strLen-1);
        //System.out.println("first: "+firstPart+" last: "+lastPart);
        return lastPart+reverser(firstPart);
    }

    public static void main(String[] args)
    {
        String result = "";
```

```
String[] names = new String[]{"Dave", "Nancy", "Dominic"};

for(int idx=0; idx<names.length; idx++)
{
  result = reverser(names[idx]);
  System.out.println(
      "=> Word: "+names[idx]+" reverse: "+result+"\n");
}
}
}
```

Listing 2.12 starts with a static method reverser() that returns the variable str if str has length 1. If str has length greater than 1, then the variable lastPart is initialized with the right-most letter of str, and the variable firstPart is initialized with all the other characters ("all but last") in the variable str. Next the return statement is invoked with the concatenation of lastPart and reverser(firstPart).

The next portion of Listing 2.12 defines the main() method that initializes the scalar variables result to an empty string and the string-based array names to a set of three string values.

Next, a loop iterates through each element of the names array and invokes the reverser() method with the current string. The result of the method invocation is assigned to the variable result, which is then printed. Launch the code in Listing 2.8 and you will see the following output:

```
all-but-first chars: ['a', 'n', 'c', 'y']
all-but-first chars: ['n', 'c', 'y']
all-but-first chars: ['c', 'y']
all-but-first chars: ['y']
all-but-first chars: []
=> Word:  Nancy  reverse:  ['y', 'c', 'n', 'a', 'N']

all-but-first chars: ['a', 'v', 'e']
all-but-first chars: ['v', 'e']
all-but-first chars: ['e']
all-but-first chars: []
=> Word:  Dave  reverse:  ['e', 'v', 'a', 'D']

all-but-first chars: ['o', 'm', 'i', 'n', 'i', 'c']
all-but-first chars: ['m', 'i', 'n', 'i', 'c']
all-but-first chars: ['i', 'n', 'i', 'c']
all-but-first chars: ['n', 'i', 'c']
all-but-first chars: ['i', 'c']
all-but-first chars: ['c']
all-but-first chars: []
=> Word:  Dominic  reverse:  ['c', 'i', 'n', 'i', 'm', 'o', 'D']
```

TASK: CHECK FOR BALANCED PARENTHESES

This task can arise as a computer science interview question, and here are some examples:

```
S1 = "()()()"
S2 = "(()()())"
S3 = "()("
S4 = "(())"
S5 = "()()("
```

As you can see, S1, S3, and S4 have balanced parentheses, whereas S2 and S5 have unbalanced parentheses.

https://stackoverflow.com/questions/31849977/balanced-parenthesis-how-to-count-them

Listing 2.13 displays the contents of `BalancedParentheses.java` that illustrate how to determine whether or not a string consists of balanced parentheses.

LISTING 2.13: BalancedParentheses.java

```java
// https://stackoverflow.com/questions/31849977/balanced-parenthesis-how-
to-count-them
public class BalancedParens
{
    public BalancedParens(){}

    public static void main(String[] args)
    {
        String[] exprs = new String[]{"(){}[]","(({","(())"};

        for(int idx=0; idx<exprs.length; idx++)
        {
            String str = exprs[idx];
            int counter = 0;

            for (char ch : str.toCharArray())
            {
                if (ch == '(') counter++;
                else if (ch == ')') counter--;

                if (counter < 0) break;
            }

            if (counter == 0) {
                System.out.println("balanced string:"+str+"\n");
            } else {
                System.out.println("unbalanced string:"+str+"\n");
            }
        }
    }
}
```

The key idea involves the integer variable counter: increase counter if a left parenthesis is encountered, and decrease counter if the current character is a right parenthesis.

Listing 2.13 defines the `main()` method that initializes the string-based array exprs with three string values consisting of combinations of parentheses and curly braces. Next, an outer loop iterates through each element of the exprs array and then an inner loop iterates through the characters of the current string via the variable ch. The loop contains conditional logic that increments the variable counter if ch equals "(" and decrements the variable counter if ch equals ")". In addition, there is an early exit from the loop if counter is negative.

The final code portion of Listing 2.13 involves conditional logic: if counter equals 0, then the current string is well-balanced, otherwise the current string is unbalanced. Launch the code in Listing 2.8 and you will see the following output:

```
balanced string:(){}[]

unbalanced string:((}

balanced string:(())
```

TASK: CALCULATE THE NUMBER OF DIGITS

Listing 2.14 displays the contents of CountDigits.java that illustrates how to calculate the number of digits in positive integers.

LISTING 2.14: CountDigits.java

```java
public class CountDigits
{
    public CountDigits(){}

    public static int countDigits(int num, int result)
    {
        if(num == 0)
        {
          return result;
        }
        else
        {
          //print("new result:",result+1)
          //print("new number:",int(num/10))
          return countDigits((int)Math.floor(num/10), result+1);
        }
    }

    public static void main(String[] args)
    {
        int[] numbers = new int[]{1234, 767, 1234321, 101};

        for (int num : numbers)
        {
            int result = countDigits(num, 0);
            System.out.println("Digits in "+num+" = "+result);
        }
    }
}
```

Listing 2.14 starts with a static method countDigits() that contains conditional logic to return num if num equals 0, and otherwise return the recursive invocation of countDigits() with the integer portion of num/10 and result+1, which are based on the parameters num and result of this recursive function.

The next portion of Listing 2.9 defines the `main()` method that initializes the integer-valued array numbers with four integer values. Next, a loop iterates through the elements of the numbers array, and then invokes the method countDigits() with the current element num and the number 0. The result of the invocation is assigned to the integer-valued variable result, and then the value of result is printed. Launch the code in Listing 2.8 and you will see the following output:

Note that the code in Listing 2.14 can be made even more concise: however, the current listing is slightly easier to understand. Launch the code in Listing 2.14 and you will see the following output:

```
Digits in  1234    =  4
Digits in  767   =  3
Digits in  1234321   =  7
Digits in  101  =  3
```

TASK: DETERMINE IF A POSITIVE INTEGER IS PRIME

Listing 2.15 displays the contents of the Java file `CheckPrime.java` that illustrates how to calculate the number of digits in positive integers.

LISTING 2.15: CheckPrime.java

```java
public class CheckPrime
{
   public CheckPrime(){}

   public static int isPrime(int num)
   {
      int PRIME = 1, COMPOSITE = 0;
      int div = 2, num2 = (int)(num/2);

      while(div <= num2)
      {
        if(num % div != 0) {
          div += 1;
        } else {
          return COMPOSITE;
        }
      }

      //print("found prime:",num)
      return PRIME;
   }

   public static void main(String[] args)
   {
      String result = "";
      int upperBound = 20;
      int[] numbers = new int[]{1234, 767, 1234321, 101};
```

```
      for(int num = 2; num < upperBound; num++)
      {
         result = findPrimeDivisors(num);
         System.out.println("Prime divisors of "+num+": "+result);
      }
   }
}
```

Listing 2.15 starts with a static method `isPrime()` with an integer-valued parameter num. The scalar-valued variables PRIME, COMPOSITE, div, and num2 are initialized with the values 1, 0, 2, and the integer portion of num/2, respectively.

Next, a while loop executes as long as the value of div is not greater than num2. A conditional block of code inside the loop checks of the remainder of num2 divided by div is non-zero: if so, then the variable div is incremented, otherwise the value of COMPOSITE is returned.

The next portion of Listing 2.9 defines the `main()` method that initializes the variables result, upperBound, and numbers to an empty string, the integer 20, and an array of four integer values, respectively. Next, a loop iterates from 2 to upperBound, and during each iteration, the method findPrimeDivisors() is invoked with the value of num. The result of the invocation is assigned to the variable result, which is then printed. Launch the code in Listing 2.8 and you will see the following output:

```
2 : is prime
3 : is prime
4 : is not prime
5 : is prime
6 : is not prime
7 : is prime
8 : is not prime
9 : is not prime
10 : is not prime
11 : is prime
12 : is not prime
13 : is prime
14 : is not prime
15 : is not prime
16 : is not prime
17 : is prime
18 : is not prime
19 : is prime
```

TASK: FIND THE PRIME DIVISORS OF A POSITIVE INTEGER

Listing 2.16 displays the contents of the `Java` file `CheckPrime.java` that illustrates how to find the prime divisors of a positive integer.

LISTING 2.16: FindPrimeDivisors.java

```
public class CheckPrime
{
   public CheckPrime(){}

   public static int isPrime(int num)
```

```java
{
   int PRIME = 1, COMPOSITE = 0;

   int div = 2, num2 = (int)(num/2);

   while(div < num2)
   {
     if(num2 % div != 0) {
       div += 1;
     } else {
       return COMPOSITE;
     }
   }

  //print("found prime:",num)
  return PRIME;
}

public static String findPrimeDivisors(int num)
{
  int div = 2;
  String prime_divisors = "";

  while(div <= num)
  {
    int prime = isPrime(div);
    if(prime == 1)
    {
      //print("=> prime number:",div)
      if(num % div == 0)
      {
        prime_divisors += " "+div;
        num = (int)(num/div);
        //System.out.println("2prime_divisors:"+prime_divisors);
      }  else {
        div += 1;
      }
    } else {
      div += 1;
    }
  }

  return prime_divisors;
}

public static void main(String[] args)
{
  int result = 0, upperBound = 20;
  for(int num = 2; num < upperBound; num++)
  {
     result = isPrime(num);
     if(result == 1) System.out.println(num+" is prime");
     if(result == 0) System.out.println(num+" is not prime");
  }
}
```

Listing 2.16 starts with a static method isPrime() that is identical to the method in Listing 2.15.

The next portion of Listing 2.16 defines the findPrimeDivisors() method that initializes the variables div and prime_divisors with the values 2 and "", respectively. The next portion of the code is a while loop that executes as long as div is less than or equal to num, where the latter is the parameter of this method.

During each iteration, the variable prime is initialized with the result of invoking the isPrime() method with the variable div. If prime equals 1, then we check if div is a divisor of num. Specifically, if num divided by div is 0, we have found a divisor, which we append to the string variable prime_divisors, and then set num equal to the integer portion of dividing num by div. If num divided by div is *not* 0, simply increment the value of div. In addition, if prime does not equal 1, then again we increment the value of div. After the loop has completed execution, return the variable prime_divisors, which consists of a string of the prime divisors of the integer num.

The next portion of Listing 2.9 defines the main() method that initializes the variables result and upperBound with the values 0 and 20, respectively. Next, a loop iterates from 2 to upper-Bound, and during each iteration, the variable result is initialized with the result of invoking the method isPrime() with the loop variable num. If the value of result equals 1, then a message is displayed that num is a prime number; otherwise, a message is displayed that num is *not* a prime number. Launch the code in Listing 2.8 and you will see the following output:

```
Prime divisors of  2 :   2
Prime divisors of  3 :   3
Prime divisors of  4 :   2 2
Prime divisors of  5 :   5
Prime divisors of  6 :   2 3
Prime divisors of  7 :   7
Prime divisors of  8 :   2 2 2
Prime divisors of  9 :   3 3
Prime divisors of 10 :   2 5
Prime divisors of 11 :   11
Prime divisors of 12 :   2 2 3
Prime divisors of 13 :
Prime divisors of 14 :   2 7
Prime divisors of 15 :   3 5
Prime divisors of 16 :   2 2 2 2
Prime divisors of 17 :
Prime divisors of 18 :   2 3 3
Prime divisors of 19 :
```

TASK: GOLDBACH'S CONJECTURE

Goldbach's conjecture states that every even number greater than 3 can be expressed as the sum of two odd prime numbers.

Listing 2.17 displays the contents of GoldbachConjecture.java that illustrates how to determine a pair of prime numbers whose sum equals a given even number.

LISTING 2.17: GoldbachConjecture.java

```
public class GoldbachConjecture
{
    public GoldbachConjecture(){}
```

```
public static int isPrime(int num)
{
    int PRIME = 1, COMPOSITE = 0;
    int div = 2;

    while(div < num)
    {
        if(num % div != 0) {
            div += 1;
        } else {
            return COMPOSITE;
        }
    }
    return PRIME;
}

public static void findPrimeFactors(int even_num)
{
    int halfway = (int)(even_num/2);
    for(int num=0; num<halfway; num++)
    {
        if(isPrime(num) == 1) {
            if(isPrime(even_num-num) == 1) {
                System.out.println(even_num+" = "+num+" + "+(even_num-num));
            }
        }
    }
}

public static void main(String[] args)
{
    int upperBound = 20;
    for(int num=0; num<upperBound; num++) {
        findPrimeFactors(num);
    }
}
}
```

Listing 2.17 starts with a static method isPrime() it that is identical to the method in Listing 2.15.

The next portion of Listing 2.17 defines the findPrimeFactors() method that initializes the variable half_way as the integer portion of even_num/2, where even_num is a parameter of this method. The next portion of the code is a loop that executes from 0 to halfway with the loop variable num. During each iteration, if the result of invoking isPrime(num) equals 1, isPrime(even_num-num) is checked to see if it also equals 1: if the latter is true, then even_num and num satisfy Goldbach's conjecture, so their values are printed.

The next portion of Listing 2.9 defines the main() method that initializes the variable upperBound with the value 20. Next, a loop iterates from 0 to upperBound, and during each iteration, the method findPrimeFactors() is involved with the current value of the loop variable num. Launch the code in Listing 2.8 and you will see the following output:

```
8  =  3 + 5
10 =  3 + 7
12 =  5 + 7
14 =  3 + 11
16 =  3 + 13
16 =  5 + 11
18 =  5 + 13
18 =  7 + 11
20 =  3 + 17
20 =  7 + 13
22 =  3 + 19
22 =  5 + 17
24 =  5 + 19
24 =  7 + 17
24 =  11 + 13
26 =  3 + 23
26 =  7 + 19
28 =  5 + 23
28 =  11 + 17
```

TASK: CALCULATE THE GCD (GREATEST COMMON DIVISOR)

Listing 2.18 displays the contents of GCD.java that illustrates how to calculate the GCD of two positive integers.

LISTING 2.18: GCD.java

```java
public class GCD
{
    public GCD() {}

    public int gcd(int num1, int num2)
    {
        if(num1 % num2 == 0) {
            return num2;
        }
        else if (num1 < num2) {
            System.out.println("Switching "+num1+" and "+num2);
            return gcd(num2, num1);
        }
        else {
            System.out.println("Reducing "+num1+" and "+num2);
            return gcd(num1-num2, num2);
        }
    }

    public static void main(String args[])
    {
        GCD g = new GCD();
```

```
      int result = g.gcd(24,10);
      System.out.println("The GCD of 24 and 10 = "+result);
    }
}
```

Listing 2.19 starts with a method `gcd()` that takes two integer-valued parameters num1 and num2. The first section of conditional logic checks if the remainder of num1 divided by num2 is zero: if so, then num2 is returned.

The second section of conditional logic checks if num1 is less than num2: if so, then the method gcd() is recursively invoked with the parameter values num2 and num1, and the result is returned.

The third section of conditional logic returns the result of a recursively invocation of the method gcd() with the parameter values num1-num2 and num2, and the result is returned.

The next portion of Listing 2.19 defines the `main()` method that instantiates the variable g as an instance of the GCD class. Next, the variable result is initialized with the result of invoking the gcd() method with the value 24 and 10, and then its value is printed. Launch the code in Listing 2.19 and you will see the following output:

```
gcd of 10 and 24 = 2
gcd of 24 and 10 = 2
gcd of 50 and 15 = 5
gcd of 17 and 17 = 17
gcd of 100 and 1250 = 50
```

Now that we can calculate the GCD of two positive integers, we can use this code to easily calculate the LCM (lowest common multiple) of two positive integers, as discussed in the next section.

TASK: CALCULATE THE LCM (LOWEST COMMON MULTIPLE)

Listing 2.20 displays the contents of `LCM.java` that illustrates how to calculate the LCM of two positive integers. Keep in mind that LCM(x,y) = (x*y)/GCD(x,y) for any positive integers x and y.

LISTING 2.20: LCM.java

```
public class LCM
{
    public LCM() {}

    public int gcd(int num1, int num2)
    {
        if(num1 % num2 == 0) {
            return num2;
        }
        else if (num1 < num2) {
            return gcd(num2, num1);
        }
        else {
            return gcd(num1-num2, num2);
```

```
        }
    }

    public int lcm(int num1, int num2)
    {
        int gcd1 = gcd(num1, num2);
        int lcm1 = num1*num2/gcd1;

        return lcm1;
    }

    public static void main(String args[])
    {
        LCM lcm1 = new LCM();
        int result = lcm1.lcm(24,10);
        System.out.println("The LCM of 24 and 10 = "+result);
    }
}
```

Listing 2.20 starts with a method gcd() that is identical to the method that is defined in Listing 2.19. The next portion of Listing 2.20 defines the method lcm() that takes parameters num1 and num2. This method the GCD of num1 and num2 and assigns the result to the variable gcd1. Next, the quantity num1*num2/gcd1 is calculated and assigned to the variable lcm1, which is then returned.

The next portion of Listing 2.20 defines the main() method that instantiates the variable lcm1 as an instance of the LCM class. Next, the variable result is initialized with the result of invoking the lcm() method with the value 24 and 10, and then its value is printed. Launch the code in Listing 2.20 and you will see the following output:

```
The LCM of 24 and 10 = 120
```

This concludes the portion of the chapter regarding recursion. The next section introduces you to combinatorics (a well-known branch of mathematics).

WHAT IS COMBINATORICS?

In simple terms, combinatorics involves finding formulas for counting the number of objects in a set. For example, how many different ways can five books can be ordered (i.e., displayed) on a bookshelf? The answer involves permutations, which in turn is a factorial value; in this case, the answer is 5! = 120.

As a second example, suppose how many different ways can you select three books from a shelf that contains five books? The answer to this question involves combinations. Keep in mind that if you select three books labeled A, B, and C, then any permutation of these three books is considered the same (the set A, B, and C and the set B, A, and C are considered the same selection).

As a third example, how many five-digit binary numbers contain exactly three 1 values? The answer to this question also involves calculating a combinatorial value. In case you're wondering, the answer is C(5,3) = 5!/[3! * 2!] = 10, provided that we allow for leading zeroes. In fact, this is also the answer to the preceding question about selecting different subsets of books.

You can generalize the previous question by asking how many four-digit, five-digit, and six-digit numbers contain exactly three 1s? The answer is the sum of these values (provided that leading zeroes are permitted):

```
C(4,3) + C(5,3) + C(6,3) = 4 + 10 + 20 = 34
```

Working With Permutations

Consider the following task: given six books, how many ways can you display them side by side? The possibilities are listed here:

position #1: 6 choices
position #2: 5 choices
position #3: 4 choices
position #4: 3 choices
position #5: 2 choices
position #6: 1 choices

The answer is 6x5x4x3x2x1 = 6! = 720. In general, if you have n books, there are n! different ways that you can order them (i.e., display them side by side).

Working With Combinations

Let's look at a slightly different question: how many ways can you select three books from those six books? Here's the first approximation:

position #1: 6 choices
position #2: 5 choices
position #3: 4 choices

Since the number of books in any position is independent of the other positions, the first answer might be 6x5x4 = 120. However, this answer is incorrect because it includes different orderings of three books; however, the sequence of books (A,B,C) is the same as (B,A,C) and every other recording of the letters A, B, and C.

As a concrete example, suppose that the books are labeled book #1, book #2, ..., book #6, and suppose that you select book #1, book #2, and book #3. Here list a list of all the different orderings of those three books:

```
123
132
213
231
312
321
```

The number of different orderings of three books is 3x2x1 = 3! = 6. However, from the standpoint of purely selecting three books, we must treat all six orderings as the same. Hence the correct answer is 6x5x4/[3x2x1] = 120/3! = 120/6 = 20.

Multiply the numerator and the denominator by 3x2x1, and the result is this number: 6x5x4x3x2x1/[3x2x1 * 3x2x1] = 6!/[3! * 3!].

If we perform the preceding task of selecting three books from eight books instead of six books, we get this result:

8x7x6/[3x2x1] = 8x7x6x5x4x3x2x1/[3x2x1 * 5x4x3x2x1] = 8!/[3! * 5!]

Now suppose you select twelve books from a set of thirty books. The number of ways that this can be done is shown here:

```
30x29x28x...x19/[12x11x...x2x1]
= 30x29x28x...x19x18x17x16x...x2x1/[12x11x...x2x1 * 18x17x16x...x2x1]
= 30!/[12! * 18!]
```

The general formula for calculating the number of ways to select k books from n books is n!/ [k! * (n-k)!], which is denoted by the term C(n,k). Incidentally, if we replace k by n-k in the preceding formula we get this result:

n!/[(n-k)! * (n-(n-k))!] = n!/[(n-k)! * k)!] = C(n,k)

Notice that the left side of the preceding snippet equals C(n,n-k), and therefore we have shown that C(n,n-k) = C(n,k).

THE NUMBER OF SUBSETS OF A FINITE SET

In the preceding section, if we allow k to vary from 0 to n inclusive, then we are effectively looking at all possible subsets of a set of n elements, and the number of such sets equals 2^n. We can derive the preceding result in two ways.

Solution #1.

The first way is the shortest explanation (and might seem like clever hand waving) and it involves visualizing a row of n books. In order to find every possible subset of those n books, we need only consider that there are two actions for the first position: either the book is selected or it is not selected.

Similarly, there are two actions for the second position: either the second book is selected or it is not selected. In fact, for every book in the set of n books there are the same two choices. Keeping in mind that the selection (or not) of a book in a given position is independent of the selection of the books in every other position, the number of possible choices equals 2x2x...x2 (n times) = 2^n.

Solution #2.

Recall the following formulas from algebra:

```
(x+y)^2 = x^2 + 2*x*y + y^2
        = C(2,0)*x^2 + C(2,1)*x*y + C(2,2)*y^2

(x+y)^3 = x^3 + 3*x^2*y + 3*x*y^2 + y^3
        = C(3,0)*x^3 + C(3,1)*x^2*y + C(3,2)*x*y^2 + C(3,3)*y^3
```

In general, we have the following formula:

```
             n
(x+y)^n =   SUM C(n,k)*x^k*y^(n-k)
            k=0
```

Set x=y=1 in the preceding formula and we get the following result:

```
        n
2^n =   SUM  C(n,k)
        k=0
```

The right-side of the preceding formula is the sum of the number of all possible subsets of a set of n elements, which the left side shows is equal to 2^n.

TASK: SUBSETS CONTAINING A VALUE LARGER THAN K

The more complete description of the task for this section is as follows: given a set N of numbers and a number k, find the number of subsets of N that contain at least one number that is larger than k. This *counting* task is an example of a coding task that can easily be solved as a combinatorial problem: you might be surprised to discover that the solution involves a single (and simple) line of code. Let's define the following set of variables:

```
N      = a set of numbers
|N|    = # of elements in N (= n)
NS     = the non-empty subsets of N
P(NS)  = the number of non-empty subsets of N (= |NS|)
M      = the numbers {n| n < k} where n is an element of N
|M|    = # of elements in M (= m)
MS     = the non-empty subsets of M
P(MS)  = the number of non-empty subsets of M (= |MS|)
Q      = subsets of N that contain at least one number larger than k
```

Note that the set NS is partitioned into the sets Q and M, and that the union of Q and M is NS. In other words, a nonempty subset of N is either in Q or in M, but not in both. Therefore, the solution to the task can be expressed as: |Q| = P(NS) – P(MS).

Moreover, the sets in M do not contain any number that is larger than k, which means that no element (i.e., subset) in M is an element of Q, and conversely, no element of Q is an element of M.

Recall from a previous result in this chapter that if a set contains m elements, then the number of subsets is $2^{**}m$, and the number of *non-empty* subsets is $2^{**}m - 1$. Hence, the answer for this task is $(2^{**}n - 1) - (2^{**}m - 1)$.

Listing 2.22 displays the contents of subarrays_max_k.py that calculates the sum of a set of binomial coefficients.

LISTING 2.22: SubarraysMaxK.java

```java
public class SubarraysMaxK
{
   //#############################################
   // N = a set with n elements
   // M = a set with m elements
   //
   // N has 2^n - 1 non-empty subsets
   // M has 2^m - 1 non-empty subsets
```

```
    //
    // O = subsets of N with at least one element > k
    // P = subsets of N with all numbers <= k
    //
    // |P| = 2**m-1
    // and |O| = |N| - |P| = (2**n-1) - (2**m-1)
    //###############################################

    // number of subarrays whose maximum element > k
    public static int count_subsets(int n, int m) {
      //System.out.println("n = "+n+" m = "+m);
      int count = (int)(Math.pow(2,n) - 1) - (int)(Math.pow(2,m) - 1);
      return count;
    }

    public static void main(String[] args)
    {
      //int[] arr = new int[]{ 1, 2, 3, 4, 5, 6, 7, 8 };
      int[] arr = new int[]{ 1, 2, 3, 4 };

      System.out.println("Array elements:");
      for (int num : arr)
        System.out.print(num+" ");
      System.out.println();

      int arr_len = arr.length;

      int[] arrk = new int[]{1, 2, 3, 4};
      for (int overk : arrk) {
        int count = count_subsets(arr_len, overk);

        System.out.println("overk:    "+overk);
        System.out.println("count:    "+count);
        System.out.println("--------------");
      }
    }
}
```

Listing 2.22 contains the `Java` code that implements the details that are described at the beginning of this section. Launch the code and you will see the following output:

```
Array elements:
1 2 3 4
overk:    1
count:    14
--------------
overk:    2
count:    12
--------------
overk:    3
count:    8
--------------
overk:    4
count:    0
--------------
```

Although the set N in Listing 2.22 contains a set of consecutive integers from 1 to n, the code works correctly for unsorted arrays or arrays that do not contain consecutive integers. In the latter case, you would need a code block to count the number of elements that are less than a given value of k.

SUMMARY

This chapter started with an introduction to recursion, along with various code samples that involve recursion, such as calculating factorial values, Fibonacci numbers, the sum of an arithmetic series, the sum of a geometric series, the GCD of a pair of positive integers, and the LCM of a pair of positive integers.

Moreover, you learned about concepts in combinatorics, and how to derive the formula for permutations and combinations of sets of objects.

CHAPTER 3

STRINGS AND ARRAYS

This chapter contains `Java`-based code samples that solving various tasks involving strings and arrays. The code samples in this chapter consists of the following sequence: examples that involve scalars and strings, followed by examples involving vectors (explained further at the end of this introduction), and then some examples involving 2D matrices. Note that the first half of Chapter 2 is relevant for the code samples in this chapter that involve recursion.

The first part of this chapter starts with a quick overview of the time complexity of algorithms, followed by various `Java` code samples, such as finding palindromes, reversing strings, and determining if the characters in a string unique.

The second part of this chapter discusses 2D arrays, along with `NumPy`-based code samples that illustrate various operations that can be performed on 2D matrices. This section also discusses 2D matrices, which are 2D arrays, along with some tasks that you can perform on them. This section also discusses multidimensional arrays, which have properties that are analogous to lower dimensional arrays.

One other detail to keep in mind pertains to the terms vectors and arrays. In mathematics, a vector is a one-dimensional construct, whereas an array has at least two dimensions. In software development, an array can refer to a one-dimensional array or a higher dimensional array (depending on the speaker). In this book a vector is always a one-dimensional construct. However, the term array always refers to a one-dimensional array; higher dimensional arrays will be referenced as "2D array," "3D array," and so forth. Therefore, the tasks involving 2D arrays start from the section titled "Working With 2D Arrays."

TIME AND SPACE COMPLEXITY

Algorithms are assessed in terms of the amount of space (based on input size) and the amount of time required for the algorithms to complete their execution, which is represented by "big O" notation. There are three types of time complexity: best case, average case, and worst case. Keep in mind that an algorithm with very good best case performance can have a relatively poor worse case performance.

Recall that O(n) means that an algorithm executes in linear time because its complexity is bounded above and below by a linear function. For example, if three algorithms require 2*n, 5*n, or n/2 operations, respectively, then all of them have O(n) complexity.

Moreover, if the best, average, and worst time performance for a linear search is 1, n/2, and n operations, respectively, then those operations have O(1), O(n), and O(n), respectively. In general, if there are two solutions T1 and T2 for a given task such T2 is more efficient than T1, then T2 requires either less time or less memory. For example, if T1 is an iterative solution for calculating factorial values (or Fibonacci numbers) and T2 involves a recursive solution, then T1 is more efficient than T2 in terms of time, but T1 also requires an extra array to store intermediate values.

The *time-space trade-off* refers to reducing either the amount of time or the amount of memory that is required for executing an algorithm, which involves choosing one of the following:

- execute in less time and more memory
- execute in more time and less memory

Although reducing both time and memory is desirable, it's also a more challenging task. Another point to keep in mind is the following inequalities (logarithms can be in any base that is greater than or equal to 2) for any positive integer n > 1:

```
O(log n) < O(n) < O(n*log n) < O(n^2)
```

In addition, the following inequalities with powers of n, powers of 2, and factorial values are also true:

```
O(n**2) < O(n**3) < O(2**n) < O(n!)
```

If you are unsure about any of the preceding inequalities, perform an online search for tutorials that provide the necessary details.

TASK: MAXIMUM AND MINIMUM POWERS OF AN INTEGER

The code sample in this section shows you how to calculate the largest (smallest) power of a number num whose base is k that is less than (greater than) num, where num and k are both positive integers.

For example, 16 is the largest power of two that is *less* than 24 and 32 is the smallest power of two that is *greater* than 24. As another example, 625 is the largest power of five that is *less* than 1000 and 3125 is the smallest power of five that is *greater* than 1000.

Listing 3.1 displays the contents of MaxMinPowerk2.java that illustrates how to calculate the largest (smallest) power of a number whose base is k that is less than (greater than) a given number. Just to be sure that the task is clear: num and k are positive integers, and the purpose of this task is two-fold:

- find the *largest* number powk such that k**powk <= num
- find the *smallest* number powk such that k**powk >= num

LISTING 3.1: MaxMinPowerk2.java

```java
public class MaxMinPowerk2
{
    public static int[] MaxMinPowerk(int num, int k)
    {
        int powk = 1;
        while(powk <= num)
        {
            powk *= k;
        }

        if(powk > num) powk /= k;

        return new int[]{(int)powk, (int)powk*k};
    }

    public static void main(String[] args)
    {
        int lowerk, upperk;
        int[] nums = new int[]{24,17,1000};
        int[] powers = new int[]{2,3,4,5};

        for(int num : nums)
        {
            for(int k : powers)
            {
                int[] results = max_min_powerk(num, k);
                lowerk = results[0];
                upperk = results[1];
                System.out.println("num: "+num+" lower "+lowerk+" upper: "+upperk);
            }

            System.out.println();
        }
    }
}
```

Listing 3.1 starts with the function MaxMinPowerk() that contains a loop that repeatedly multiplies the local variable powk (initialized with the value 1) by k. When powk exceeds the parameter num, then powk is divided by k so that we have the lower bound solution.

Note that this function returns powk *and* powk*k because this pair of numbers is the lower bound and higher bound solutions for this task. Launch the code in Listing 3.1 and you will see the following output:

```
num: 24 lower 16 upper: 32
num: 24 lower 9 upper: 27
num: 24 lower 16 upper: 64
num: 24 lower 5 upper: 25
```

```
num: 17 lower 16 upper: 32
num: 17 lower 9 upper: 27
num: 17 lower 16 upper: 64
num: 17 lower 5 upper: 25

num: 1000 lower 512 upper: 1024
num: 1000 lower 729 upper: 2187
num: 1000 lower 256 upper: 1024
num: 1000 lower 625 upper: 3125
```

TASK: BINARY SUBSTRINGS OF A NUMBER

Listing 3.2 displays the contents of the BinaryNumbers.java that illustrates how to display all binary substrings whose length is less than or equal to a given number.

LISTING 3.2: BinaryNumbers.java

```java
public class BinaryNumbers
{
    public static void binary_values(int width)
    {
        System.out.println("Binary values of width "+width+":");

        String bin_value = "";
        int power = (int)java.lang.Math.pow(2,width);

        for(int i=0; i<power; i++)
        {
            bin_value = Integer.toBinaryString(i);
            System.out.println(bin_value);
        }
        System.out.println("");
    }

    public static void main(String[] args)
    {
        int max_width = 4;
        for (int i=1; i<max_width; i++) {
            //System.out.print(el + " ");
            binary_values(i);
        }
    }
}
```

Listing 3.2 starts with the function binary_values() whose loop iterates from 0 to 2**width, where width is the parameter for this function. The loop variable is i, and during each iteration bin_value is initialized with the binary value of i.

Next, the variable str_value is the string-based value of bin_value, which is stripped of the two leading characters 0b. Launch the code in Listing 3.2 and you will see the following output:

```
Binary values of width 1:
0
1
Binary values of width 2:
0
1
10
11

Binary values of width 3:
0
1
10
11
100
101
110
111
```

TASK: COMMON SUBSTRING OF TWO BINARY NUMBERS

Listing 3.3 displays the contents of CommonBits.java that illustrates how to find the longest common substring of two binary strings.

LISTING 3.3: CommonBits.java

```java
public class CommonBits
{
    public static int commonBits(int num1, int num2)
    {
        String bin_str1 = Integer.toBinaryString(num1);
        String bin_str2 = Integer.toBinaryString(num2);

        if(bin_str2.length() < bin_str1.length())
        {
            while(bin_str2.length() < bin_str1.length())
                bin_str2 = "0" + bin_str2;
        }

        if(bin_str1.length() < bin_str2.length())
        {
            while(bin_str1.length() < bin_str2.length())
                bin_str1 = "0" + bin_str1;
        }

        System.out.println(num1+"="+bin_str1);
        System.out.println(num2+"="+bin_str2);

        int common = 0;
        String common_bits2 = "";
        for(int i=0; i<bin_str1.length(); i++)
        {
            if((bin_str1.charAt(i) == bin_str2.charAt(i)) &&
                (bin_str1.charAt(i) =='1'))
```

```
            {
                common_bits2 = common_bits2 + "1";
                common++;
            }
        }
        return common;
    }

    public static void main(String[] args)
    {
        int[] nums1 = new int[]{61,28, 7,100,189};
        int[] nums2 = new int[]{51,14,28,110, 14};

        for(int idx=0; idx<nums1.length; idx++)
        {
          int num1 = nums1[idx];
          int num2 = nums2[idx];
          int common = commonBits(num1, num2);

          System.out.println(
              num1+" and "+num2+" have "+common+" bits in common\n");
        }
    }
}
```

Listing 3.3 starts with the function commonBits() that initializes the binary strings bin_str1 and bin_str2 with the binary values of the two input parameters. The next two loops left-pad the strings bin_str1 and bin_str2 to ensure that they have the same number of digits.

The next portion of Listing 3.3 is a loop iterates from 0 to the length of the string bin_str1 in order to compare each digit to the corresponding digit in bit_str2 to see if they are both equal and also equal to 1. Each time that the digit 1 is found, the value of common (initialized with the value 0) is incremented. When the loop terminates, the variable common equals the number of common bits in bin_num1 and bin_num2.

The final portion of Listing 3.3 is the main() method that initializes two arrays with integer values, followed by a loop that iterates through these two arrays in order to count the number of common bits in each pair of numbers. Launch the code in Listing 3.3 and you will see the following output:

```
61=111101
51=110011
61 and 51 have 3 bits in common

28=11100
14=01110
28 and 14 have 2 bits in common

7=00111
28=11100
7 and 28 have 1 bits in common

100=1100100
110=1101110
```

```
100 and 110 have 3 bits in common
189=10111101
14=00001110
189 and 14 have 2 bits in common
```

TASK: MULTIPLY AND DIVIDE VIA RECURSION

Listing 3.4 displays the contents of the RecursiveMultiply.java that illustrates how to compute the product of two positive integers via recursion.

LISTING 3.4: RecursiveMultiply.java

```java
class RecursiveMultiply
{
    public static int add_repeat(int num, int times, int sum)
    {
        if(times == 0)
            return sum;

        return add_repeat(num, times-1, num+sum);
    }

    public static void main(String args[])
    {
        int[] arr1 = {9,13,25,17,100};
        int[] arr2 = {5,10,25,10,100};

        for(int i=0; i<arr1.length; i++) {
            int num1 = arr1[i];
            int num2 = arr2[i];
            int prod = add_repeat(num1, num2, 0);
            System.out.println("remainder of "+num1+"/"+num2+" = "+prod);
        }
    }
}
```

Listing 3.4 starts with the function add_repeat(num,times,sum) that performs repeated addition by recursively invokes itself. Note that this function uses tail recursion: each invocation of the function replaces times with times-1 and also replaces sum with num+sum (the latter is the tail recursion). The terminating condition is when times equals 0, at which point the function returns the value of sum. Launch the code in Listing 3.4 and you will see the following output:

```
product of 5 and 9 = 45
product of 13 and 10 = 130
product of 25 and 25 = 625
product of 17 and 10 = 170
product of 100 and 100 = 10000
```

Listing 3.5 displays the contents of the RecursiveDivide.java that illustrates how to compute the quotient of two positive integers via recursion.

LISTING 3.5: RecursiveDivide.java

```java
class RecursiveDivide
{
   public static int sub_repeat(int num1, int num2, int remainder)
   {
      if(num1 < num2)
        return num1;
      else
        //print("num1-num2:",num1-num2,"num2:",num2)
        return sub_repeat(num1-num2, num2, remainder);
   }

   public static void main(String args[])
   {
      int[] arr1 = {9,13,25,17,100};
      int[] arr2 = {5,10,25,10,100};

      for(int i=0; i<arr1.length; i++) {
         int num1 = arr1[i];
         int num2 = arr2[i];
         int prod = sub_repeat(num1, num2, 0);
         System.out.println("remainder of "+num1+"/"+num2+" = "+prod);
      }
   }
}
```

Listing 3.5 contains code that is very similar to Listing 3.4: the difference involves replacing addition with subtraction. Launch the code in Listing 3.5 and you will see the following output:

```
remainder of 9 / 5 = 4
remainder of 13 / 10 = 3
remainder of 25 / 25 = 0
remainder of 17 / 10 = 7
remainder of 100 / 100 = 0
```

TASK: SUM OF PRIME AND COMPOSITE NUMBERS

Listing 3.6 displays the contents of the PairSumSorted.java that illustrates how to determine whether or not a sorted array contains the sum of two specified numbers.

LISTING 3.6: PairSumSorted.java

```java
//given two numbers num1 and num2 in a sorted array,
//determine whether or not num1+num2 is in the array

public class PairSumSorted
{
   public static void check_sum(int[] arr1,int num1,int num2)
   {
      int ndx1 = 0;
      int ndx2 = arr1.length-1;
      //System.out.println("Anum1: "+num1+" num2: "+num2);
```

```java
      while(arr1[ndx1] < num1)
        ndx1 += 1;
      //System.out.println("Bndx1: "+ndx1+" ndx2: "+ndx2);

      int sum = num1+num2;
      while(arr1[ndx2] > num2)
        ndx2 -= 1;

      System.out.print("Array: ");
      for(int i=0; i< arr1.length; i++) {
        System.out.print(arr1[i]+" ");
      }
      System.out.println("");

      //System.out.println("Cndx1: "+ndx1+" ndx2: "+ndx2);
      System.out.println("num1:  "+num1+" num2: "+num2);
      System.out.println("ndx1:  "+ndx1+" ndx2: "+ndx2);
      /* NOTE: arr1[ndx1] >= num1 AND arr1[ndx2] >= sum */

      if(arr1[ndx1]+arr1[ndx2] == sum)
        System.out.println(
          "=> FOUND sum "+sum+" for ndx1 = "+ndx1+" ndx2 = "+ndx2);
      else
        System.out.println("=> NOT FOUND "+sum);
      System.out.println();
   }

   public static void main(String args[])
   {
      int[] arr1 = { 20,50,100,120,150,200,250,300 };
      int num1 = 60;
      int num2 = 90;
      check_sum(arr1,num1,num2);

      num1 = 60;
      num2 = 100;
      check_sum(arr1,num1,num2);

      int[] arr2 = { 3,3 };
      num1 = 3;
      num2 = 3;
      check_sum(arr2,num1,num2);
   }
}
```

Listing 3.6 starts with the method `check_sum()` that determines whether or the sum of num1 and num2 is an element in the array arr1. The "left index" ndx1 has the initial value 0, and it's incremented as long as `arr1[ndx1] < num1`. In an analogous manner, the "right index" ndx2 has the initial value equal to the number of elements in the array arr1, and it's decremented as long as `arr1[ndx2] > num2`.

The next portion of code in Listing 3.6 contains conditional logic that checks whether or not the sum of arr1[ndx1] and arr1[ndx2] equals the value of sum, and then prints an appropriate message.

Launch the code in Listing 3.6 and you will see the following output:

```
num1: 60 num2:90
ndx1: 2  ndx2: 1
=> FOUND sum 150 for ndx1=2 ndx2=1

num1: 60 num2:100
ndx1: 2  ndx2: 2
=> NOT FOUND 160

num1: 3 num2: 3
ndx1: 0 ndx2: 1
=> FOUND sum 6 for ndx1=0ndx2=1
```

The next portion of this chapter contains various examples of string-related tasks. If need be, you can review the relevant portion of Chapter 1 regarding some of the Java built-in string functions, such as int() and len().

TASK: COUNT WORD FREQUENCIES

Listing 3.7 displays the contents of the WordFrequency.java that illustrates how to determine the frequency of each word in an array of sentences.

LISTING 3.7: WordFrequency.java

```java
import java.util.ArrayList;
import java.util.Arrays;
import java.util.Hashtable;
import java.util.Enumeration;

public class WordFrequency
{
   public static void main(String[] args)
   {
      String[] sent1 =
        new String[]{"I", "love", "thick", "pizza"};
      String[] sent2 =
        new String[]{"I", "love", "deep", "dish","pizza"};
      String[] sent3 =
        new String[]{"Pepperoni","and","sausage","pizza"};
      String[] sent4 =
        new String[]{"Pizza", "with", "mozzarrella"};

      ArrayList<String> sents =
        new ArrayList<String>(Arrays.asList(sent1));
      sents.addAll(Arrays.asList(sent2));
      sents.addAll(Arrays.asList(sent3));
      sents.addAll(Arrays.asList(sent4));

      ArrayList<String> words = new ArrayList<String>();
      ArrayList<String> tokens = new ArrayList<String>();
```

```
Hashtable<String,Integer> ht = new Hashtable<String,Integer>();

for(int idx=0; idx<sents.size(); idx++)
{
    String word = sents.get(idx);
    tokens.add(word);

    // remove this snippet if you want case sensitivity:
    word = word.toLowerCase();

    if (!ht.contains(word)) {
      ht.put(word,0);
    }
    int count = ht.get(word);
    ht.put(word,count+1);
}
//System.out.println("tokens: "+tokens);

Enumeration enumer = ht.keys();

System.out.println("Words and their frequency:");
while (enumer.hasMoreElements()) {
    String key = (String)enumer.nextElement();
    System.out.println("key: "+key+" occurrences: "+ht.get(key));
}
    }
}
```

Listing 3.7 starts with the main() method that initializes the string arrays sent1, sent2, sent3, and sent4 with various text strings, after which these arrays are appended to the variable sents that is an instance of the Java class ArrayList.

The next portion of Listing 3.7 instantiates the variable ht that is an instance of the Java Hashtable class. Next, a loop iterates through the tokens (words) in sents converts them to lowercase, after which the latter word is added to the hash table ht. Notice that the number of occurrences of each lowercase word is also incremented so that we can count the frequency of each word.

The final portion of Listing 3.7 contains a loop that displays each word in ht, along with its frequency. Launch the code in Listing 3.7 and you will see the following output:

```
Words and their frequency:
key: dish occurrences: 1
key: pepperoni occurrences: 1
key: i occurrences: 1
key: and occurrences: 1
key: thick occurrences: 1
key: love occurrences: 1
key: sausage occurrences: 1
key: pizza occurrences: 1
key: deep occurrences: 1
key: with occurrences: 1
key: mozzarrella occurrences: 1
```

TASK: CHECK IF A STRING CONTAINS UNIQUE CHARACTERS

The solution involves keeping track of the number of occurrences of each ASCII character in a string, and returning False if that number is greater than 1 for any character (otherwise return True). Hence, one constraint for this solution is that it's restricted to Indo-European languages that do not have accent marks.

Listing 3.8 displays the contents of UniqueChars.java that illustrates how to determine whether or not a string contains unique letters.

LISTING 3.8: UniqueChars.java

```
//128 characters for ASCII and 256 characters for extended ASCII
public class UniqueChars
{
   public static Boolean unique_chars(String str)
   {
     boolean result = false;
     if (str.length() > 128)
       return result;

     str = str.toLowerCase();

     int[] char1_set = new int[128];

     for(int idx=0; idx<str.length(); idx++)
     {
       char char1 = str.charAt(idx);
       int val = 'z' - char1; // # error
       //System.out.println("val: "+val);

       if (char1_set[val] == 1)
         return result;
       else
         char1_set[val] = 1;
     }

     return !result;
   }

   public static void main(String[] args)
   {
     String[] arr1 =
       new String[]{"a string", "second string", "hello world"};

     for(String str : arr1)
     {
       System.out.println("string: "+str);
       boolean result = unique_char1s(str);
       System.out.println("unique: "+result);
       System.out.println();
     }
   }
}
```

Listing 3.8 starts with the function `unique_chars()` that converts its parameter `str` to low-ercase letters and then initializes the 1x128 integer array `char_set` whose values are all 0. The next portion of this function iterates through the characters of the string `str` and initializes the integer variable `val` with the offset position of each character from the character `z`.

If this position in `char_set` equals 1, then a duplicate character has been found; otherwise, this position is initialized with the value 1. Note that the value `False` is returned if the string `str` contains duplicate letters, whereas the value `True` is returned if the string str contains unique characters. Launch the code in Listing 3.8 and you will see the following output:

```
string: a string
unique: True

string: second string
unique: False

string: hello world
unique: False
```

TASK: INSERT CHARACTERS IN A STRING

Listing 3.9 displays the contents of `InsertChars.java` that illustrates how to insert each character of one string in every position of another string.

LISTING 3.9: InsertChars.java

```java
import java.io.*;
import java.util.*;

public class InsertChars
{
   public static String insertChar(String str1, char chr)
   {
     String inserted="", left="", right="", result = str1;

     result = chr + str1;
     for(int i=0;i<str1.length(); i++)
     {
        left  = str1.substring(0,i+1);
        right = str1.substring(i+1);
        inserted = left + chr + right;
     }

     result = result + " " + inserted;
     return result;
   }

   public static void main(String[] args)
   {
      String str1 = "abc";
      String str2 = "def";
      System.out.println("str1: "+str1);
      System.out.println("str2: "+str2);
```

```
        String newStr="", insertions = "";
        for(int i=0; i<str2.length(); i++)
        {
            newStr = insertChar(str1, str2.charAt(i));
            insertions = insertions+ " " + newStr;
        }

        System.out.println("result:"+insertions);
    }
}
```

Listing 3.9 starts with the function insertChar() that has a string str1 and a character chr as input parameters. The next portion of code is a loop whose loop variable is i, which is used to split the string str1 into two strings: the left substring from positions 0 to i, and the right substring from position i+1. A new string with three components is constructed: the left string, the character chr, and the right string.

The next portion of Listing 3.9 contains a loop that iterates through each character of str2; during each iteration, the code invokes insert_char() with string str1 and the current character. The number of new strings generated by this code equals the following product: (len(str1)+1)*len(str2).

Launch the code in Listing 3.9 and you will see the following output:

```
str1: abc
str2: def
result:  dabc adbc abdc abcd eabc aebc abec abce fabc afbc abfc abcf
```

TASK: STRING PERMUTATIONS

There are several ways to determine whether or not two strings are permutations of each other. One way involves sorting the strings alphabetically: if the resulting strings are equal, then they are permutations of each other.

A second technique is to determine whether or not they have the same number of occurrences for each character. A third way is to add the numeric counterpart of each letter in the string: if the numbers are equal and the strings have the same length, then they are permutations of each other.

Listing 3.10 displays the contents of the StringPermute.java that illustrates how to determine whether or not two strings are permutations of each other.

LISTING 3.10: StringPermute.java

```
import java.util.Arrays;

public class StringPermute
{
    public static void permute(String str1,String str2)
    {
        char temp1[] = str1.toCharArray();
        char temp2[] = str2.toCharArray();
```

```
        Arrays.sort(temp1);
        Arrays.sort(temp2);

        String str1d = new String(temp1);
        String str2d = new String(temp1);
        Boolean permute = (str1d == str2d);

        System.out.println("string1: "+str1);
        System.out.println("string2: "+str2);
        System.out.println("permuted:"+permute);
        System.out.println();
    }
    public static void main(String[] args)
    {
        String[] strings1 = new String[]{"abcdef", "abcdef"};
        String[] strings2 = new String[]{"efabcf", "defabc"};

        for(int idx=0; idx<strings1.length; idx++) {
            String str1 = strings1[idx];
            String str2 = strings2[idx];
            permute(str1,str2);
        }
    }
}
```

Listing 3.10 starts with the function `permute()` that takes the two strings `str1` and `str2` as parameters. Next, the strings `str1d` and `str2d` are initialized with the result of sorting the characters in the strings `str1` and `str2`, respectively. At this point, we can determine whether or not `str1` and `str2` are permutations of each other by determining whether or not the two strings `str1d` and `str2d` are equal. Launch the code in Listing 3.10 and you will see the following output:

```
string1:  abcdef
string2:  efabcf
permuted: False

string1:  abcdef
string2:  defabc
permuted: True
```

TASK: CHECK FOR PALINDROMES

One way to determine whether or not a string is a palindrome is to compare the string with the reverse of the string: if the two strings are equal, then the string is a palindrome. Moreover, there are two ways to reverse a string: one way involves the Java `reverse()` function, and another way is to process the characters in the given string in a right-to-left fashion, and to append each character to a new string.

Another technique involves iterating through the characters in a left-to-right fashion and compares each character with its corresponding character that is based on iterating through the string in a right-to-left fashion.

Listing 3.11 displays the contents of the `Palindrome1.java` that illustrates how to determine whether or not a string or a positive integer is a palindrome.

LISTING 3.11: Palindrome1.java

```java
public class Palindrome1
{
    public static Boolean palindrome1(String str) {
        int full_len = str.length();
        int half_len = str.length()/2;

        for(int i=0; i<half_len; i++) {
            char lchar = str.charAt(i);
            char rchar = str.charAt(full_len-1-i);
            if(lchar != rchar)
                return false;
        }
        return true;
    }

    public static void main(String[] args)
    {
        String[] arr1 = new String[]{"rotor", "tomato", "radar","maam"};
        String[] arr2 = new String[]{"123", "12321", "555"};

        // CHECK FOR STRING PALINDROMES:
        for(String str : arr1)
        {
            Boolean result = palindrome1(str);
            System.out.println("String: "+str+ " palindrome: "+result);
        }

        // CHECK FOR NUMERIC PALINDROMES:
        for(String num : arr2)
        {
            System.out.print("Number: "+num);
            String str1 = num;
            String str2 = "";
            for(int i=0; i<str1.length(); i++) {
                str2 = str2 + str1.charAt(i);
            }

            Boolean result = palindrome1(str2);
            System.out.println(" palindrome:  "+result);
        }
    }
}
```

Listing 3.11 starts with the function `palindrome1()` with parameter `str` that is a string. This function contains a loop that starts by comparing the left-most character with the right-most character of the string `str`. The next iteration of the loop advances to the second position of the left-side of the string and compares that character with the character whose position is second from the right end of the string. This step-by-step comparison continues until the middle of the string is reached. During each iteration of the loop, the value `False` is returned if the pair of characters is different. If all pairs of characters are equal, then the string must be a palindrome, in which case the value `True` is returned.

The next portion of Listing 3.11 contains an array `arr1` of strings and an array `arr2` of positive integers. Next, another loop iterates through the elements of `arr1` and invokes the `palindrome1` function to determine whether or not the current element of `arr1` is a palindrome. Similarly, a second loop iterates through the elements of `arr2` and invokes the `palindrome1` function to determine whether or not the current element of `arr2` is a palindrome. Launch the code in Listing 3.11 and you will see the following output:

```
String: rotor palindrome: true
String: tomato palindrome: false
String: radar palindrome: true
String: maam palindrome: true
Number: 123 palindrome:  false
Number: 12321 palindrome:  true
Number: 555 palindrome:  true
```

TASK: CHECK FOR LONGEST PALINDROME

This section extends the code in the previous section by examining substrings of a given string. Listing 3.12 displays the contents of `LongestPalindrome.java` that illustrates how to determine the longest palindrome in a given string. Note that a single character is always a palindrome, which means that every string has a substring that is a palindrome (in fact, any single character in any string is a palindrome).

LISTING 3.12: LongestPalindrome.java

```java
public class LongestPalindrome1
{
    public static String check_string(String str)
    {
      int result = 0; // 0 = palindrome 1 = not palindrome
      int str_len  = str.length();
      int str_len2 = str.length()/2;

      for(int i=0; i<str_len2; i++) {
        if(str.charAt(i) != str.charAt(str_len-i-1)) {
          result = 1;
          break;
        }
      }

      if(result == 0)
        return str;
      else
        return "";
```

```
    }

    public static Boolean palindrome1(String str)
    {
      int full_len = str.length();
      int half_len = str.length()/2;

      for(int i=0; i<half_len; i++) {
        char lchar = str.charAt(i);
        char rchar = str.charAt(full_len-1-i);
        if(lchar != rchar)
          return false;
      }
      return true;
    }
    public static void main(String[] args)
    {
        String[] my_strings = new String[]
            {"abc","abb","abccba","azaaza","abcdefgabccbax"};

        String max_pal_str = "";
        int max_pal_len = 0;
        String sub_str = "";

        for(String my_str : my_strings) {
          max_pal_str = "";
          max_pal_len = 0;
          int my_str_len = my_str.length();

          for(int i=0; i<my_str.length()-1; i++) {
            for(int j=1; j<my_str.length()-i+1; j++) {
                sub_str = my_str.substring(i,i+j);
                String a_str = check_string(sub_str);

                if(a_str != "") {
                  if(max_pal_len < a_str.length()) {
                    max_pal_len = a_str.length();
                    max_pal_str = a_str;
                  }
                }
            }
          }
        System.out.println("string: "+my_str);
        System.out.println("maxpal: "+max_pal_str);
        System.out.println();
      }
    }
}
```

Listing 3.12 contains logic that is very similar to Listing 3.11. However, the main difference is that there is a loop that checks if *substrings* of a given string are palindromes. The code also keeps track of the longest palindrome and then prints its value and its length when the loop finishes execution.

Note that it's possible for a string to contain multiple palindrome of maximal length: the code in Listing 3.12 finds only the first such palindrome. However, it might be a good exercise to modify the code in Listing 3.12 to find all palindromes of maximal length. Launch the code in Listing 3.12 and you will see the following output:

```
string: abc
maxpal: a

string: abb
maxpal: bb

string: abccba
maxpal: abccba
string: azaaza
maxpal: azaaza

string: abcdefgabccbax
maxpal: abccba
```

WORKING WITH SEQUENCES OF STRINGS

This section contains `Java` code samples that search strings to determine the following:

- The maximum length of a sequence of consecutive 1s in a string.
- Find a given sequence of characters in a string.
- The maximum length of a sequence of unique characters.

After you complete this section, you can explore variations of these tasks that you can solve using the code samples in this section.

The Maximum Length of a Repeated Character in a String

Listing 3.13 displays the contents of `MaxCharSequence.java` that illustrates how to find the maximal length of a repeated character in a string.

LISTING 3.13: MaxCharSequence.java

```java
public class MaxCharSequence
{
    public static void max_seq(String my_str,char ch)
    {
        int max = 0, left = 0, right = 0, counter = 0;
        for(int i=0; i<my_str.length(); i++) {
            char curr_ch = my_str.charAt(i);
```

```
          if(curr_ch == ch) {
            counter += 1;
            right = i;
            if(max < counter)
              max = counter;
              //System.out.println("new max:",max)
          } else {
            counter = 0;
            left = i;
            right = i;
          }
        }

      System.out.println("my_str: "+my_str);
      System.out.println("max sequence of "+ch+": "+max);
      System.out.println();
    }
    public static void main(String[] args)
    {
      String[] str_list   = new String[]
                    {"abcdef","aaaxyz","abcdeeefghij"};

      String[] char_list = new String[]{"a","a","e"};

      for(int idx=0; idx<str_list.length; idx++) {
          String my_str = str_list[idx];
          String str    = char_list[idx];
          char ch       = char_list[idx].charAt(0);
          max_seq(my_str,ch);
      }
    }
}
```

Listing 3.13 starts with the function max_seq() whose parameters are a string my_str and a character char. This function contains a loop that iterates through each character of my_str and performs a comparison with char. As long as the characters equal char, the value of the variables right and counter are incremented: right represents the right-most index and counter contains the length of the substring containing the same character.

However, if a character in my_str differs from char, then counter is reset to 0, and left is reset to the value of right, and the comparison process begins anew. When the loop has completed execution, the variable counter equals the length of the longest substring consisting of equal characters.

The next portion of Listing 3.13 initializes the array str_list that contains a list of strings and the array char_list with a list of characters. The final loop iterates through the elements of str_list and invokes the function max_seq() with the current string and the corresponding character in the array char_list. Launch the code in Listing 3.13 and you will see the following output:

```
my_str: abcdef
max sequence of a: 1
```

```
my_str: aaaxyz
max sequence of a: 3

my_str: abcdeeefghij
max sequence of e: 3
```

Find a Given Sequence of Characters in a String

Listing 3.14 displays the contents of MaxSubstrSequence.java that illustrates how to find the right-most substring that matches a given string.

LISTING 3.14: MaxSubstrSequence.java

```java
public class MaxSubstrSequence
{
    public static void rightmost_substr(String my_str,String substr)
    {
        int left = -1;
        int len_substr = substr.length();
        System.out.println("initial substr: "+substr);

        // check for substr from right to left:
        for(int i=my_str.length()-len_substr; i>=0; i--) {
            //String curr_str = my_str[i:i+len_substr];
            String curr_str = my_str.substring(i,i+len_substr);

            if(substr.equals(curr_str)) {
                left = i;
                break;
            }
        }

        if(left >= 0)
            System.out.println(
                substr+" is in index "+left+" of: "+my_str);
        else
            System.out.println(
                substr+" does not appear in "+my_str);
        System.out.println();
    }

    public static void main(String[] args)
    {
        String[] str_list    =
                new String[]{"abcdef","aaaxyz","abcdeeefghij"};

        String[] substr_list = new String[]{"bcd","aaa","cde"};

        for(int idx=0; idx<str_list.length; idx++) {
            String my_str = str_list[idx];
            String substr = substr_list[idx];
            rightmost_substr(my_str,substr);
```

```
            }
        }
    }
```

Listing 3.14 starts with the function `rightmost_substr` whose parameters are a string `my_str` and a substring `sub_str`. This function contains a loop that performs a right-most comparison of `my_str` and `sub_str`, and iteratively moves leftward one position until the loop reaches the first index position of the string `my_str`.

After the loop has completed its execution, the variable `left` contains the index position at which there is a match between `my_str` and `sub_str`, and its value will be nonnegative. If there is no matching substring, then the variable `left` will retain its initial value of -1. In either case, the appropriate message is printed. Launch the code in Listing 3.14 and you will see the following output:

```
initial substr: bcd
bcd is in index 1 of: abcdef
initial substr: aaa
aaa is in index 0 of: aaaxyz

initial substr: cde
cde is in index 2 of: abcdeeefghij
```

TASK: LONGEST SEQUENCES OF SUBSTRINGS

This section contains `Java` code samples that search strings to determine the following:

• the longest subsequence of unique characters in a given string
• the longest subsequence that is repeated in a given string

After you complete this section you can explore variations of these tasks that you can solve using the code samples in this section.

The Longest Sequence of Unique Characters

Listing 3.15 displays the contents of `LongestUnique.java` that illustrates how to find the longest sequence of unique characters in a string.

LISTING 3.15: LongestUnique.java

```java
import java.util.Hashtable;

public class LongestUnique
{
    public static void rightmost_substr(String my_str)
    {
        int left = 0, right = 0;
        String sub_str = "", longest = "";
        Hashtable<String, Integer> ht = new Hashtable<String,Integer>();

        for(int pos=0; pos<my_str.length(); pos++) {
```

```
    String ch_str = "" + my_str.charAt(pos);

    Integer count = 0;
    if (ht.containsKey(ch_str))
      count = ht.get(ch_str);

    if (count > 0) {
      ht = new Hashtable<String,Integer>();
      left = pos+1;
      right = pos+1;
    } else {
      ht.put(ch_str, 1);

      String unique = my_str.substring(left,pos+1);
      //System.out.println("unique string: "+unique);

      if(longest.length() < unique.length()) {
        longest = unique;
        right = pos;
      } else {
        //System.out.println("new hashtable:");
        ht = new Hashtable<String,Integer>();
        left = pos+1;
        right = pos+1;
      }
    }
  }

  System.out.println("original string: "+my_str);
  System.out.println("longest unique:  "+longest);
}

public static void main(String[] args)
{
  //String [] str_list = new String[]{"ACCC"};
  String [] str_list =
    new String[]{"abcdef","aaaxyz","abcdeeefghij"};

  for(int idx=0; idx<str_list.length; idx++) {
    String my_str = str_list[idx];
    rightmost_substr(my_str);
  }
}
}
```

Listing 3.15 starts with the function `rightmost_substr` whose parameter is a string `my_str`. This function contains a right-to-left loop and stores the character in the current index position in the dictionary `my_dict`. If the character has already been encountered, then it's a duplicate character, at which point the length of the current substring is compared with the length of the longest substring that has been found thus far, at which point the variable `longest` is updated with the new value. In addition, the left position `left` and the right position `right` are reset to `pos+1`, and the search for a unique substring begins anew.

After the loop has completed its execution, the value of the variable `longest` equals the length of the longest substring of unique characters.

The next portion of Listing 3.15 initializes the variable `str_list` as an array of strings, followed by a loop that iterates through the elements of `str_list`. The function `right-most_substr()` is invoked during each iteration in order to find the longest unique substring of the current string. Launch the code in Listing 3.15 and you will see the following output:

```
checking: abcdef
longest unique: abcdef

checking: aaaxyz
longest unique: axyz

checking: abcdeeefghij
longest unique: efghij
```

The Longest Repeated Substring

Listing 3.16 displays the contents of `MaxRepeatedSubstr.java` that illustrates how to find the longest substring that is repeated in a given string.

LISTING 3.16: MaxRepeatedSubstr.java

```java
public class MaxRepeatedSubstr
{
   public static String[] check_string(String my_str, String sub_str,
int pos)
   {
     String match = "", part_str = "";
     int left = 0, right = 0;

     int str_len = my_str.length();
     int sub_len = sub_str.length();
     //System.out.println("my_str: "+my_str+" sub_str: "+sub_str);

     for(int i=0; i<str_len-sub_len-pos; i++) {
       left  = pos+sub_len+i;
       right = left+sub_len;
       //System.out.println("left: "+left+" right: "+right);

       if(right > str_len) {
         //System.out.println("right too large: "+right);
         break;
       }

       part_str = my_str.substring(left,right);

       if(part_str.equals(sub_str)) {
```

```
            match = part_str;
            break;
        }
    }
}

    return new String[]{match,Integer.toString(left)};
}

public static void main(String[] args)
{
    System.out.println("==> Repeating substrings have length >= 2");
    String [] my_strings =
    new String[]{"abc","abab","abccba","azaaza","abcdefgabccbaxyz"};

    for(String my_str : my_strings) {
        System.out.println("=> Checking current string:      "+my_str);
        int half_len = (int)(my_str.length()/2);
        int max_len = 0;
        String max_str = "";

        for(int i=0; i<half_len+1; i++) {
          for(int j=2; j<half_len+1; j++) {
            String sub_str = my_str.substring(i,i+j);
            String[] result = check_string(my_str, sub_str,i);
            String a_str = result[0];
            int left     = Integer.parseInt(result[1]);

            if(a_str != "") {
             if(max_len < a_str.length()) {
                max_len = a_str.length();
                max_str = a_str;
              }
            }
          }
        }

        if(max_str != "")
            System.out.println("=> Maximum repeating substring: "+max_
str+"\n");
        else
            System.out.println("No maximum repeating substring: "+my_
str+"\n");
    }
  }
}
```

Listing 3.16 starts with the function check_string() that checks whether or not the string sub_str is a substring of my_str whose lengths are assigned to the integer variables sub_len and str_len, respectively. The next portion of Listing 3.16 consists of a loop that iterates through the characters in the string substr whose index position is at most str_len-sub_len-pos so that it does not exceed the length of substr. Notice that the loop uses a "sliding window" to compare a substring of my_str whose length equals the length of sub_str: if they are equal than a repeated string exists in my_str, and the results are returned.

The next portion of Listing 3.16 defines the `main()` method that starts by initialing the string array my_strings with a set of strings, each of which will be examined to determine whether or not it contains a repeated substring of length at least 2. The next portion of the `main()` method consists of an outer loop that iterates through each element of the my_strings array.

During each iteration, a nested loop processes the current element contains a nested loop that iterates from index position 0 up to the midpoint of the current element. Next, a substring of the current element is extracted and processed by the check_string() method to determine whether or not there is a matching substring. In addition, the returned values are compared with the current "candidate" for the maximum repeated substring, and the values are updated accordingly.

A final conditional code block displays a message depending on whether or not the current element in my_strings contains a maximum repeated substring. Launch the code in Listing 3.16 and you will see the following output:

```
==> Repeating substrings have length >= 2
=> Checking current string:      abc
No maximum repeating substring: abc

=> Checking current string:      abab
=> Maximum repeating substring: ab
=> Checking current string:      abccba
No maximum repeating substring: abccba

=> Checking current string:      azaaza
=> Maximum repeating substring: aza

=> Checking current string:      abcdefgabccbaxyz
=> Maximum repeating substring: abc
```

This concludes the portion of the chapter regarding strings-related code samples. The next section introduces you to 1D arrays and related code samples.

WORKING WITH 1D ARRAYS

A *one-dimensional array* in Java is a one-dimensional construct whose elements are homogeneous (i.e., mixed data types are not permitted). Given two arrays A and B, you can add or subtract them, provided that they have the same number of elements. You can also compute the inner product of two vectors by calculating the sum of their component-wise products.

Now that you understand some of the rudimentary operations with one-dimensional matrices, the following subsections illustrate how to perform various tasks on arrays in Java.

Rotate an Array

Listing 3.17 displays the contents of `RotateArray.java` that illustrates how to rotate the elements in an array.

LISTING 3.17: RotateArray.java

```java
import java.util.ArrayList;

public class RotateArray
{
   public static void main(String[] args)
   {
      int temp=0, item=0, saved=0;
      int[] arr1 = new int[]{5,10,17,23,30,47,50};
      int arr1_len = arr1.length;
      System.out.println("arr1_len: "+arr1_len);

      System.out.println("original:");
      for(int j=0; j<arr1.length; j++) {
         System.out.print(arr1[j]+" ");
      }

      System.out.println();
      int shift_count = 2;
      for(int i=0; i<shift_count; i++) {
        saved = arr1[0];
        for(int j=1; j<arr1.length; j++) {
          arr1[j-1] = arr1[j];
        }
        arr1[arr1.length-1] = saved;
      }

      System.out.println("rotated:");
      for(int j=0; j<arr1.length; j++) {
         System.out.print(arr1[j]+" ");
      }
      System.out.println();
   }
}
```

Listing 3.17 initializes the variable `list` as a list of integers and the variable `shift_count` with the value 2: the latter is the number of positions to shift leftward the elements in `list`. The next portion of Listing 3.17 is a loop that performs two actions:

- "pop" the left-most element of list
- append that element to list so that it becomes the new right-most element

The loop is executed `shift_count` iterations, after which the elements in list have been rotated the specified number of times. Launch the code in Listing 3.18 and you will see the following output:

```
original: [5, 10, 17, 23, 30, 47, 50]
rotated:  [17, 23, 30, 47, 50, 5, 10]
```

TASK: INVERT ADJACENT ARRAY ELEMENTS

Listing 3.18 displays the contents of InvertItems.java that illustrates how to perform a pairwise inversion of adjacent elements in an array. Specifically, index 0 and index 1 are switched, then index 2 and index 3 are switched, and so forth until the end of the array.

LISTING 3.18: InvertItems.java

```java
import java.util.Arrays;

public class InvertItems
{
    public static void main(String[] args)
    {
        int temp=0, mid_point=0;
        int[] arr1 = new int[]{5,10,17,23,30,47,50};

        System.out.println("Original: "+Arrays.toString(arr1));

        mid_point = (int)(arr1.length/2);

        for(int idx=0; idx<mid_point+2; idx+=2)
        {
            temp = arr1[idx];
            arr1[idx] = arr1[idx+1];
            arr1[idx+1] = temp;
        }

        System.out.println("Inverted: "+Arrays.toString(arr1));
    }
}
```

Listing 3.18 starts with the array arr1 of integers and the variable mid_point that is the midpoint of arr1. The next portion of Listing 3.18 contains a loop that iterates from index 0 to index mid_point+2, where the loop variable ndx is incremented by 2 (not by 1) after each iteration. As you can see, the code performs a standard "swap" of the contents of arr1 in index positions ndx and ndx+1 by means of a temporary variable called temp. Launch the code in Listing 3.18 and you will see the following output:

```
original: [ 5 10 17 23 30 47 50]
inverted: [10  5 23 17 47 30 50]
```

Listing 3.20 displays the contents of the Java file Swap.java that illustrates how to invert adjacent values in an array without using an intermediate temporary variable. Notice that Listing 3.18 does not require a temporary variable temp to switch adjacent values, whereas Listing 3.19 depends on a temporary intermediate variable.

LISTING 3.19: Swap.java

```java
import java.util.Arrays;

public class Swap
{
   public static int[] swap(int num1, int num2)
   {
     int delta;
     delta = num2 - num1;
     //print("num1:",num1,"num2:",num2)

     num2 = delta;
     num1 = num1+delta;
     num2 = num1-delta;
     return new int[]{num1,num2};
   }

   public static void main(String[] args)
   {
      int num1, num2;
      int[] result;

      int[] arr1 = new int[] {15,4,23,35,80,50};
      System.out.println("BEFORE: "+Arrays.toString(arr1));


      for(int idx=0; idx<arr1.length; idx+=2)
      {
        result = swap(arr1[idx],arr1[idx+1]);
        num1 = result[0];
        num2 = result[1];
        arr1[idx]   = num1;
        arr1[idx+1] = num2;
      }

      System.out.println("AFTER:  "+Arrays.toString(arr1));
   }
}
```

Listing 3.19 starts with the function swap that switches the values of two numbers. If this section of code is not clear to you, try manually executing this code with hard-coded values for num1 and num2. The next portion of Listing 3.19 initializes the array arr1 with integers, followed by a loop that iterates through the values of arr1, and invoking the function swap during each iteration. Launch the code in Listing 3.19 and you will see the following output:

```
BEFORE arr1: [15  4 23 35 80 50]
AFTER  arr1: [ 4 15 35 23 50 80]
```

TASK: SHIFT NONZERO ELEMENTS LEFTWARD

Listing 3.20 displays the contents of ShiftZeroesLeft.java that illustrates how to shift nonzero values toward the left while maintaining their relative positions.

LISTING 3.20: ShiftZeroesLeft.java

```java
public class ShiftZeroesLeft
{
    public static void main(String[] args)
    {
        int left=-1;
        int[] arr1 = new int[]{0,10,0,0,60,30,0,200,0};

        System.out.println("Initial:");
        for(int i=0;i<arr1.length; i++) {
            System.out.print(arr1[i]+" ");
        }
        System.out.println("\n");

        // find the left-most index with value 0:
        for(int i=0;i<arr1.length; i++) {
            if(arr1[i] == 0) {
                left = i;
            } else {
                left += 1;
                break;
            }
        }
        System.out.println("non-zero index: "+left);

        // ex: 0 10 0 0 30 60 0 200 0
        // right shift positions left-through-(idx-1):
        for(int idx=left+1; idx<arr1.length; idx++) {
            if(arr1[idx] == 0) {
                for(int j=idx-1;j>=left; j--) {
                    arr1[j+1] = arr1[j];
                }
                arr1[left] = 0;
                System.out.println("shifted non-zero position "+left);
                left += 1;
            }
        }

        System.out.println("\nSwitched:");
        for(int i=0;i<arr1.length; i++) {
            System.out.print(arr1[i]+" ");
        }
        System.out.println();
    }
}
```

Listing 3.20 starts with a main() function that initializes the array arr1 with a set of ten integers, followed by a loop that displays the contents of arr1. The second loop iterates through the values of arr1 in order to determine the index of the left-most nonzero value in arr1, which is assigned to the variable left.

The third loop starts from index left+1 and performs a right-shift of the nonzero values in arr1 that have a smaller index position (i.e., on the left side). Next, the value of arr1[left] is initialized with 0, thereby completing the right-shift of nonzero values. This process continues until the right-most element of arr1 has been processed. Launch the code in Listing 3.20 and you will see the following output:

```
Initial:
0 10 0 0 30 60 0 200 0
non-zero index:   1
shifted non-zero position   1
shifted non-zero position   2
shifted non-zero position   3
shifted non-zero position   4
switched:
0 0 0 0 0 10 30 60 200
```

TASK: SORT ARRAY IN-PLACE IN O(N) WITHOUT A SORT FUNCTION

Listing 3.21 displays the contents of SimpleSort.java that illustrates a very simple way to sort an array containing an *equal number* of values 0, 1, and 2 without using another data structure.

LISTING 3.21: SimpleSort.java

```java
public class SimpleSortColors
{
    public static void main(String[] args)
    {
        int[] arr1 = new int[]{0,1,2,2,1,0,0,1,2};
        int zeroes = 0;

        System.out.println("Initial:");
        for(int i=0;i<arr1.length; i++) {
            System.out.print(arr1[i]+" ");
        }
        System.out.println();

        int third=arr1.length/3;
        for(int i=0;i<third; i++) {
            arr1[i]         = 0;
            arr1[third+i]   = 1;
            arr1[2*third+i] = 2;
        }

        System.out.println("Sorted:");
        for(int i=0;i<arr1.length; i++) {
            System.out.print(arr1[i]+" ");
        }
        System.out.println();
    }
}
```

Listing 3.21 contains a main() method that initializes the array arr1 with an equal number of entries for 0, 1, and 2. So, if arr1 must have length 3*n, where n is a positive integer. Therefore, we use a loop that sets the first third of arr1 with 0, the second third with the value 1, and the "third third" with the value 2.

We can execute the preceding loop because the key word in this task description is *equal*, and therefore there is no need for another data structure, or temporary variables, or any comparisons between pairs of elements in the array arr1. Launch the code in Listing 3.21 and you will see the following output:

```
Initial:
0 1 2 2 1 0 0 1 2
Sorted:
0 0 0 1 1 1 2 2 2
```

TASK: GENERATE 0 THAT IS THREE TIMES MORE LIKELY THAN A 1

This solution to this task is based on the observation that an AND operator with two inputs generates three 0s and a single 1: we only need to randomly generate a 0 and a 1 and supply those random values as input to the AND operator.

Listing 3.22 displays the contents of GenerateZeroOrOne.java that illustrates how to generate 0s and 1s with the expected frequency.

LISTING 3.22: GenerateZeroOrOne.java

```
public class GenerateZeroOrOne
{
    public static void main(String[] args)
    {
        int zeroes=0, ones=0, max=100;

        for(int i=0; i<max; i++) {
            int x  = (int)Math.floor(Math.random()*2);
            int y  = (int)Math.floor(Math.random()*2);
            int xy = (x & y);

            if(xy == 0) ones++;
            if(xy == 1) zeroes++;
        }

        System.out.println("Percentages ("+max+" iterations):");
        System.out.println("ones:  "+(100*ones/max));
        System.out.println("zeoes: "+(100*zeroes/max));
    }
}
```

Listing 3.22 defines a main() method that initializes the integer-valued variables zeroes, ones, and max with the values 0, 0, and 100, respectively. The next portion of code contains a loop that iterates from 0 to max. Each iteration initializes the variables x and y with a random integer value that is either 0 or 1, and then initializes the variable xy with the logical OR of x and y. The next portion of the loop increments either ones or zeroes depending on whether xy equals 0 or 1, respectively. The last code block in Listing 3.22 displays the values of max, ones, and zeros. Launch the code in Listing 3.22 and you will see the following output:

```
Percentages (100 iterations):
ones:   74
zeoes: 26
```

TASK: INVERT BITS IN EVEN AND ODD POSITIONS

This solution to this task involves two parts: the first part "extracts" the bits in the even positions and shifts the result one bit to the right, followed by the second part that extracts the bits in the odd positions and shifts the result one bit to the left. Listing 3.23 displays the contents of SwitchBitPairs.java that illustrates how to solve this task.

LISTING 3.23: SwitchBitPairs.java

```
public class SwitchBitPairs
{
   public static void main(String[] args)
   {
     // This task involves two binary masks:
     // A for even bits and 5 for odd bits
     // hex A = 8 + 2 = 1010
     // hex 5 = 4 + 1 = 0101
     // 01010101 1+4+16+64 = 85
     // 10101010 2+8+32+128 = 170
     int[] numbers = new int[]{42, 37, 52, 63};
     for(int num : numbers) {
         String bnum =  Integer.toBinaryString(num);
         int rnum = ((num & 0xaa) >> 1) | ((num & 0x55) << 1);
         String srnum = Integer.toBinaryString(rnum);

         String srnum2 = String.format("%6s",
                 Integer.toBinaryString(rnum)).replace(' ','0');

         System.out.println("num: "+num+ " bnum:   "+bnum);
         System.out.println("rnum: "+rnum+
                         " srnum: "+srnum+" srnum2: "+srnum2);
         System.out.println("---------------\n");
     }
   }
}
```

Listing 3.23 defines a main() method that initializes the integer-valued variable numbers with an array of four integers. The next portion of code contains a loop that iterates through the elements of the array numbers. Each iteration initializes the variables bnum as the binary representation of num (the loop variable). Next, the integer-valued variable rum is initialized as the logical OR of two quantities, as shown here:

```
int rnum = ((num & 0xaa) >> 1) | ((num & 0x55) << 1);
```

The left term in the preceding code snippet performs a logical AND of num and the hexadecimal number 0xaa, and then performs a right shift. The right term in the preceding code snippet performs a logical AND of num and the hexadecimal number 0x55, and then performs a left shift.

The next code snippet in Listing 3.23 initializes the variable sum with the string-based binary representation of rnum, followed by a code snippet that replaces blank spaces in rnum with "0."

The final portion of Listing 3.24 displays the values of all the variables that are initialized in the loop. Launch the code in Listing 3.23 and you will see the following output:

```
num:  42 bnum:  101010
rnum: 21 srnum: 10101 srnum2: 010101
----------------


num:  37 bnum:  100101
rnum: 26 srnum: 11010 srnum2: 011010
----------------


num:  52 bnum:  110100
rnum: 56 srnum: 111000 srnum2: 111000
----------------


num:  63 bnum:  111111
rnum: 63 srnum: 111111 srnum2: 111111
----------------
```

TASK: CHECK FOR ADJACENT SET BITS IN A BINARY NUMBER

This solution to this task involves Listing 3.24, and displays the contents of the Java file CheckAdjacentBits.java that illustrates how to solve this task.

LISTING 3.24: CheckAdjacentBits.java

```java
// true if adjacent bits are set in num:

public class CheckAdjacentBits
{
   // true if adjacent bits are set in bin(num):
   public static boolean check(int num) {
      return (num & (num << 1)) != 0;
   }

   public static void main(String[] args)
   {
      int[] arr = new int[]{9,18,31,67,88,100};

      for(int num : arr) {
         System.out.println(num+" (binary): "+
                            Integer.toBinaryString(num));

         if (check(num)) {
            System.out.println(num+": found adjacent set bits\n");
         }
         else {
            System.out.println(num+": no pair of adjacent set bits\n");
         }
      }
   }
}
```

Listing 3.24 defines the static method check() with a single line of code that returns a Boolean value, which determines whether or not the logical AND of the integer num with the right-shifted result of num is nonzero.

The next portion of Listing 3.24 defines a main() method that initializes the integer-valued variable arr with an array of six integers. The next portion of code contains a loop that iterates through the elements of the array arr. Each iteration tests the result of invoking the method check() with the variable num (the loop variable). A suitable message is printed depending on whether or not the return value is True or False. Launch the code in Listing 3.24 and you will see the following output:

```
9 (binary): 1001
9: no pair of adjacent set bits

18 (binary): 10010
18: no pair of adjacent set bits

31 (binary): 11111
31: found adjacent set bits
67 (binary): 1000011
67: found adjacent set bits

88 (binary): 1011000
88: found adjacent set bits

100 (binary): 1100100
100: found adjacent set bits
```

TASK: COUNT BITS IN A RANGE OF NUMBERS

This solution to this task involves Listing 3.25 displays the contents of the Java file BitCount.java that illustrates how to solve this task.

LISTING 3.25: BitCount.java

```java
public class BitCount
{
    public static void main(String[] args)
    {
        int bits = 0;
        int[] numbers = new int[]{1,7,8,15,16,17,33,64,256};

        for(int num : numbers) {
            bits = (int)Math.ceil((Math.log(num+1)/ Math.log(2)));
            if((num == 1) && (bits == 0)) bits = 1;
            System.out.println("Number: "+num+" bit count: "+bits);
        }
    }
}
```

Listing 3.25 defines a `main()` method that initializes the integer-valued variable bits as 0 and the integer-valued array numbers with an array of nine integers. The next portion of code contains a loop that iterates through the elements of the array numbers. Each iteration initializes the variable bits with the integer-valued portion of ceiling of the ratio of two logarithmic values, as shown here:

```
bits = (int)Math.ceil((Math.log(num+1)/ Math.log(2)));
```

The next code snippet sets bits equal to 1 if num equals 1 and bits is equal to 0 (this is a "corner case" for the loop). The final code snippet is a print statement that displays the values of num and bits. Launch the code in Listing 3.25 and you will see the following output:

```
Number: 1 bit count: 1
Number: 7 bit count: 3
Number: 8 bit count: 4
Number: 15 bit count: 4
Number: 16 bit count: 5
Number: 17 bit count: 5
Number: 33 bit count: 6
Number: 64 bit count: 7
Number: 256 bit count: 9
```

TASK: FIND THE RIGHT-MOST SET BIT IN A NUMBER

This solution to this task involves Listing 3.26 displays the contents of the Java script `RightMostSetBit.java` that illustrates how to solve this task.

LISTING 3.26: RightMostSetBit.java

```java
public class RightMostSetBit
{
    public static void main(String[] args)
    {
        int[] numbers = new int[]{42, 37, 52, 63};

        for(int num : numbers) {
            int two1 =  ~(num-1);
            int two2 =  (num & ~(num-1));

            String padn = String.format("%6s",
                    Integer.toBinaryString(num)).replace(' ', '0');

            System.out.println(
                "num: "+num+" two1: "+two1+" two2: "+two2+" padn: "+padn);
        }

        System.out.println();
    }
}
```

Listing 3.26 defines a `main()` method that initializes the integer-valued array numbers with an array of four integers. The next portion of code contains a loop that iterates through the elements of the array numbers. Each iteration initializes the variables two1 and two2 based on a bit-based operation involving the complement of (num–1) and the logical and of num and the preceding quantity for two1 and two2, respectively.

The nest portion of listing 3.26 initializes the string-valued variable padn that replaces space characters in num with the string "0." The final code snippet print the values of num, two, and two. Launch the code in Listing 3.26 and you will see the following output:

```
num: 42 two1: -42 two2: 2 padn: 101010
num: 37 two1: -37 two2: 1 padn: 100101
num: 52 two1: -52 two2: 4 padn: 110100
num: 63 two1: -63 two2: 1 padn: 111111
```

TASK: THE NUMBER OF OPERATIONS TO MAKE ALL CHARACTERS EQUAL

This solution to this task involves Listing 3.27 displays the contents of the Java file FlipBitCount.java that illustrates how to solve this task.

LISTING 3.27: FlipBitCount.java

```java
public class FlipBitCount
{
    // determine the minimum number of operations
    // to make all characters of the string equal
    public static int minOperations(String the_string)
    {
        int count = 0; // track the # of changes

        for(int i=1; i<the_string.length(); i+=2) {
            // are adjacent characters equal?
            if (the_string.charAt(i) != the_string.charAt(i-1))
                count += 1;
        }

        return(count);
    }

    public static void main(String[] args)
    {
        String[] arr1 = new String[]
            {"0101010101", "1111010101", "100001", "111111"};

        for(String str1 : arr1)
        {
            System.out.println("String: "+str1);
            System.out.println("Result: "+ minOperations(str1));
            System.out.println("----------------\n");
        }
    }
}
```

Listing 3.27 defines the static method cminOperations() that counts the number of adjacent (contiguous) characters that are different via a loop that iterates through the characters in the string the_string and performs a simple comparison of adjacent characters.

The next portion of Listing 3.27 initializes the string-based variable arr1 and then defines a main() method that iterates through the elements of the array numbers. Each iteration displays the current string and the result of invoking the minOperations() method with the current string. Launch the code in Listing 3.27 and you will see the following output:

```
String:   0101010101
Result:   9
----------------

String:   1111010101
Result:   6
----------------

String:   100001
Result:   2
----------------

String:   111111
Result:   0
----------------
```

TASK: COMPUTE XOR WITHOUT XOR FOR TWO BINARY NUMBERS

This solution to this task involves Listing 3.28 displays the contents of the Java file XORWithoutXOR.java that illustrates how to solve this task.

LISTING 3.28: XORWithoutXOR.java

```java
class XORWithoutXOR
{
   public static int findBits(int x, int y)
   {
     return (x | y) - (x & y);
   }

   public static void main(String[] args)
   {
      int[] arrx = new int[]{65,15};
      int[] arry = new int[]{80,240};

      for(int i=0; i<arrx.length; i++)
      {
         int x = arrx[i];
         int y = arry[i];

         String xstr  = Integer.toBinaryString(x);
         String ystr  = Integer.toBinaryString(y);
         String xory  = Integer.toBinaryString(x|y);
```

```
String xandy = Integer.toBinaryString(x&y);
String xxory = Integer.toBinaryString(findBits(x,y));

System.out.println("Decimal x: "+x);
System.out.println("Decimal y: "+y);

System.out.println("Binary x:   "+xstr);
System.out.println("Binary y:   "+ystr);

System.out.println("x OR y:     "+xory);
System.out.println("x AND y:    "+xandy);
System.out.println("x XOR y:    "+xxory);
System.out.println("------------------\n");
        }
    }
}
```

Listing 3.28 starts with the static method findBits() that returns the XOR of two number with the following code snippet that does not require an XOR operation:

```
return (x | y) - (x & y);
```

The next portion of Listing 3.28 defines a `main()` method that initializes two integer arrays arrx and arry, followed by a loop that processes the elements of `arrx` and `arry` in a pair-wise fashion. During each iteration, the variables x and y are initialized to the current pair of values in `arrx` and `arry`, followed by the variables xstr and ystr that are initialized as the string-based counterparts of the variables x and y.

The next portion of the loop initializes the variables `xory` and `xandy` as the string-based values for the OR and AND of the variables x and y, respectively. In addition, the variable and `xxory` is initialized by the result of invoking the findBits() method with x and y, which is simply the XOR of x and y. The next portion of the loop displays the decimal and binary values of x and y, followed by the values of `xory`, `xandy`, and `xxory`. Launch the code in Listing 3.28 and you will see the following output:

```
Decimal x: 65
Decimal y: 80
Binary x:   1000001
Binary y:   1010000
x OR y:     1010001
x AND y:    1000000
x XOR y:    10001
------------------

Decimal x: 15
Decimal y: 240
Binary x:   1111
Binary y:   11110000
x OR y:     11111111
x AND y:    0
x XOR y:    11111111
------------------
```

TASK: SWAP ADJACENT BITS IN TWO BINARY NUMBERS

Listing 3.29 displays the contents of `SwapAdjacentBits.java` that illustrates how to solve this task.

LISTING 3.29: SwapAdjacentBits.java

```java
public class SwapAdjacentBits
{
   public static String toBinaryString(int n)
   {
      return String.format("%32s", Integer.toBinaryString(n))
                .replaceAll(" ", "0");
   }

   // Function to swap adjacent bits of a given number
   public static int swapAdjacentBits(int n) {
       return (((n & 0xAAAAAAAA) >>1)|((n & 0x55555555) <<1));
   }

   public static void main(String[] args)
   {
      int[] numbers = new int[]{17, 761622921, 123};
      for (int num : numbers)
      {
        System.out.println(num + " binary: " +
                       toBinaryString(num));

        int num2 = swapAdjacentBits(num);
        System.out.println("After Swapping:");
        System.out.println(num + " binary: " +
                       toBinaryString(num2)+"\n");
      }
   }
}
```

Listing 3.29 starts with the definition of the function `toBinaryString()` and generates a binary 32-bit string that is left-padded with 0. The next portion of Listing 3.29 defines the function `swapAdjacentBits()` that swaps adjacent bits by performing an OR operation on two quantities. The left quantity calculates the AND of an integer n with the value `0xAAAAAAAA` and then shifts the result one bit to the right. The right quantity calculates the AND of an integer n with the value `0x55555555` and then shifts the result one bit to the left. The result is returned by the `swapAdjacentBits()` method, as shown here:
```java
return (((n & 0xAAAAAAAA) >>1)|((n & 0x55555555) <<1));
```
The next portion of Listing 3.29 defines the main() method that initializes the array numbers with a set of numbers, followed by a loop that iterates through the values in numbers. During each iteration, the binary value of the current number is displayed, followed by the binary value of the "flipped" number. Launch the code in Listing 3.29 and you will see the following output:

```
17 binary: 00000000000000000000000000010001
After Swapping:
17 binary: 00000000000000000000000000100010

761622921 binary: 00101101011001010111000110001001
After Swapping:
761622921 binary: 00011110100110101011001001000110

123 binary: 00000000000000000000000001111011
After Swapping:
123 binary: 00000000000000000000000010110111
```

WORKING WITH 2D ARRAYS

A *two-dimensional array* in Java is a two-dimensional construct whose elements are homogeneous (i.e., mixed data types are not permitted). Given two arrays A and B, you can add or subtract them, provided that they have the same number of rows and columns.

Multiplication works differently: if A is an mxn matrix that you want to multiply (on the right of A) by B, then B must be an nxp matrix. The rule for matrix multiplication is as follows: the number of columns of A must equal the number of rows of B.

In addition, the *transpose* of matrix A is another matrix At such that the rows and columns are interchanged. Thus, if A is an mxn matrix then At is an nxm matrix. The matrix A is symmetric if A = At. The matrix A is the identity matrix I if the values in the main diagonal (upper left to lower right) are 1 and the other values are 0. The matrix A is invertible if there is a matrix B such that A*B = B*A = I. Based on the earlier discussion regarding the product of two matrices, both A and B must be square matrices with the same number of rows and columns.

Now that you understand some of the rudimentary operations with strings, the following subsections illustrate how to perform various tasks on matrices in Java.

THE TRANSPOSE OF A MATRIX

As a reminder, the transpose of matrix A is matrix At, where the rows and columns of A are the columns and rows, respectively, of matrix At.

Listing 3.30 displays the contents of MatTranspose.java that illustrates how to find the transpose of an mxn matrix.

LISTING 3.30: MatTranspose.java

```java
public class MatTranspose
{
   public static int[][] transpose(int[][]A, int rows, int cols)
   {
      for(int i=0; i<rows; i++) {
        for(int j=i; j<cols; j++) {
          //System.out.println("switching "+A[i][j]+" and "+A[j][i]);
          int temp = A[i][j];
          A[i][j] = A[j][i];
          A[j][i] = temp;
```

```
            }
        }
        return A;
    }
    public static void main(String[] args)
    {
        int[][] A1 = new int[][]{{100,3},{500,7}};
        System.out.println("=> original:");
        System.out.println(A1);

        int[][] At1 = transpose(A1, 2, 2);
        System.out.println("=> transpose:");
        System.out.println(At1);
        System.out.println();

        // example 2:
        int[][] A2 = new int[][]{{100,3,-1},{30,500,7},{123,456,789}};
        System.out.println("=> original:");
        System.out.println(A2);

        int[][] At2 = transpose(A2, 3, 3);
        System.out.println("=> transpose:");
        System.out.println(At2);
    }
}
```

Listing 3.30 is actually straightforward: the function `transpose()` contains a nested loop that uses a temporary variable `temp` to perform a simple swap of the values of `A[i,j]` and `A[j,i]` in order to generate the transpose of the matrix `A`. The next portion of Listing 3.30 initializes a 2x2 array `A` and then invokes the function `transpose` to generate its transpose. Launch the code in Listing 3.30 and you will see the following output:

```
=> original:
[[100    3]
 [500    7]]
=> transpose:
[[100 500]
 [  3   7]]

=> original:
[[100    3   -1]
 [ 30 500    7]
 [123 456 789]]
=> transpose:
[[100   30 123]
 [  3 500 456]
 [ -1    7 789]]
```

It should be noted that the transpose `At` of a matrix `A` is actually a 90 degree rotation of matrix `A`. Hence, if `A` is a square matrix of pixels values for a PNG, then `At` is a 90 degree rotation of the PNG. However, if you take the transpose of `At`, the result is the original matrix `A`.

SUMMARY

This chapter started with an introduction to one-dimensional vectors, and how to calculate their length and the inner product of pairs of vectors. Then you saw how to perform various tasks involving numbers, such as multiplying and dividing two positive integers via recursive addition and subtraction, respectively.

In addition, you learned about working with strings, and how to check a string for unique characters, how to insert characters in a string, and how to find permutations of a string. Next, you learned about determining whether or not a string is a palindrome.

Moreover, you learned how to calculate the transpose of a matrix, which is the equivalent of rotating a bitmap of an image by 90 degrees.

CHAPTER 4

SEARCH AND SORT ALGORITHMS

The first half of this chapter provides an introduction to some well-known search algorithms, followed by the second half that discusses various sorting algorithms.

The first section of this chapter introduces search algorithms such as linear search and binary search, that you can use when searching for an item (which can be numeric or character-based) in an array. A linear search is inefficient because it requires an average of $n/2$ (which has complexity $O(n)$) comparisons to determine whether or not the search element is in the array, where n is the number of elements in the list or array.

By contrast, a binary search required $O(\log n)$ comparisons, which is vastly more efficient with larger sets of items. For example, if an array contains 1,024 items, a most ten comparisons are required in order to find an element because 2**10 = 1024, so log(1024) = 10. However, a binary search algorithm requires a sorted list of items.

The second part of this chapter discusses some well-known sorting algorithms, such as the bubble sort, selection sort, insertion sort, the merge sort, and the quick sort that you can perform on an array of items.

SEARCH ALGORITHMS

The following list contains some well-known search algorithms that will be discussed in several subsections:

- linear search
- binary search
- jump search
- Fibonacci search

A *linear search* algorithm is probably the simplest of all the search algorithms: this algorithm checks every element in an array until either the desired item is located or the end of the array is reached.

However, as you learned in the introduction for this chapter, a linear search is inefficient when an array contains a large number of values. If the array is very small, the difference in performance between a linear search and a binary search can also be very small. In this case, a linear search might be an acceptable choice of algorithms.

In the RDBMS (relational database management system) world, tables often have an index (and sometimes more than one) in order to perform a table search more efficiently. However, there is some additional computational overhead involving the index, which is a separate data structure that is stored on disk. However, a linear search involves only the data in the table. As a rule of thumb, an index-based search is more efficient when tables have more than 300 rows (but results can vary). The next section contains a code sample that performs a linear search on an array of numbers.

Linear Search

Listing 4.1 displays the contents of the LinearSearch.java that illustrates how to perform a linear search on an array of numbers.

LISTING 4.1: LinearSearch.java

```
public class LinearSearch
{
    public static void main(String[] args)
    {
        int found = -1, item = 123;
        int[] arr1 = new int[]{1,3,5,123,400};

        for(int i=0; i<arr1.length; i++) {
          if (item == arr1[i]) {
             found = i;
             break;
          }
        }

        if (found >= 0)
           System.out.println("found "+item+" in position "+found);
        else
           System.out.println(item+" not found");
    }
}
```

Listing 4.1 starts with the variable found that is initialized with the value -1, followed by the search item 123, and also the array arr1 that contains an array of numbers. Next, a loop that iterates through the elements of the array arr1 of integers, comparing each element with the value of item. If a match occurs, the variable found is set equal to the value of the loop variable i, followed by an early exit.

The last portion of Listing 4.1 checks the value of the variable found: if it's nonnegative, then the search item was found (otherwise it's not in the array). Launch the code in Listing 4.1 and you will see the following output:

```
found 123 in position 3
```

Keep in mind the following point: although the array `arr1` contains a sorted list of numbers, the code works correctly for an unordered list as well.

Binary Search Walk-Through

A *binary search* requires a sorted array and can be implemented via an iterative algorithm as well as a recursive solution. The key idea involves comparing the middle element of an array of sorted elements with a search element. If they are equal, then the item has been found; if the middle element is smaller than the search element then repeat the previous step with the right half of the array; if the middle element is larger than the search element then repeat the previous step with the left half of the array. Eventually the element will be found (if it appears in the array) or the repeated splitting of the array terminates when the subarray has a single element (i.e., no further splitting can be performed).

Let's perform a walk-through of a binary search that searches for an item in a sorted array of integers.

Example #1: Let `item` = 25 and `arr1` = `[10,20,25,40,100]`, so the midpoint of the array is 3. Since `arr1[3]` == `item`, the algorithm terminates successfully.

Example #2: Let `item` = 25 and `arr1` = `[1,5,10, 15, 20, 25, 40]`, which means that the midpoint is 4.
First iteration: since arr1[4] < item, we search the array [20, 25, 40]
Second iteration: the midpoint is 1, and the corresponding value is 25.
Third iteration: 25 and the array is the single element [25], which matches the item.

Example #3: item = 25 and `arr1` = `[10, 20, 25, 40, 100,150,400]`, so the midpoint is 4.
First iteration: since arr1 [4] > 25, we search the array [10, 20, 25].
Second iteration: the midpoint is 1, and the corresponding value is 20.
Third iteration: 25 and the array is the single element [25], which matches the item.

Example #4: item = 25 and `arr1` = `[1,5,10, 15, 20, 30, 40]`, so the midpoint is 4.

First iteration: since arr1[4] < 25, we search the array [20, 30, 40].
Second iteration: the midpoint is 1, and the corresponding value is 30.
Third iteration: 25 and the array is the single element [20], so there is no match.

As mentioned in the first paragraph of this section, a binary search can be implemented with an interactive solution, which is the topic of the next section.

Binary Search (Iterative Solution)

Listing 4.2 displays the contents of `BinarySearch.java` that illustrates how to perform a binary search with an array of numbers.

LISTING 4.2: BinarySearch.java

```
public class BinarySearch
{
    public static void main(String[] args)
    {
```

```
int[] arr1 = new int[]{1,3,5,123,400};
int left = 0, found = -1, item = 123;
int right = arr1.length-1;

System.out.print("array: ");
for(int i=0; i<arr1.length; i++) {
  System.out.print(arr1[i]+" ");
}
System.out.println("");

while(left <= right) {
  int mid = (int)(left + (right-left)/2);

  if(arr1[mid] == item) {
    found = mid;
    break;
  } else if (arr1[mid] < item) {
    left = mid+1;
  } else {
    right = mid-1;
  }
}

if(found >= 0)
  System.out.println("found "+item+" in position "+found);
else
  System.out.println(item+" not found");
  }
}
```

Listing 4.2 initializes an array of numbers and some scalar variables to keep track of the left and right index positions of the subarray that we will search each time that we split the array. The next portion of Listing 4.2 contains conditional logic that implements the sequence of steps that you saw in the examples in the previous section. Launch the code in Listing 4.2 and you will see the following output:

```
array: [1   3   5 123 400]
found 123 in position 3
```

Binary Search (Recursive Solution)

Listing 4.3 displays the contents of BinarySearchRecursive.java that illustrates how to perform a binary search recursively with an array of numbers.

LISTING 4.3: BinarySearchRecursive.java

```
public class BinarySearchRecursive
{
    public static Boolean binary_search(int[] data, int item, int left,
int right)
    {
      if(left > right) {
        return false;
      } else {
```

```
      //incorrect (can result in overflow):
      //int mid = (left + right) / 2
      int mid = (int)(left + (right-left)/2);

      if(item == data[mid]) {
        return true;
      } else if(item < data[mid]) {
        //recursively search the left half
        return binary_search(data, item, left, mid-1);
      } else {
        //recursively search the right half
        return binary_search(data, item, mid+1, right);
      }
    }
  }

  public static void main(String[] args)
  {
     int[] items = new int[]{-100, 123, 200, 400};
     int[] arr1 = new int[]{1,3,5,123,400};
     int[] arr2 = new int[]{1,3,5,123,400};
     int found = -1, item = 123;
     int left = 0, right = arr1.length-1;

     System.out.print("array: ");
     for(int i=0; i<arr1.length; i++) {
       System.out.print(arr1[i]+" ");
     }
     System.out.println("");

     for(Integer item2 : items) {
       arr1 = arr2;
       System.out.println("searching for item:  "+item2);
       left  = 0;
       right = arr1.length-1;
       Boolean result = binary_search(arr1, item2, left, right);
       System.out.println("item:  "+item2+ " found: "+result);
     }

     if(found >= 0)
       System.out.println("found "+item+" in position "+found);
     else
       System.out.println(item+" not found");
  }
}
```

Listing 4.3 starts with the function `binary_search()` with parameters `data`, `item`, `left`, and `right`) that contain the current array, the search item, the left index of `data`, and the right index of `data`, respectively. If the left index `left` is greater than the right index `right` then the search item does not exist in the original array.

However, if the left index `left` is *less than* the right index `right` then the code assigns the middle index of `data` to the variable `mid`. Next, the code performs the following three-part conditional test:

If `item == data[mid]` then the search item has been found in the array.

If `item < data[mid]` then the function `binary_search()` is invoked with the left-half of the `data` array.

If `item > data[mid]` then the function `binary_search()` is invoked with the right-half of the `data` array.

The next portion of Listing 4.3 initializes the sorted array `arr1` with numbers and initializes the array `items` with a list of search items, and also initializes some scalar variables to keep track of the left and right index positions of the subarray that we will search each time that we split the array.

The final portion of Listing 4.3 consists of a loop that iterates through each element of the items array and invokes the function `binary_search()` to determine whether or not the current item is in the sorted array. Launch the code in Listing 4.3 and you will see the following output:

```
array: 1 3 5 123 400
searching for item:  -100
item:  -100 found: false
searching for item:  123
item:  123 found: true
searching for item:  200
item:  200 found: false
searching for item:  400
item:  400 found: true
123 not found
```

WELL-KNOWN SORTING ALGORITHMS

Sorting algorithms have a best case, average case, and worst case in terms of performance. Interestingly, sometimes an efficient algorithm (such as quick sort) can perform the worst when a given array is already sorted.

The following subsections contain code samples for the following well-known sort algorithms:

- bubble sort
- selection sort
- insertion sort
- merge sort
- quick sort
- bucketSort
- Shell Sort
- Shell Sort 108
- heap Sort 108
- inplaceSort
- countingSort
- radixSort

If you want to explore sorting algorithms in more depth, perform an Internet search for additional sorting algorithms.

Bubble Sort

A *bubble sort* involves a nested loop whereby each element of an array is compared with the elements to the right of the given element. If an array element is less than the current element, the values are interchanged ("swapped"), which means that the contents of the array will eventually be sorted from smallest to largest value.

Here is an example:

```
arr1 = np.array([40, 10, 30, 20]);
Item = 40;
Step 1: 40 > 10 so switch these elements:
arr1 = np.array([10, 40, 30, 20]);
Item = 40;
Step 2: 40 > 30 so switch these elements:
arr1 = np.array([10, 30, 40, 20]);
Item = 40;
Step 3: 40 > 20 so switch these elements:
arr1 = np.array([10, 30, 20, 40]);
```

As you can see, the smallest element is in the left-most position of the array `arr1`. Now repeat this process by comparing the second position (which is index 1) with the right-side elements.

```
arr1 = np.array([10, 30, 20, 40]);
Item = 30;
Step 4: 30 > 20 so switch these elements:
arr1 = np.array([10, 20, 30, 40]);
Item = 30;
Step 4: 30 < 40 so do nothing
```

As you can see, the smallest elements two elements occupy the first two positions in the array `arr1`. Now repeat this process by comparing the third position (which is index 2) with the right-side elements.

```
arr1 = np.array([10, 20, 30, 40]);
Item = 30;
Step 4: 30 < 40 so do nothing
```

The array `arr1` is now sorted in increasing order (in a left-to-right fashion). If you want to reverse the order so that the array is sorted in decreasing order (in a left-to-right fashion), simply replace the ">" operator with the "<" operator in the preceding steps.

Listing 4.4 displays the contents of the `BubbleSort.java` that illustrates how to perform a bubble sort on an array of numbers.

LISTING 4.4: BubbleSort.java

```
public class BubbleSort
{
    public static void main(String[] args)
    {
        int[] arr1 = new int[]{40, 10, 30, 20};
        System.out.print("Initial: ");
```

```
      for(int i=0; i<arr1.length; i++) {
        System.out.print(arr1[i]+" ");
      }
      System.out.println("");

      for(int i=0; i<arr1.length-1; i++) {
        for(int j=i+1; j<arr1.length; j++) {
          if(arr1[i] > arr1[j]) {
            int temp = arr1[i];
            arr1[i] = arr1[j];
            arr1[j] = temp;
          }
        }
      }

      System.out.print("Sorted:   ");
      for(int i=0; i<arr1.length; i++) {
        System.out.print(arr1[i]+" ");
      }
      System.out.println("");
    }
}
```

You can manually perform the code execution in Listing 4.4 to convince yourself that the code is correct. (Hint: it's the same sequence of steps that you saw earlier in this section). Launch the code in Listing 4.4 and you will see the following output:

```
initial: [40 10 30 20]
sorted:  [10 20 30 40]
```

Find Anagrams in a List of Words

Recall that the variable word1 is an anagram of word2 if word2 is a permutation of word1. Listing 4.5 displays the contents of the Anagrams2.java that illustrates how to check if two words are anagrams of each other.

LISTING 4.5: Anagrams2.java

```
import java.util.Arrays;

public class Anagrams2
{
    public static String myStringSort(String str)
    {
        char[] arr = str.toCharArray();
        Arrays.sort(arr);
        String sorted = String.valueOf(arr);
        return sorted;
    }

    public static Boolean is_anagram(String str1, String str2)
    {
        String sorted1 = myStringSort(str1);
```

```
      String sorted2 = myStringSort(str2);
      return (sorted1.equals(sorted2));
   }


  public static void main(String[] args)
   {
      String[] words = new String[]{"abc","evil","Z","cab","live","xyz",
"zyx","bac"};
      System.out.println("INITIAL: "+Arrays.toString(words));
      System.out.println();


      for(int i=0; i<words.length-1; i++) {
        for(int j=i+1; j<words.length; j++) {
          Boolean result = is_anagram(words[i], words[j]);
          if(result == true)
            System.out.println(words[i]+" and "+words[j]+" are
anagrams");
          //else
          //  System.out.println(words[i]+" and "+words[j]+" are NOT
anagrams");
        }
      }
   }
}
```

Listing 4.5 starts with the definition of the static method myStringSort() that sorts the letters in an input string and then returns a string consisting of the sorted letters. The next portion of Listing 4.5 defines the static method is_anagram() that invokes the myStringSort() method in order to compare its two parameters. The sorted versions of the two parameters are compared and the return statement returns either true or false depending on whether the sorted strings are equal or unequal, respectively.

The next portion of Listing 4.5 contains a main() method that initializes the variable words as an array of strings and then displays the contents of words. The next portion of code consists of a nested loop that compares each string in words with the subsequent strings in the variable words. For example, the first string is compared with the second through last (right-most) string, the second string is compared with the third through last (right-most) string, and so forth.

Each pair of strings in the nested loop is compared by invoking the method is_anagran() and a message is printed if any pair strings is indeed a pair of anagrams. Launch the code in Listing 4.5 and you will see the following output:

```
=> Initial words:
['abc', 'evil', 'Z', 'cab', 'live', 'xyz', 'zyx', 'bac']

abc   and   cab   are anagrams
abc   and   bac   are anagrams
evil  and   live  are anagrams
cab   and   bac   are anagrams
xyz   and   zyx   are anagrams
```

SELECTION SORT

Listing 4.6 displays the contents of `SelectionSort.java` that illustrates how to perform a selection sort on an array of numbers.

LISTING 4.6: SelectionSort.java

```java
public class SelectionSort
{
    public static void main(String[] args)
    {
        int[] arr1 = new int[]{64, 25, 12, 22, 11};

        System.out.print("Initial: ");
        for(int i=0; i<arr1.length; i++) {
          System.out.print(arr1[i]+" ");
        }
        System.out.println ("");

        //Traverse through all array elements
        for(int i=0; i<arr1.length; i++) {
          //Find the minimum element in remaining unsorted array
          int min_idx = i;
          for(int j=i+1; j<arr1.length; j++) {
            if(arr1[min_idx] > arr1[j])
              min_idx = j;
          }

          //Swap the found minimum element with the first element
          int temp = arr1[i];
          arr1[i] = arr1[min_idx];
          arr1[min_idx] = temp;
        }

        System.out.print("Sorted:   ");
        for(int i=0; i<arr1.length; i++) {
          System.out.print(arr1[i]+" ");
        }
        System.out.println();
    }
}
```

Listing 4.6 starts by initializing the array `arr1` with some integers, followed by a loop that iterates through the elements of `arr1`. During each iteration of this loop, another inner loop compares the current array element with each element that appears to the right of the current array element. If any of those elements is smaller than the current array element, then the index position of the former is maintained in the variable `min_idx`. After the inner loop has completed execution, the current element is "swapped" with the small element (if any) that has been found via the following code snippet:

```
arr1[i], arr1[min_idx] = arr1[min_idx], arr1[i]
```

In the preceding snippet, `arr1[i]` is the "current" element and `arr1[min_idx]` is element (to the right of index `i`) that is smaller than `arr1[i]`. If these two values are the same, then the code snippet swaps `arr1[i]` with itself. Now launch the code in Listing 4.6 and you will see the following output:

```
Initial: 64 25 12 22 11
Sorted:  11 12 22 25 64
```

INSERTION SORT

Listing 4.7 displays the contents of `InsertionSort.java` that illustrates how to perform a selection sort on an array of numbers.

LISTING 4.7: InsertionSort.java

```java
public class InsertionSort
{
    public static void insertionSort(int[] arr1)
    {
      // Traverse through 1 to len(arr1)
      for(int i=1; i<arr1.length; i++) {
         int key = arr1[i];

         //Move elements of arr1[0..i-1], that are
         //greater than key, to one position ahead
         //of their current position
         int j = i-1;
         while((j >=0) && (key < arr1[j])) {
            arr1[j+1] = arr1[j];
            j -= 1;
         }
         arr1[j+1] = key;
         //System.out.println("New order: "+arr1);
      }
    }

    public static void main(String[] args)
    {
        int[] arr1 = new int[]{12, 11, 13, 5, 6};
        System.out.print("Initial:  ");
        for(int i=0; i<arr1.length; i++) {
           System.out.print(arr1[i]+" ");
        }
        System.out.println();

        insertionSort(arr1);
        System.out.print("Sorted:   ");
        for(int i=0; i<arr1.length; i++) {
           System.out.print(arr1[i]+" ");
        }
        System.out.println();
    }
}
```

Listing 4.7 starts with the function `insertionSort()` that contains a loop that iterates through the elements of the array `arr1`. During each iteration of this loop, the variable key is assigned the value of the element of array `arr1` whose index value is the loop variable `i`. Next, a `while` loop shift a set of elements to the right of index `j`, as shown here:

```
j = i-1
while j >=0 and key < arr1[j] :
  arr1[j+1] = arr1[j]
  j -= 1
arr1[j+1] = key
```

For example, after the first iteration of the inner while loop we have the following output:

```
Initial:    [12, 11, 13, 5, 6]
New order: [11, 12, 13, 5, 6]
```

The second iteration of the inner loop does not produce any changes, but the third iteration shifts some of the array elements, at which point we have the following output:

```
Initial:    [12, 11, 13, 5, 6]
New order: [11, 12, 13, 5, 6]
New order: [11, 12, 13, 5, 6]
New order: [5, 11, 12, 13, 6]
```

The final iteration of the outer loop results in an array with sorted elements. Now launch the code in Listing 4.7 and you will see the following output:

```
Initial:   12 11 13 5 6
Sorted:     5 6 11 12 13
New order: [5, 6, 11, 12, 13]
```

COMPARISON OF SORT ALGORITHMS

A bubble sort is rarely used: it's most effective when the data value are already almost sorted. A selection sort is used infrequently: while this algorithm is effective for very short lists, the insertion sort is often superior. An insertion sort is useful if the data are already almost sorted, or if the list is very short (e.g., at most 50 items).

Among the three preceding algorithms, only insertion sort is used in practice, typically as an auxiliary algorithm in conjunction with other more sophisticated sorting algorithms (e.g., quick sort or merge sort).

MERGE SORT

A *merge sort* involves merging two arrays of sorted values. In the following subsections you will see three different ways to perform a merge sort. The first code sample involves a third array, whereas the second and third code samples do not require a third array. Moreover, the third code sample involves one `while` loop whereas the second code sample involves a pair of nested loops, which means that the third code sample is simpler and also more memory efficient.

Merge Sort With a Third Array

The simplest way to merge two arrays involves copying elements from those two arrays to a third array, as shown here:

```
      A              B              C
  +-----+        +-----+        +-----+
  |  20 |        |  50 |        |  20 |     A
  |  80 |        |  70 |        |  50 |     B
  | 200 |    +   | 100 |    =   |  70 |     B
  | 300 |        +-----+        |  80 |     A
  | 500 |                       | 100 |     B
  +-----+                       | 200 |     A
                                | 300 |     A
                                | 500 |     A
                                +-----+
```

The right-most column in the preceding diagram lists the array (either A or B) that contains each number. As you can see, the order ABBABAAA switches between array A and array B. However, the final three elements are from array A because all the elements of array B have been processed.

Two other possibilities exist: array A is processed and B still has some elements, or both A and B have the same size. Of course, even if A and B have the same size, it's still possible that the final sequence of elements are from a single array.

For example, array A is longer than array B in the example below, which means that the final values in array C are from A:

```
A = [20,80,200,300,500]
B = [50,70,100]
```

The following example involves array A and array B with the same length:

```
A = [20,80,200]
B = [50,70,300]
```

The next example also involves array A and array B with the same length, but all the elements of A are first copied to C and then all the elements of B are copied to C:

```
A = [20,30,40]
B = [50,70,300]
```

Listing 4.8 displays the contents of MergeSort1.java that illustrates how to perform a merge sort on two arrays of numbers.

LISTING 4.8: MergeSort1.java

```
public class MergeSort1
{

    public static void MergeSort1(){}
```

```java
    public static int[] MergeItems(int[] items1, int[] items2, int[]
items3)
    {
      int ndx1 = 0, ndx2 = 0, ndx3 = 0;

      // => always add the smaller element first:
      while(ndx1 < items1.length && ndx2 < items2.length)
      {
        //System.out.println(
        //"items1 data:"+items1[ndx1]+" items2 data:"+items2[ndx2]);

        int data1 = items1[ndx1];
        int data2 = items2[ndx2];
        if(data1 < data2) {
          //System.out.println("adding data1: "+data1);
          items3[ndx3] = data1;
          ndx1 += 1;
        } else {
          //System.out.println("adding data2: "+data2);
          items3[ndx3] = data2;
          ndx2 += 1;
        }
        ndx3 += 1;
      }

      // append any remaining elements of items1:
      while(ndx1 < items1.length) {
          //System.out.println("MORE items1: "+items1[ndx1]);
          items3[ndx3] = items1[ndx1];
          ndx1 += 1;
      }

      // append any remaining elements of items2:
      while(ndx2 < items2.length) {
          //System.out.println("MORE items2: "+items2[ndx2]);
          items3[ndx3] = items2[ndx2];
          ndx2 += 1;
      }

      return items3;
    }

    public static void display_items(int[] items)
    {
       for(int item : items)
         System.out.print(item+" ");
       System.out.println("");
    }
    public static void main(String[] args)
    {
       int[] items1 = new int[]{20, 30, 50, 300};
```

```
            int[] items2 = new int[]{80, 100, 200};
            int[] items3 = new int[items1.length+items2.length];

            // display the initial and merged lists:
            System.out.println("First sorted array:");
            display_items(items1);
            System.out.println("");

            System.out.println("Second sorted array:");
            display_items(items2);
            System.out.println("");

            System.out.println("Merged array:");
            items3 = MergeItems(items1, items2, items3);
            display_items(items3);
      }
}
```

Listing 4.8 defines the static methods `merge_items()` and `display_items()` that perform the merge operation on two sorted arrays and display the initial arrays and merged array, respectively.

The `merge_items()` method contains three loops. The first loop iterates through the elements of `items1` and `items2` and performs a comparison: whichever element is smaller is added to the array `items3`. The second loop adds any remaining elements in items1 to `arr3`, and the third loop adds any remaining elements in `items2` to `arr3`. The `display_items()` method displays the contents of the array that is passed to this method.

The next portion of Listing 4.8 defines the method main() that initializes the sorted arrays `items1` and `items2` with integer and allocates storage for the "target" array items3. The next three (short) code blocks display the contents of `items1` and `items2`, and then invoke the method `merge_items()` to merge these two arrays, after which the merged contents are displayed. Launch the code in Listing 4.8 and you will see the following output:

```
First sorted array:
20 30 50 300

Second sorted array:
80 100 200

Merged array:
20 30 50 80 100 200 300
```

Merge Sort Without a Third Array

Listing 4.9 displays the contents of `MergeSort2.java` that illustrates how to perform a merge sort on two *sorted* arrays without using a third array.

LISTING 4.9: MergeSort2.java

```java
public class MergeSort2
{
   public static void display_items(int[] items)
   {
      for(int item : items)
        System.out.print(item+" ");
      System.out.println("");
   }


   public static void merge_arrays()
   {
      int[] items1 = new int[] {20, 30, 50, 300, 0, 0, 0, 0};
      int[] items2 = new int[] {80, 100, 200,999};

      System.out.println("=> Merge items2 into items1");
      System.out.println("Sorted array items1:");
      display_items(items1);
      System.out.println("");
      System.out.println("Sorted array items2:");
      display_items(items2);
      System.out.println("");

      int ndx1 = 0, ndx2 = 0, ndx3 = 0;
      int last1 = 4; // do not count the 0 values in items1

    // merge elements of items2 into items1:
    while(ndx2 < items2.length)
    {
       //System.out.println(
       //"items1 data: "+items1[ndx1]+" items2 data: "+items2[ndx2]);
       int data1 = items1[ndx1];
       int data2 = items2[ndx2];

       // skip over elements in items1 that
       // are < their counterpart in items2:
       while(data1 < data2 )
       {
          if (ndx1 < items1.length-1) {
             //System.out.println("incrementing ndx1: "+ndx1);
             ndx1  += 1;
             data1 = items1[ndx1];
          } else {
             //System.out.println("past length of array items1");
             break;
          }
       }

       // right-shift elements in items1 by one position
       // in order to insert an element from items2:
       for(int idx3=last1; idx3 >ndx1; idx3--) {
         //System.out.println("shift "+items1[idx3]+" to the right");
```

```
            items1[idx3] = items1[idx3-1];
        }

        // insert data2 into items1:
        items1[ndx1] = data2;
        ndx1  = 0;
        ndx2  += 1;
        last1 += 1;
        // System.out.println("=> shifted items1: "+items1);
    }

    System.out.println("Merged sorted array items3:");
    display_items(items1);
}

public static void main(String[] args)
{
    merge_arrays();
}
}
```

Listing 4.9 defines the static methods merge_arrays() and display_items() that perform the merge operation on two sorted arrays and display the initial arrays and merged array, respectively.

The merge_arrays() initializes the sorted arrays items1 and items2 and then displays their contents by invoking the display_items() method with each array. The next portion of merge_arrays() contains an outer loop that iterates through the values of items2. During each iteration, an inner loop is executed that increments the index ndx1 for items1 until the value in the items1 array is greater than the current value in the items2 array. At this point another loop performs a right-shift of the elements in the items1 array in order to insert the current element of the items2 array. The outer loop terminates when all of the elements in items2 have been processed: remember that the purpose of the code is to insert the elements from the array items2 into the array items1 so that the result is a sorted array.

The next portion of Listing 4.9 defines the method main() that invokes the merge_arrays() method. Now launch the code in Listing 4.9 and you will see the following output:

```
=> Merge items2 into items1
Sorted array items1:
20 30 50 300 0 0 0 0

Sorted array items2:
80 100 200 999

System.out.println("Merged sorted array items3:");
20 30 50 80 100 200 300 999
```

Merge Sort: Shift Elements From End of Lists

In this scenario we assume that matrix A has enough uninitialized elements at the end of the matrix in order to accommodate all the values of matrix B, as shown in Figure 4.1.

```
        A                B                A
   +-----+          +-----+          +-----+
   |  20 |          |  50 |          |  20 |   A
   |  80 |          |  70 |          |  50 |   B
   | 200 |    +     | 100 |    =     |  70 |   B
   | 300 |          +-----+          |  80 |   A
   | 500 |                           | 100 |   B
   | xxx |                           | 200 |   A
   | xxx |                           | 300 |   A
   | xxx |                           | 500 |   A
   +-----+                           +-----+
```

FIGURE 4.1. Merging two arrays.

HOW DOES QUICK SORT WORK?

The *quick sort* algorithm uses a divide-and-conquer approach to sort an array of elements. The key idea involves selecting an item in a given list as the *pivot* item (which can be any item in the list) that is used for partitioning the given list into two sublists and then recursively sorting the two sublists.

Due to the recursive nature of this algorithm, each recursive invocation results in smaller sublists. Hence, the sublists eventually reach the base cases where the sublists have either 0 or 1 elements (which are obviously sorted).

Another key point: one sublist contains values that are less than the pivot item, and the other sublist contains values that are greater than the pivot item. In the ideal case, both sublists have approximately the same length. This results in a binary-like splitting of the sublists, which involves log N invocations of the quick sort algorithm, where N is the number of elements in the list.

There are several points to keep in mind regarding the quick sort. First, the case in which the two sublists are approximately the same length is the more efficient case. However, this case involves a prior knowledge of the data distribution in the given list in order to achieve optimality.

Second, if the list contains values that are close to randomly distributed, in which case the first value or the last value are common choices for the pivot item. Third, quick sort has its worst performance when the values in a list are already sorted. In this scenario, select the pivot item in one of the following ways:

- Select the middle item in the list.
- Select the median of the first, middle, and last items in the list.

Quick Sort Code Sample

Listing 4.10 displays the contents of QuickSort.java that illustrates how to perform a quick sort on an array of numbers.

LISTING 4.10: QuickSort.java

```java
public class QuickSort
{
    public static void sort(int[] values) {
```

```
      quicksort(values);
    }

public static void quicksort(int[] arr) {
  if(arr.length == 0)
    return;
  else
    quicksort(arr, 0, arr.length - 1);
}

// Sort interval [lo, hi] inplace recursively
public static void quicksort (int[] arr, int lo, int hi)
{
  if (lo < hi) {
    int splitPoint = partition(arr, lo, hi);
    quicksort(arr, lo, splitPoint);
    quicksort(arr, splitPoint + 1, hi);
  }
}

// Performs Hoare partition algorithm for quicksort
public static int partition(int[] arr, int lo, int hi)
{
  int pivot = arr[lo];
  int i = lo - 1;
  int j = hi + 1;

  while (true) {
    do {
      i += 1;
    }
    while (arr[i] < pivot);

    do {
      j -= 1;
    }
    while (arr[j] > pivot);

    if (i < j) swap(arr, i, j);
    else return j;
  }
}

// Swap two elements
public static void swap(int[] arr, int i, int j)
{
  int tmp = arr[i];
  arr[i] = arr[j];
  arr[j] = tmp;
}

public static void main(String[] args)
{
    int[] array = new int[]{10, 4, 6, 4, 8, -13, 2, 3};
```

```
        System.out.println("Initial array:");
        for (int num : array )
          System.out.print(num+" ");
        System.out.println();

        sort(array);
        System.out.println("Sorted  array:");
        for (int num : array )
          System.out.print(num+" ");
        System.out.println();
    }
}
```

Listing 4.10 contains the definition of the following static methods, followed by the `main()` method:

- `sort()`
- `quicksort()`
- `partition()`
- `swap()`

The method `sort()` invokes the overloaded method `quicksort()`, which in turn invokes the second `quicksort()` method if the parameter `arr` (which is an array) has nonzero length.

Next, the second `quicksort()` method contains conditional logic that is executed when the parameter `lo` is less than the parameter `hi`, which involves three code snippets. The first code snippet initializes the value `splitPoint` with the result of executing the method `partition()`, which is discussed later. The second code snippet recursively invokes the current `quicksort()` method with one set of arguments, followed by another recursive invocation of executes the the current `quicksort()` method with a second set of arguments.

The next portion of Listing 4.10 is the method `partition()` that performs the "heavy lifting" of the quick sort algorithm. This method starts by initializing the variables pivot, i, and j, with the values of `arr[lo]`, `lo-1`, and `hi+1`, respectively, which are the parameters of the current method.

The remaining code in the method `partition()` consists of a `while` loop that contains two `do-while` loops and an `if/else` statement. The first `while` loop increments the value of i as long as the value of `arr[i]` is less than the value of `pivot`, whereas the second `while` loop *decrements* the value of j as long as the value of `arr[i]` is greater than the value of `pivot`. Next, the `if/else` statement invokes the method `swap()` if i is less than j; otherwise, this method returns the value of j. The method `swap()` is a standard method for swapping the values of two variables.

The next portion of Listing 4.10 is the `main()` method that initializes the variable `array` with a list of 8 integer values, followed by a code block that displays the contents of the variable `array`.

The next portion of the main() method invokes the `sort()` method, followed by another code block that displays the contents of the sorted array. Now launch the code in Listing 4.10 and you will see the following output:

```
Sorted array: [1, 5, 7, 8, 9, 10]
```

SHELL SORT

The *Shell sort* (by Donald L. Shell) is similar to bubble sort: both algorithms compare pairs of elements and then swap them if they are out of order. However, unlike bubble sort, Shell sort does not compare adjacent elements until the last iteration. Instead, it first compares elements that are widely separated, shrinking the size of the gap with each pass. In this way, it deals with elements that are significantly out of place early on, reducing the number of computations that subsequent passes through the array must perform.

Listing 4.11 displays the contents of `ShellSort.java` that illustrates how to implement the Shell sort algorithm in `Java`.

LISTING 4.11: ShellSort.java

```java
public class ShellSort
{
   public static int[] shellSort(int num, int[] arr)
   {
     int gap = (int)(num/2);

     while(gap > 0) {
       //for i in range(gap,num-1):
       for(int i=gap; i<num; i++) {
         int j = i-gap;

         while(j >= 0 && arr[j] > arr[j+gap]) {
           // swap arr[j] and arr[j+gap]
           int temp = arr[j];
           arr[j] = arr[j+gap];
           arr[j+gap] = temp;
           j = j-gap ;
         }
       }
       gap = (int)(gap/2);
     }

   return arr;
   }

   public static void main(String[] args)
   {
      int num = 6;
      int[] arr = new int[]{50,20,80,-100,500,200};

      System.out.println("Original:");
      for (int num1 : arr )
        System.out.print(num1+" ");
      System.out.println();

      int[] result = shellSort(num, arr);
      System.out.println("Sorted:");
      for (int num2 : result )
        System.out.print(num2+" ");
      System.out.println();
   }
}
```

Listing 4.11 defines the static method `shellSort()` that contains the Shell sort algorithm. The first line of code initializes the integer-valued variable `gap` as the midpoint of the array `arr` that contains integer values. Next, a `while` loop executes as long as the variable `gap` is greater than 0. During each iteration, a nested `for` loop and another `while` loop are executed. The `for` loop initializes the loop variable `i` with the value of `gap` and increments the value of `i` up to the value `num-1`, and also initializes the variable `j` with the value `i-gap`, as shown here:

```
for(int i=gap; i<num; i++) {
  int j = i-gap;
```

Next, the nested `while` loop swaps the elements in index positions `j` and `j+gap` and replaces the value of `j` with `j-gap`. When the nested `for` loop has completed execution, the value of `gap` divided by 2, and the outer loop executes again.

The next portion of Listing 4.11 defines the `main()` method that initializes the array `arr` with six integer values, and initializes the variable `num` with the length of `arr`. The remaining portion of the `main()` method displays the values of area, invokes the `shellSort()` method, and then displays the sorted values in the array `arr`. Launch the code in Listing 4.11 and you will see the following output:

```
Original:
50 20 80 -100 500 200 orted:
-100 20 50 80 200 500
```

TASK: SORTED ARRAYS AND THE SUM OF TWO NUMBERS

Listing 4.12 displays the contents of the `PairSumTarget.java` that illustrates how to determine whether or not a sorted array contains the sum of two specified numbers.

LISTING 4.12: PairSumTarget.java

```java
// given two numbers num1 and num2 in a sorted array,
// determine whether or not num1+num2 is in the array
public class PairSumTarget
{
    public static void check_sum(int[] arr1, int num1, int num2)
    {
        int ndx1 = 0;
        int ndx2 = arr1.length-1;
        //System.out.println("Anum1: "+num1+" num2: "+num2);

        while(arr1[ndx1] < num1)
          ndx1 += 1;
        //System.out.println("Bndx1: "+ndx1+" ndx2: "+ndx2);

        while(arr1[ndx2] > num2)
          ndx2 -= 1;
        //System.out.println("Cndx1: "+ndx1+" ndx2: "+ndx2);
```

```
      System.out.println("Contents of array:");
      for (int num3 : arr1 )
        System.out.print(num3+" ");
      System.out.println("\n");


      int sum = num1+num2;
      System.out.println("Checking for the sum => "+sum);


      //System.out.println("num1: "+num1+" num2: "+num2);
      //System.out.println("ndx1: "+ndx1+" ndx2: "+ndx2);
      // NOTE: arr1[ndx1] >= num1 AND arr1[ndx2] >= sum

      if(arr1[ndx1]+arr1[ndx2] == sum) {
        System.out.println("=> FOUND the sum "+sum);
        System.out.println("indexes: "+ndx1+" and "+ndx2);
      } else {
        System.out.println("=> SUM NOT FOUND: "+sum);
      }
      System.out.println();
    }

  public static void main(String[] args)
  {
      int[] arr1 = new int[]{20,50,100,120,150,200,250,300};
      int num1 = 60;
      int num2 = 90;
      check_sum(arr1,num1,num2);

      arr1 = new int[] {20,50,100,120,150,200,250,300};
      num1 = 60;
      num2 = 100;
      check_sum(arr1,num1,num2);

      arr1 = new int[]{3,3};
      num1 = 3;
      num2 = 3;
      check_sum(arr1,num1,num2);
    }
}
```

Listing 4.12 defines the static method check_sum() that calculate the sum of pairs of array elements to determine whether or not that sum is equal to a given value. This calculation is performed in a loop that *increments* a lower index ndx1 while the array value in arr is less than num1, and then *decrements* an upper index ndx2 while the array value is larger than num2. If the sum of arr[ndx1] and arr[ndx2] equals the value in the variable sum, then a target sum has been found, and an appropriate message is displayed.

The next portion of Listing 4.12 defines the main() method that initializes the array arr1 with a sorted list of integers and then displays the contents of arr1. The remaining portion of the `main()` method initializes the variables `num1` and `num2` and then invokes the n method. Now launch the code in Listing 4.12 and you will see the following output:

```
Original:
50 20 80 -100 500 200
Sorted:
-100 20 50 80 200 500
```

SUMMARY

This chapter started with search algorithms, such as linear search and binary search (iterative and recursive). You also learned about well-known sort algorithms such as the bubble sort, the merge sort (with three variations), and the quick sort.

Finally, you learned about the Shell sort, along with checking whether or not the sum of two array elements is an element in an array of numbers.

CHAPTER 5

LINKED LISTS (1)

T his chapter introduces you to a data structure called a *linked list*, which includes singly linked lists, doubly linked lists, and circular lists. Linked lists support various operations, such as create, traverse, insert, and delete operations. This chapter shows you how to implement linked lists and how to perform some operations on linked lists. Chapter 6 contains various task-related code samples that involve more than just the basic operations on linked lists. Keep in mind that algorithms for linked lists often involve recursion, which is discussed in Chapter 2.

The first part of this chapter introduces you to linked lists, followed by examples of performing various operations on singly linked lists, such as creating and displaying the contents of linked lists, as well as updating nodes and deleting nodes in a singly linked list.

The second part of this chapter introduces you to doubly linked lists, followed by examples of performing various operations on doubly linked lists, which are the counterpart to the code samples for singly linked lists.

One other point to keep in mind for this chapter as well as other chapters: the code samples provide a solution that prefers clarity over optimization. In addition, many code samples contain "commented out" `print()` statements. If the code samples confuse you, uncomment the `print()` statements in order to trace the execution path of the code: doing so can make the code easier to follow and also save you debugging time. Indeed, after you have read each code sample and you fully understand the code, try to optimize the code, or perhaps use a different algorithm, which will enhance your problem solving skills as well as increase your confidence level.

If you are already comfortable with linked lists, then you might already be prepared for Chapter 6 that contains well-known tasks that pertain to linked lists.

TYPES OF DATA STRUCTURES

This section introduces you to the concept of linear data structures, such as stacks and queues (and briefly describes nonlinear data structures such as trees and graphs), which is the focus of Chapters 5, 6, and 7.

Linear Data Structures

Linear data structures are data structures whose elements are occur in sequential memory locations or are logically connected, such as stacks and queues. As you will see in Chapter 7, stacks are last-in-first-out (LIFO) data structures, which means that the last element inserted is the first element removed. Moreover, operations are performed from one end of the stack. A real-life counterpart to a stack is an elevator that has a single entrance that is also the lone exit.

In Chapter 7, you will also learn about queues, which are first-in-first-out (FIFO) data structures, which means that the first element inserted is the first element removed. By contrast with a stack, insert operations are performed at the so-called "front" of the queue and delete operations are performed at the "rear" of the queue. A real-life counterpart to a queue is a line of people waiting to purchase tickets to a movie.

Nonlinear Data Structures

Nonlinear data structures are data structures whose elements are not sequential, such as trees and graphs. Trees have a single node called the root node that has no parent node, whereas every other node has exactly one parent node. Two nodes are related if there is edge connecting the two nodes. In fact, the nodes in a tree have a hierarchical relationship. Trees can have undirected edges, directed edges, and cycles.

A graph is a generalization of a tree, and nodes in a graph can have multiple parent nodes. Instead of a root node, a graph has a node called a "source" and a node called the "sink" that are somewhat analogous to a "start" node and an "end" node. This designation appears in graphs that represent transport networks in which edges can have weights assigned to them. Think of trucks that transport food or other commodities from a warehouse (the "source") and have multiple routes to reach their destination (the "sink").

DATA STRUCTURES AND OPERATIONS

In this book, the data structure for singly linked lists is a custom `Node` structure that consists of the following:

1. a key/value pair
2. a pointer to next node

The data structure for doubly linked lists is a custom `Node` that consists of the following:

1. a key/value pair
2. a pointer to next node
3. a pointer to previous node

The data structure for a stack and also for a queue is a `Java` list.
The data structure for trees is a custom node that consists of the following:

1. a key/value pair
2. a pointer to left node
3. a pointer to right node

The data structure for a hash table is a `Java` dictionary. The preceding structures are based on simplicity; however, please keep in mind that other structures are possible as well. For example, you can use an array to implement a list, a stack, a queue, and even a tree.

Operations on Data Structures

As you will see later in this chapter as well as other chapters, the operations on these data structures usually involve the following:

1. insert (includes append)
2. delete
3. search
4. update (an existing element)
5. check for empty structure
6. check for full structure (queues and stacks)

WHAT ARE SINGLY LINKED LISTS?

Although arrays are useful data structures, one of their disadvantages is that the size or the number of elements in an array must be known in advance. One alternative that does not have this advantage is a "linked list," which is the topic of this chapter.

A singly linked list is a collection of data elements, which are commonly called nodes. Given a node, it contains two things:

```
1. a value that is stored in the node, and
2. a reference to the next node (called its successor)
```

By way of analogy, think of a conga line of dances: each dancer is a node, and the dancer places his or her hands on the hips of another dancer: the latter dancer is the location of the next node.

Unlike arrays, linked lists are dynamically created on an as-needed basis. Moreover, the preceding analogy makes the following point clear: there is a "last" node that does not have a next node. Thus, the last node in a list has None as its successor (i.e., next node).

In general, a node in a singly linked list can be one of the following three types:

```
1) the "root" node
2) an intermediate node
3) the last node (no next element)
```

Of course, when a linked list is empty, then the nodes in the preceding list are all None.

Tradeoffs for Linked Lists

Every data structure has tradeoffs, which is to say, advantages and disadvantages. In particular, linked lists have the following advantages:

1. easy to append an element to a list
2. easy to insert an element in a list
3. easy to delete an element from a list
4. the node count for the list is not required in advance

Unlike arrays, the operations in the preceding bullet items do not require "shifting over" the elements of an array: only the references are updated.

However, linked lists do have disadvantages:

1. more difficult (time-consuming) to search for an element
2. a larger amount of memory is required

Thus, arrays work better when the number of elements is known in advance and there are no insertions or deletions (only updates), whereas linked lists work better when the number of data elements is not known in advance.

Unlike arrays, the elements of a linked list can be stored in noncontiguous memory locations: the value of the next field provides the location of the next node in the linked list (except for the LAST node that has None as its next node).

SINGLY LINKED LISTS: CREATE AND APPEND OPERATIONS

Linked lists support several operations, including insert (add a new node), delete (an existing node), update (change the value of an existing node), and traverse (list all the nodes). The following subsections discuss the preceding operations in more detail.

A Node Class for Singly Linked Lists

Listing 5.1 displays the contents of SLNode.java that illustrates how to define a simple Java class that represents a single node in a linked list.

LISTING 5.1: SLNode.py

```
public class SLNode
{
    static class Node {
      String data = "";
      public Node(String data) {
        this.data = data;
        Node next = null;
      }
    }

    public static void main(String[] args)
    {
        Node node1 = new Node("Jane");
        Node node2 = new Node("Dave");
        Node node3 = new Node("Stan");
        Node node4 = new Node("Alex");
```

```
            System.out.println("node1.data: "+node1.data);
            System.out.println("node2.data: "+node2.data);
            System.out.println("node3.data: "+node3.data);
            System.out.println("node4.data: "+node4.data);
    }
}
```

Listing 5.1 is straightforward: it initializes the variables msg and num with the specified values. Launch the following command from the command line and you will see the following output:

```
node1.data: Jane
node2.data: Dave
node3.data: Stan
node4.data: Alex
```

Java Code for Appending a Node

Listing 5.2 displays the contents of AppendSLNode.java that illustrates a better way to create a linked list and append nodes to that list.

LISTING 5.2: AppendSLNode.java

```
public class AppendSLNode
{
    static class Node {
      String data = "";
      Node next = null;

      public Node(String data) {
        this.data = data;
        this.next = null;
      }
    }

    public static Node[] append_node(Node ROOT, Node LAST, String item)
    {
      if(ROOT == null) {
        ROOT = new Node(item);
        //System.out.println("1Node:", ROOT.data);
      } else {
        if(ROOT.next == null) {
          Node NEWNODE = new Node(item);
          LAST = NEWNODE;
          ROOT.next = LAST;
          //System.out.println("2Node:", NEWNODE.data);
        } else {
          Node NEWNODE = new Node(item);
          LAST.next = NEWNODE;
          LAST = NEWNODE;
          //System.out.println("3Node: "+NEWNODE.data);
        }
      }
```

```
        Node[] results = new Node[2];
        results[0] = ROOT;
        results= LAST;
        return results;
    }

    public static void main(String[] args)
    {
        Node[] results = new Node[2];
        Node ROOT  = null;
        Node LAST  = null;

        // append items to list:
        String[] items = new String[]{"Stan", "Steve", "Sally", "Alex"};
        for(String item : items) {
          results = append_node(ROOT, LAST, item);
          ROOT = results[0];
          LAST = results[1];
        }

        // display items in list:
        Node CURR = ROOT;
        while(CURR != null) {
          System.out.println("Node: "+CURR.data);
          CURR = CURR.next;
        }
    }
}
```

Listing 5.2 defines a Node class as before, followed by the Java function append_node() that contains the logic for initializing a singly linked list and also for appending nodes to that list. Launch the code in Listing 5.2 from the command line and you will see the following output:

```
Node: Stan
Node: Steve
Node: Sally
Node: Alex
```

FINDING A NODE IN A LINKED LIST

Listing 5.3 displays the contents of FindSLNode2.java that illustrates how to find a node in a linked list.

LISTING 5.3: FindSLNode2.java

```
public class FindSLNode2
{
    static class Node {
      String data = "";
      Node next = null;

      public Node(String data) {
        this.data = data;
```

```java
      this.next = null;
   }
}

public static Node[] append_node(Node ROOT, Node LAST, String item)
{
   if(ROOT == null) {
      ROOT = new Node(item);
      //System.out.println("1Node:", ROOT.data);
   } else {
      if(ROOT.next == null) {
         Node NEWNODE = new Node(item);
         LAST = NEWNODE;
         ROOT.next = LAST;
         //System.out.println("2Node:", NEWNODE.data);
      } else {
         Node NEWNODE = new Node(item);
         LAST.next = NEWNODE;
         LAST = NEWNODE;
         //System.out.println("3Node:", NEWNODE.data);
      }
   }

   Node[] results = new Node[2];
   results[0] = ROOT;
   results= LAST;
   return results;
}

public static void find_item(Node ROOT,String item)
{
   Boolean found = false;
   Node CURR = ROOT;
   System.out.println("=> Search for: "+item);
   while (CURR != null) {
      System.out.println("Checking: "+CURR.data);
      if(CURR.data == item) {
         System.out.println("=> Found "+item);
         found = true;
         break;
      } else {
         CURR = CURR.next;
      }
   }

   if(found == false) {
      System.out.println("* "+item+" not found *");
   }
   System.out.println("------------------\n");
}

public static void display_list(Node ROOT)
{
    Node CURR = ROOT;
    while (CURR != null) {
```

```
            System.out.print(CURR.data+" ");
            CURR = CURR.next;
        }
        System.out.println("\n");
    }

    public static void main(String[] args)
    {
        Node[] results = new Node[2];
        Node ROOT  = null;
        Node LAST  = null;

        String[] items = new String[]{"Stan", "Steve", "Sally", "Alex"};
        for(String item : items) {
            results = append_node(ROOT, LAST, item);
            ROOT = results[0];
            LAST = results[1];
        }

        System.out.println("List of Items:");
        display_list(ROOT);

        for(String item : items)
            find_item(ROOT,item);
    }
}
```

Listing 5.3 defines the static methods append_node(), find_item(), and display_list() that append nodes to a linked list, find items in a linked list, and display the contents of a linked list, respectively.

The append_node() method contains the same code that you saw in a previous example, and the find_item() iterates through the linked list and compares the contents of each node with a given string. An appropriate message is displayed depending on whether or not the given string was found in the linked list.

The main() method starts by initializing the string-based array items with a list of strings, followed by a loop that iterates through the elements of items and invokes the append_node() method in order to append each string to the linked list. The final portion of the main() method displays the contents of the linked list, followed by a loop that iterates through the elements in the items variable and checks whether or not each element is present in the linked list. Launch the code in Listing 5.3 from the command line and you will see the following output:

```
List of Items:
Stan Steve Sally Alex

=> Search for: Stan
Checking: Stan
=> Found Stan
--------------------

=> Search for: Steve
Checking: Stan
Checking: Steve
=> Found Steve
```

```
-------------------
=> Search for: Sally
Checking: Stan
Checking: Steve
Checking: Sally
=> Found Sally
-------------------

=> Search for: Alex
Checking: Stan
Checking: Steve
Checking: Sally
Checking: Alex
=> Found Alex
-------------------
```

Listing 5.3 works fine for a small number of nodes. For linked lists that contain more nodes, we need a scalable way to construct a list of nodes, which is discussed in the next section.

APPENDING A NODE IN A LINKED LIST

When you create a linked list, you must *always* check if the root node is empty: if so, then you create a root node, otherwise you append the new node to the last node. Let's translate the preceding sentence into pseudocode that describes how to add a new element to a linked list:

```
Let ROOT be the root node (initially NULL) of the linked list
Let LAST be the last node (initially NULL) of the linked list
Let NEW be a new node and let NEW->next = NULL

// decide where to insert the new node:
if (ROOT == NULL)
{
   ROOT = NEW;
   LAST = NEW;
}
else
{
   LAST->next = NEW;
   LAST = NEW;
}
```

The last node in a linked list always points to a NULL element.

Finding a Node in a Linked List (Method 2)

Listing 5.4 displays the contents of FindSLNode.java that illustrates how to find a node in a linked list.

LISTING 5.4: FindSLNode.java

```java
public class FindSLNode
{
   static class Node {
```

```java
    String data = "";
    Node next = null;
    public Node(String data) {
      this.data = data;
      this.next = null;
    }
  }


  public static void find_item(Node ROOT, String item)
  {
     Boolean found = false;
     Node CURR = ROOT;
     System.out.println("=> Search for: "+item);

     while (CURR != null) {
       System.out.println("Checking: "+CURR.data);
       if(CURR.data == item) {
         System.out.println("=> Found "+item);
         found = true;
         break;
       } else {
         CURR = CURR.next;
       }
     }

     if(found == false)
       System.out.println("* "+item+" not found *");
     System.out.println("------------------\n");
  }

  public static Node[] append_node(Node ROOT, Node LAST, String item)
  {
    if(ROOT == null) {
      ROOT = new Node(item);
      //print("1Node:", ROOT.data);
    } else {
      if(ROOT.next == null) {
        Node NEWNODE = new Node(item);
        LAST = NEWNODE;
        ROOT.next = LAST;
        //print("2Node:", NEWNODE.data);
      } else {
        Node NEWNODE = new Node(item);
        LAST.next = NEWNODE;
        LAST = NEWNODE;
        //print("3Node:", NEWNODE.data)
      }
    }

    Node[] results = new Node[2];
    results[0] = ROOT;
    results= LAST;
    return results;
  }
```

```java
public static void main(String[] args)
{
    Node[] results = new Node[2];

    Node ROOT  = null;
    Node LAST  = null;

    Node node1 = new Node("Jane");
    ROOT  = node1;

    Node node2 = new Node("Dave");
    LAST = node2;
    ROOT.next = LAST;

    Node node3 = new Node("Stan");
    LAST.next = node3;
    LAST  = node3;

    Node node4 = new Node("Alex");
    LAST.next = node4;
    LAST  = node4;

    ROOT  = null;
    LAST  = null;

    String[] items = new String[]{"Stan", "Steve", "Sally", "Alex"};
    for(String item : items) {
      results = append_node(ROOT, LAST, item);
      ROOT = results[0];
      LAST = results[1];
    }

    for(String item : items)
      find_item(ROOT,item);
  }
}
```

Listing 5.4 is straightforward: it initializes the variables msg and num with the specified values. Launch the code in Listing 5.4 from the command line and you will see the following output:

```
=> Search for: Stan
Checking: Jane
Checking: Dave
Checking: Stan
=> Found Stan
-------------------

=> Search for: Steve
Checking: Jane
Checking: Dave
Checking: Stan
Checking: Alex
* Steve not found *
-------------------
```

```
=> Search for: Sally
Checking: Jane
Checking: Dave
Checking: Stan
Checking: Alex
* Sally not found *
-------------------

=> Search for: Alex
Checking: Jane
Checking: Dave
Checking: Stan
Checking: Alex
=> Found Alex
```

SINGLY LINKED LISTS: UPDATE AND DELETE OPERATIONS

In the previous section, you saw how to create a linked list, display its contents, and search for a specific node. In this section, you will learn how to update a node in a linked list as also how to delete a node in a linked list.

UPDATING A NODE IN A SINGLY LINKED LIST

The following pseudocode explains how to search for an element, and update its contents if the element is present in a linked list:

```
CURR = ROOT
Found = False
OLDDATA = "something old";
NEWDATA = "something new";

if (ROOT == NULL)
{
    print("* EMPTY LIST *");
}

while (CURR != NULL)
{
    if(CURR->data == OLDDATA)
    {
        print("found node with value",OLDDATA);
        CURR->data = NEWDATA;
        Found = True;
    }

    if(Found == True) { break; }

    PREV = CURR;
    CURR = CURR->next;
}
```

Java Code to Update a Node

Listing 5.5 displays the contents of `UpdateSLNode.java` that illustrates how to update a node in a linked list.

LISTING 5.5: UpdateSLNode.java

```java
public class UpdateSLNode
{
    static class Node {
      String data = "";
      Node next = null;

      public Node(String data) {
        this.data = data;
        this.next = null;
      }
    }

    public static Node[] append_node(Node ROOT, Node LAST, String item)
    {
      if(ROOT == null) {
        ROOT = new Node(item);
        //print("1Node:", ROOT.data);
      } else {
        if(ROOT.next == null) {
          Node NEWNODE = new Node(item);
          LAST = NEWNODE;
          ROOT.next = LAST;
          //print("2Node:"+ NEWNODE.data);
        } else {
          Node NEWNODE = new Node(item);
          LAST.next = NEWNODE;
          LAST = NEWNODE;
          //print("3Node:", NEWNODE.data)
        }
      }

      Node[] results = new Node[2];
      results[0] = ROOT;
      results= LAST;
      return results;
    }

    public static void main(String[] args)
    {
      Node[] results = new Node[2];
      Node ROOT  = null;
      Node LAST  = null;

      String[] items = new String[]{"Stan", "Steve", "Sally", "Alex"};
      for(String item : items) {
        results = append_node(ROOT, LAST, item);
        ROOT = results[0];
        LAST = results[1];
      }

      // display items in list:
      System.out.println("=> list items:");
      Node CURR = ROOT;
      while(CURR != null) {
```

```
            System.out.println("Node: "+CURR.data);
            CURR = CURR.next;
        }
        System.out.println();

        // update item in list:
        String curr_val = "Alex";
        String new_val  = "Alexander";
        Boolean found = false;

        CURR = ROOT;
        while(CURR != null)
        {
          if(CURR.data == curr_val) {
            System.out.println("Found:   "+CURR.data);
            CURR.data = new_val;
            System.out.println("Updated: "+CURR.data);
            found = true;
            break;
          } else {
            CURR = CURR.next;
          }
        }

        if(found == false)
          System.out.println("* Item "+curr_val+" not in list *");
    }
}
```

Listing 5.5 defines a `Node` class as before, followed by the Java method `append_node()` that contains the logic for initializing a singly linked list and also for appending nodes to that list.

Launch the code in Listing 5.5 from the command line and you will see the following output:

```
=> list items:
Node: Stan
Node: Steve
Node: Sally
Node: Alex

Found:   Alex
Updated: Alexander
```

DELETING A NODE IN A LINKED LIST

The following pseudocode explains how to search for an element, and delete the element if it is present in a linked list:

```
CURR = ROOT
PREV = ROOT
item = <node-value>
Found = False

if (ROOT == NULL)
{
```

```
      print("* EMPTY LIST *");
  }

  while (CURR != NULL)
  {
     if(CURR.data == item)
     {
        print("found node with value",item);

        Found = True
        if(CURR == ROOT)
        {
           ROOT = CURR.next // the list is now empty
        }
        else
        {
           PREV.next = CURR.next;
        }
     }

     if(found == True) { break; }

     PREV = CURR;
     CURR = CURR.next;
  }

  return ROOT
```

JAVA CODE FOR DELETING A NODE

Listing 5.6 displays the contents of DeleteSLNode.java that illustrates how to delete a node in a linked list. This code sample is longer than the code samples in the previous sections because the code needs to distinguish between deleting the root node versus a nonroot node.

LISTING 5.6: DeleteSLNode.java

```java
public class DeleteSLNode
{
   static class Node {
     String data = "";
     Node next = null;
     public Node(String data) {
       this.data = data;
       this.next = null;
     }
   }

   public static Node[] append_node(Node ROOT, Node LAST, String item)
   {
     if(ROOT == null) {
       ROOT = new Node(item);
     //System.out.println("1Node: "+ ROOT.data);
     } else {
       if(ROOT.next == null) {
```

```
          Node NEWNODE = new Node(item);
          LAST = NEWNODE;
          ROOT.next = LAST;
     //System.out.println("2Node: "+ NEWNODE.data);
     } else {
        Node NEWNODE = new Node(item);
        LAST.next = NEWNODE;
        LAST = NEWNODE;
     //System.out.println("3Node: "+ NEWNODE.data);
     }
   }

//System.out.println("NEW ROOT: "+ROOT.data);
//System.out.println("NEW LAST: "+LAST.data);
  Node[] results = new Node[2];
  results[0] = ROOT;
  results= LAST;
  return results;
}

public static Node delete_item(Node ROOT, String item)
{
  Node PREV = ROOT;
  Node CURR = ROOT;
  Boolean found = false;

  System.out.println("=> searching for item: "+item);
  while (CURR != null) {
     if(CURR.data == item) {
        //System.out.println("=> Found node with value: "+item);
        found = true;

        if(CURR == ROOT) {
          ROOT = CURR.next;
        //System.out.println("NEW ROOT");
        } else {
        //System.out.println("REMOVED NON-ROOT");
          PREV.next = CURR.next;
        }
     }

     if(found == true)
       break;

     PREV = CURR;
     CURR = CURR.next;
  }

  if(found == false)
    System.out.println("* Item "+item+" not in linked list *\n");
  else
    System.out.println("* Removed "+item+" from linked list *\n");

  return ROOT;
}
```

```java
    public static void display_items(Node ROOT)
    {
      System.out.println("=> Items in Linked List:");
      Node CURR = ROOT;
      while(CURR != null) {
        System.out.println("Node: "+CURR.data);
        CURR = CURR.next;
      }
      System.out.println();
    }

    public static Node initialize_list(Node ROOT)
    {
        Node LAST = ROOT;
        // initialize linked list:
        String[] items = new String[]{"Stan", "Steve", "Sally", "Alex"};

        Node[] results = new Node[2];
        for(String item : items) {
          results = append_node(ROOT, LAST, item);
          ROOT = results[0];
          LAST = results[1];
        }

        return ROOT;
    }

    public static void main(String[] args)
    {
        Node ROOT = null;
        Node LAST = null;
        Node[] results = new Node[2];

        // construct linked list:
        ROOT = initialize_list(ROOT);

        // display items in linked list:
        display_items(ROOT);

        // remove item from linked list:
        ROOT = delete_item(ROOT, "Alex");

        display_items(ROOT);
    }
}
```

Listing 5.6 defines a `Node` class as before, followed by the Java method `append_node()` that contains the logic for initializing a singly linked list and also for appending nodes to that list.

Launch the code in Listing 5.6 from the command line and you will see the following output:

```
=> Items in Linked List:
Node: Stan
Node: Steve
Node: Sally
```

```
Node: Alex

=> searching for item: Alex
* Removed Alex from linked list *

=> Items in Linked List:
Node: Stan
Node: Steve
Node: Sally
```

JAVA CODE FOR A CIRCULAR LINKED LIST

The only structural difference between a singly linked list and a circular linked list is that the "last" node in the latter has a "next" node equal to the initial (root) node. Operations on circular linked lists are the same as operations on singly linked lists. However, the algorithms for singly linked lists need to be modified in order to accommodate circular linked lists.

Listing 5.7 displays the contents of CircularSLNode.java that illustrates how to delete a node in a linked list. This code sample is longer than the code samples in the previous sections because the code needs to distinguish between deleting the root node versus a nonroot node.

LISTING 5.7: CircularSLNode.java

```java
public class CircularSLNode
{
    static class Node {
      String data = "";
      Node next = null;

      public Node(String data) {
        this.data = data;
        this.next = null;
      }
    }

/*
The code follows these cases for inserting a node:
    NULL     (empty list)
    x        (one node)
    x<->x    (two nodes)
    x y z x (multiple nodes)
*/
    public static Node append_node(Node ROOT, String item)
    {
      System.out.println("=> processing item: "+item);

      if(ROOT == null) {
        ROOT = new Node(item);
        ROOT.next = ROOT;
        //System.out.println("1NEW initialized Root: "+ROOT.data);
      } else {
        if(ROOT.next == ROOT) {
          //System.out.println("Found SINGLE NODE Root: "+ROOT.data);
          Node NEWNODE = new Node(item);
```

```
            ROOT.next = NEWNODE;
            NEWNODE.next = ROOT;
            //System.out.println("Root: "+ROOT.data+" NEWNODE: "+NEWNODE.
data);
        } else {
            // traverse the list to find the node prior to ROOT:
            Node LAST = ROOT;
            LAST = LAST.next;
            while(LAST.next != ROOT) {
                LAST = LAST.next;
            }
            Node NEWNODE = new Node(item);
            NEWNODE.next = ROOT;
            LAST.next = NEWNODE;
            //System.out.println("3Node NEW LAST: "+NEWNODE.data);
        }
    }
    //System.out.println("Returning ROOT: "+ROOT.data);
    return ROOT;
}

public static void display_list(Node ROOT)
{
    Node CURR = ROOT;
    if( ROOT == null ) {
        System.out.print("* empty list *");
        return;
    }

    System.out.print(CURR.data+" ");
    CURR = CURR.next;

    // display items in list:
    while(CURR != ROOT) {
        System.out.print(CURR.data+" ");
        CURR = CURR.next;
    }
    System.out.println();
}

public static void main(String[] args)
{
    Node ROOT = null;

    String[] items = new String[]{"Stan","Steve","Sally","Alex","Nancy",
"Sara"};

    // append items to list:
    for(String item : items) {
        ROOT = append_node(ROOT, item);
    }

    System.out.println("Contents of circular list:");
    display_list(ROOT);
}
}
```

Listing 5.7 defines a `Node` class as before, followed by the Java method `append_node()` that contains the logic for initializing a singly linked list and also for appending nodes to that list.

Launch the code in Listing 5.7 from the command line and you will see the following output:

```
=> processing item: Stan
=> processing item: Steve
=> processing item: Sally
=> processing item: Alex
=> processing item: Nancy
=> processing item: Sara
Contents of circular list:
Stan Steve Sally Alex Nancy Sara
```

JAVA CODE FOR UPDATING A CIRCULAR LINKED LIST

The only structural difference between a singly linked list and a circular linked list is that the "last" node in the latter has a "next" node equal to the initial (root) node. Operations on circular linked lists are the same as operations on singly linked lists. However, the algorithms for singly linked lists need to be modified in order to accommodate circular linked lists.

Listing 5.8 displays the contents of `CircularUpdateSLNode.java` that illustrates how to delete a node in a linked list. This code sample is longer than the code samples in the previous sections because the code needs to distinguish between deleting the root node versus a nonroot node.

LISTING 5.8: CircularUpdateSLNode.java

```java
public class CircularUpdateSLNode
{
    static class Node {
      String data = "";
      Node next = null;

      public Node(String data) {
        this.data = data;
        this.next = null;
      }
    }

/*
The code follows these cases for inserting a node:
    NULL    (empty list)
    x       (one node)
    x<->x   (two nodes)
    x y z x (multiple nodes)
*/
    public static Node append_node(Node ROOT, String item)
    {
      //System.out.println("=> processing item: "+item);
      if(ROOT == null) {
```

```
        ROOT = new Node(item);
        ROOT.next = ROOT;
        //System.out.println("1NEW initialized Root: "+ROOT.data);
    } else {
        if(ROOT.next == ROOT) {
            //System.out.println("Found SINGLE NODE Root: "+ROOT.data);
            Node NEWNODE = new Node(item);
            ROOT.next = NEWNODE;
            NEWNODE.next = ROOT;
            //System.out.println(
            //.    "Root: "+ROOT.data+" NEW: "+NEWNODE.data);
        } else {
            // traverse the list to find the node prior to ROOT:
            Node LAST = ROOT;
            LAST = LAST.next;
            while(LAST.next != ROOT) {
                LAST = LAST.next;
            }

            Node NEWNODE = new Node(item);
            NEWNODE.next = ROOT;
            LAST.next = NEWNODE;
            //System.out.println("3Node NEW LAST: "+NEWNODE.data);
        }
    }
    //System.out.println("Returning ROOT: "+ROOT.data);
    return ROOT;
}

public static Node update_item(Node ROOT, String curr_val, String
new_val)
{
    if(ROOT == null) {
        System.out.println("=> empty list *");
        return null;
    }

    System.out.println("OLD: "+curr_val+" NEW: "+new_val);

    if(ROOT.next == ROOT) {
        System.out.println("ROOT VALUE: "+ROOT.data);
        if(curr_val.equals(ROOT.data)) {
            System.out.println(
                "Found data: "+curr_val+" new value: "+new_val);
            ROOT.data = new_val;
            return ROOT;
        }
    }

    Node CURR = ROOT;
    if(curr_val.equals(CURR.data)) {
        System.out.println(
            "Found data: "+curr_val+" new value: "+new_val);
        CURR.data = new_val;
        return ROOT;
```

```
    }

    // compare the contents of each node with the new string:
    Boolean Found = false;
    CURR = CURR.next;
    while(CURR != ROOT) {
      if(CURR.data == curr_val) {
        System.out.println(
          "Found data: "+curr_val+" new value: "+new_val);
        CURR.data = new_val;
        Found = true;
        break;
      } else {
        CURR = CURR.next;
      }
    }

    if(Found == false)
      System.out.println("* "+curr_val+" not found *");

    return ROOT;
  }

  public static void display_list(Node ROOT)
  {
    Node CURR = ROOT;
    if(ROOT == null) {
      System.out.println("* empty list *");
      return;
    }

    System.out.print("LIST: ");
    System.out.print(CURR.data+" ");
    CURR = CURR.next;

    // display items in list:
    while(CURR != ROOT) {
      System.out.print(CURR.data+" ");
      CURR = CURR.next;
    }
    System.out.println();
  }

  public static void main(String[] args)
  {
    Node ROOT = null;

    String[] items =
      new String[]{"Stan","Steve","Sally","Alex","Nancy","Sara"};

    // append items to list:
    for(String item : items) {
      ROOT = append_node(ROOT, item);
    }
    System.out.println("Contents of circular list:");
```

```
        display_list(ROOT);
        System.out.println();

        // list of update strings:
        String[] replace1 =
            new String[]{"Stan","Sally","Sara","Tomas"};
        String[] replace2 =
            new String[]{"Joe","Sandra","Rebecca","Theo"};

        for(int i=0; i<replace1.length; i++) {
            // update value of a list item:
            String curr_val = replace1[i];
            String new_val  = replace2[i];
            ROOT = update_item(ROOT, curr_val, new_val);
            display_list(ROOT);
            System.out.println();
        }
    }
}
```

Listing 5.8 defines a `Node` class as before, followed by the Java method `append_node()` that contains the logic for initializing a singly linked list and also for appending nodes to that list.

Launch the code in Listing 5.8 from the command line and you will see the following output:

```
Contents of circular list:
LIST: Stan Steve Sally Alex Nancy Sara

OLD VALUE: Stan NEW VALUE: Joe
Found data: Stan new value: Joe
LIST: Joe Steve Sally Alex Nancy Sara

OLD VALUE: Sally NEW VALUE: Sandra
Found data: Sally new value: Sandra
LIST: Joe Steve Sandra Alex Nancy Sara

OLD VALUE: Sara NEW VALUE: Rebecca
Found data: Sara new value: Rebecca
LIST: Joe Steve Sandra Alex Nancy Rebecca

OLD VALUE: Tomas NEW VALUE: Theo
* Tomas not found *
LIST: Joe Steve Sandra Alex Nancy Rebecca
```

WORKING WITH DOUBLY LINKED LISTS (DLL)

A doubly linked list is a collection of data elements, which are commonly called nodes. Given a node, it contains three items:

1. a value that is stored in the node, and
2. the location of the `next` node (called its successor)
3. the location of the previous node (called its predecessor)

Using the same "conga line" analogy as described in the previous section about singly linked lists, each person knows is touching the "next" node with one hand and is touching the "previous" node with the other hand (not the best analogy, but you get the idea).

Operations on doubly linked lists are the same as the operations on singly linked lists; however, there are two pointers (the successor and the predecessor) to update instead of just one (the successor).

A Node Class for Doubly Linked Lists

Listing 5.9 displays the contents of the Java file DLNode.java that illustrates how to define a simple Java class that represents a single node in a linked list.

LISTING 5.9: DLNode.java

```
public class DLNode
{
    public String data = "";
    public String prev = "";
    public String next = "";

    public DLNode( String data )
    {
      this.data = data;
      this.prev = "";
      this.next = "";
    }

    public static void main( String[] args)
    {
        DLNode node1 = new DLNode("Jane");
        DLNode node2 = new DLNode("Dave");
        DLNode node3 = new DLNode("Stan");
        DLNode node4 = new DLNode("Alex");

        System.out.println("node1.data: "+node1.data);
        System.out.println("node2.data: "+node2.data);
        System.out.println("node3.data: "+node3.data);
        System.out.println("node4.data: "+node4.data);
    }
}
```

Listing 5.9 is straightforward: it defines the Java class DLNode and then creates four such nodes. The final portion of Listing 5.9 displays the contents of the four nodes. Launch the following command from the command line and you will see the following output:

```
node1.data: Jane
node2.data: Dave
node3.data: Stan
node4.data: Alex
```

Once again, a node in a doubly linked list can be one of the following three types:

```
1) the "root" node
2) an intermediate node
3) the last node (no next element)
```

Of course, when a linked list is empty, then the nodes in the preceding list are all None.

APPENDING A NODE IN A DOUBLY LINKED LIST

When you create a linked list, you must always check if the root node is empty: if so, then you create a root node, otherwise you append the new node to the last node. Let's translate the preceding sentence into pseudocode that describes how to add a new element to a linked list.

```
Let ROOT be the root node (initially NULL) of the linked list
Let LAST be the last node (initially NULL) of the linked list
Let NEW be a new node with NEW->next = NULL and NEW->prev = NULL

// decide where to insert the new node:
if (ROOT == NULL)
{
   ROOT = NEW;
   ROOT->next = NULL;
   ROOT->prev = NULL;

   LAST = NEW;
   LAST->next = NULL;
   LAST->prev = NULL;
}
else
{
   NEW->prev = LAST;
   LAST->next = NEW;
   NEW->next = NULL;
   LAST = NEW;
}
```

The last node in a doubly linked list always points to a null element.

Java Code for Appending a Node

Listing 5.10 displays the contents of AppendDLNode.java that illustrates a better way to create a linked list and append nodes to that list.

LISTING 5.10: AppendDLNode.java

```
public class AppendDLNode
{
   static class DLNode {
```

```
      String data = "";
      DLNode next = null;
      DLNode prev = null;

      public DLNode(String data) {
        this.data = data;
        this.next = null;
        this.prev = null;
      }
    }

    public static DLNode construct_list()
    {
        DLNode ROOT = null;
        DLNode LAST = null;
        DLNode[] results = new DLNode[2];

        String[] items = new String[]{"Jane", "Dave", "Stan", "Alex"};

        for(String item : items) {
            results = append_node(ROOT, LAST, item);
            ROOT = results[0];
            LAST = results[1];
        }

        return ROOT;
    }

    public static DLNode[] append_node(DLNode ROOT, DLNode LAST, String
item)
    {
      if(ROOT == null) {
        ROOT = new DLNode(item);
        ROOT.next = ROOT;
        ROOT.prev = ROOT;
        LAST = ROOT;
        //System.out.println("1DLNode:", ROOT.data);
      } else {
        if(ROOT.next == null) {
          DLNode NEWNODE = new DLNode(item);
          LAST.next = NEWNODE;
          NEWNODE.prev = LAST;
          LAST = NEWNODE;
          //System.out.println("2DLNode:", NEWNODE.data);
        } else {
          DLNode NEWNODE = new DLNode(item);
          LAST.next = NEWNODE;
          NEWNODE.prev = LAST;
          NEWNODE.next = null;
          LAST = NEWNODE;
          //System.out.println("3DLNode:", NEWNODE.data);
        }
      }

      DLNode[] results = new DLNode[2];
```

```
      results[0] = ROOT;
      results= LAST;
      return results;
   }

   public static void display_list(DLNode ROOT)
   {
      System.out.println("Doubly Linked List:");
      DLNode CURR = ROOT;
      while (CURR != null) {
        System.out.println(CURR.data);
        CURR = CURR.next;
      }
   }

   public static void main( String[] args)
   {
      DLNode ROOT = null;
      ROOT = construct_list();
      display_list(ROOT);
   }
}
```

Listing 5.10 defines a `Node` class as before, followed by the method `append_node()` that contains the logic for initializing a singly linked list and also for appending nodes to that list.

Launch the code in Listing 5.10 from the command line and you will see the following output:

```
1ROOT: Stan
2ROOT: Stan
2LAST: Steve
3Node: Sally
3Node: Alex

=> list items:
Node: Stan
Node: Steve
Node: Sally
Node: Alex

=> update list items:
Found data in LAST: Alex

=> list items:
Node: Stan
Node: Steve
Node: Sally
Node: Alexander
```

Java Code for Inserting a New Root Node

Listing 5.11 displays the contents of the `Java` file `NewRootSLNode.java` that illustrates how to iterate through an array of strings and set each string as the new root node, which effectively creates a linked list in reverse order.

LISTING 5.11: NewRootSLNode.java

```java
public class NewRootSLNode
{
   static class SLNode {
     String data = "";
     SLNode next = null;

     public SLNode(String data) {
       this.data = data;
       this.next = null;
     }
   }

   public static SLNode construct_list(SLNode ROOT, SLNode LAST)
   {
      String[] items = new String[]{"Stan", "Steve", "Sally", "Alex"};

      System.out.println("Initial items:");
      for(String item : items) {
         System.out.print(item+" ");
      }
      System.out.println("\n");

      for(String item : items) {
        ROOT = new_root(ROOT, item);
      }
      return ROOT;
   }

   public static SLNode new_root(SLNode ROOT, String item)
   {
     if(ROOT == null) {
       ROOT = new SLNode(item);
       ROOT.next = null;
       //print("1SLNode:", ROOT.data);
     } else {
       SLNode NEWNODE = new SLNode(item);
       NEWNODE.next = ROOT;
       ROOT = NEWNODE;
     }
     return ROOT;
   }

   public static void display_list(SLNode ROOT)
   {
      System.out.println("Reversed Linked List:");
      SLNode CURR = ROOT;
      while(CURR != null) {
        System.out.print(CURR.data+" ");
        CURR = CURR.next;
      }
      System.out.println("\n");
   }

   public static void main(String[] args)
```

```
   {
      SLNode ROOT = null;
      SLNode LAST = null;

      // construct SL list:
      ROOT = construct_list(ROOT, LAST);

      display_list(ROOT);
   }
}
```

Listing 5.11 defines a Node class as before, followed by the definition of the methods construct_list(), new_root(), and display_list() that construct a linked list, insert a new root node, and display the contents of the constructed linked list, respectively.

The `construct_list()` displays the elements of the string array items, followed by a loop that iterates through the elements of the items array. During each iteration, the new_root() method is invoked with a string that is used to create a new node, which in turn is set as the new root node of the linked list. The display_list() method contains the same code that you have seen in previous examples.

The main() method is very simple: the ROOT and LAST nodes are initialized as null nodes and then the construct_list() method is invoked. The only other code snippet invokes the display_list() method that displayed the elements in the (reversed) list. Launch the code in Listing 5.11 from the command line and you will see the following output:

```
Initial items:
Stan Steve Sally Alex

Reversed Linked List:
Alex Sally Steve Stan
```

Java Code for Inserting an Intermediate Node

Listing 5.12 displays the contents of `NewInterSLNode.java` that illustrates a better way to create a linked list and append nodes to that list.

LISTING 5.12: NewInterSLNode.java

```java
public class NewInterSLNode
{
   static class Node {
      String data = "";
      Node next = null;

      public Node(String data) {
         this.data = data;
         this.next = null;
      }
   }

/*
The code follows these cases for deleting a node:
   NULL   (empty list)
```

```
    x      (one node)
    x x    (two nodes)
    x x x  (multiple nodes)
*/
    public static void insert_item(Node ROOT, int position, String data)
    {
       if(ROOT == null) {
          System.out.println("* empty list *");
       }

       int count=0;
       Node CURR = ROOT;
       Node PREV = CURR;

       while (CURR != null) {
         if(count == position) {
            System.out.println("=> "+data+" after position "+position);
            Node NEWNODE = new Node(data);
            if(CURR.next == null) {
               CURR.next = NEWNODE;
            } else {
               NEWNODE.next = CURR.next;
               CURR.next = NEWNODE;
            }
            break;
         }
         count += 1;
         PREV = CURR;
         CURR = CURR.next;
       }

       if(count < position) {
          System.out.println(position+" is beyond end of list");
       }
    }

    public static Node[] append_node(Node ROOT, Node LAST, String item)
    {
      if(ROOT == null) {
        ROOT = new Node(item);
        //print("1Node:", ROOT.data);
      } else {
        if(ROOT.next == null) {
          Node NEWNODE = new Node(item);
          LAST = NEWNODE;
          ROOT.next = LAST;
          //print("2Node:", NEWNODE.data);
        } else {
          Node NEWNODE = new Node(item);
          LAST.next = NEWNODE;
          LAST = NEWNODE;
          //print("3Node:", NEWNODE.data)
        }
      }

      Node[] results = new Node[2];
```

```
      results[0] = ROOT;
      results= LAST;
      return results;
   }

   public static void display_list(Node ROOT)
   {
      Node CURR = ROOT;
      while (CURR != null) {
         System.out.print(CURR.data+" ");
         CURR = CURR.next;
      }
      System.out.println("\n");
   }

   public static void main(String[] args)
   {
      Node[] results = new Node[2];
      Node ROOT  = null;
      Node LAST  = null;

      String[] items =
               new String[]{"Stan", "Steve", "Sally", "Alex"};
      for(String item : items) {
        results = append_node(ROOT, LAST, item);
        ROOT = results[0];
        LAST = results[1];
      }

      System.out.println("Initial list:");
      display_list(ROOT);

      String[] insert_items =
               new String[]{"MIKE", "PASTA", "PIZZA", "CODE"};
      int[] insert_indexes  = new int[]{0, 3, 8, 2};

      int pos = 0;
      for(String new_item : insert_items) {
         System.out.println("Inserting: "+new_item);
         insert_item(ROOT, insert_indexes[pos++], new_item);
         System.out.println("Updated list:");
         display_list(ROOT);
      }
   }
}
```

Listing 5.12 defines a Node class as before, followed by the Java method append_node() that contains the logic for initializing a singly linked list and also for appending nodes to that list.

Launch the code in Listing 5.12 from the command line and you will see the following output:

```
Initial list:
Stan Steve Sally Alex

Inserting: MIKE
=> MIKE after position 0
Updated list:
```

```
Stan MIKE Steve Sally Alex

Inserting: PASTA
=> PASTA after position 3
Updated list:
Stan MIKE Steve Sally PASTA Alex

Inserting: PIZZA
8 is beyond end of list
Updated list:
Stan MIKE Steve Sally PASTA Alex

Inserting: CODE
=> CODE after position 2
Updated list:
Stan MIKE Steve CODE Sally PASTA Alex
```

Traversing the Nodes in a Doubly Linked List

The following pseudocode explains how to traverse the elements of a linked list:

```
CURR = ROOT

while (CURR != NULL)
{
   print("contents:",CURR->data);
   CURR = CURR->next;
}

If (ROOT == NULL)
{
   print("* EMPTY LIST *");
}
```

Updating a Node in a Doubly Linked List

The following pseudocode explains how to search for an element and update its contents if the element is present in a linked list:

```
CURR = ROOT
Found = False
OLDDATA = "something old";
NEWDATA = "something new";

If (ROOT == NULL)
{
   print("* EMPTY LIST *");
}

while (CURR != NULL)
{
   if(CURR->data = OLDDATA)
   {
      print("found node with value",OLDDATA);
      CURR->data = NEWDATA;
```

```
        }

    if(Found == True) { break; }

    PREV = CURR;
    CURR = CURR->next;
}
```

As you now know, some operations on doubly linked lists involve updating a single pointer, and other operations involve updating two pointers.

Java Code to Update a Node

Listing 5.13 displays the contents of UpdateDLNode.java that illustrates how to update a node in a linked list.

LISTING 5.13: UpdateDLNode.java

```java
public class UpdateDLNode
{
    static class DLNode {
      String data = "";
      DLNode next = null;
      DLNode prev = null;

      public DLNode(String data) {
         this.data = data;
         this.next = null;
         this.prev = null;
      }
    }

    public static DLNode construct_list()
    {
        DLNode ROOT = null;
        DLNode LAST = null;
        DLNode[] results = new DLNode[2];

        String[] items = new String[]{"Jane", "Dave", "Stan", "Alex"};

        for(String item : items) {
            results = append_node(ROOT, LAST, item);
            ROOT = results[0];
            LAST = results[1];
        }

        return ROOT;
    }

    public static DLNode[] append_node(DLNode ROOT, DLNode LAST, String
item)
    {
      if(ROOT == null) {
        ROOT = new DLNode(item);
        ROOT.next = ROOT;
```

```
        ROOT.prev = ROOT;
        LAST = ROOT;
        //System.out.println("1DLNode:", ROOT.data);
    } else {
      if(ROOT.next == null) {
        DLNode NEWNODE = new DLNode(item);
        LAST.next = NEWNODE;
        NEWNODE.prev = LAST;
        LAST = NEWNODE;
        //System.out.println("2DLNode:", NEWNODE.data);
      } else {
        DLNode NEWNODE = new DLNode(item);
        LAST.next = NEWNODE;
        NEWNODE.prev = LAST;
        NEWNODE.next = null;
        LAST = NEWNODE;
        //System.out.println("3DLNode:", NEWNODE.data);
      }
    }

  DLNode[] results = new DLNode[2];
  results[0] = ROOT;
  results= LAST;
  return results;
}

public static void display_list(DLNode ROOT)
{
   System.out.println("Doubly Linked List:");
   DLNode CURR = ROOT;
   while (CURR != null) {
     System.out.println(CURR.data);
     CURR = CURR.next;
   }
   System.out.println();
}

public static void updateNode(DLNode ROOT, String item, String data)
{
   Boolean found = false;
   System.out.println("Searching for "+item+":");

   DLNode CURR = ROOT;
   while (CURR != null) {
     if(CURR.data == item) {
        System.out.println("Replacing "+item+" with "+data);
        CURR.data = data;
        found = true;
        break;
     }
     CURR = CURR.next;
   }

   if(found == false) {
      System.out.println(item+" not found in linked list");
   }
```

```
      System.out.println();
   }

   public static void main( String[] args)
   {
      DLNode ROOT = null;
      ROOT = construct_list();
      display_list(ROOT);

      updateNode(ROOT, "steve", "sally");
      updateNode(ROOT, "Dave", "Davidson");
   }
}
```

Listing 5.13 defines a `Node` class as before, followed by the `Java` method `append_node()` that contains the logic for initializing a singly linked list and also for appending nodes to that list. Launch the code in Listing 5.13 from the command line and you will see the following output:

```
Doubly Linked List:
Jane
Dave
Stan
Alex

Searching for steve:
steve not found in linked list

Searching for Dave:
Replacing Dave with Davidson
```

DELETING A NODE IN A DOUBLY LINKED LIST

The following pseudocode explains how to search for an element, and delete the element if it is present in a linked list:

```
CURR = ROOT
PREV = ROOT
ANODE = <a-node-to-delete>
Found = False

If (ROOT == NULL)
{
   print("* EMPTY LIST *");
}

while (CURR != NULL)
{
   if(CURR->data = ANODE->data)
   {
      print("found node with value",ANODE->data);

      Found = True
      if(CURR == ROOT)
```

```
      {
          ROOT = NULL; // the list is now empty
      }
      else
      {
          PREV->next = CURR->next;
      }
  }

  if(Found == True) { break; }

  PREV = CURR;
  CURR = CURR->next;
}
```

Java Code to Delete a Node

Listing 5.14 displays the contents of `DeleteDLNode.java` that illustrates how to update a node in a doubly linked list.

LISTING 5.14: DeleteDLNode.java

```java
public class DeleteDLNode
{
   static class DLNode {
     String data = "";
     DLNode next = null;
     DLNode prev = null;

     public DLNode(String data) {
        this.data = data;
        this.next = null;
        this.prev = null;
     }
   }

   public static DLNode construct_list()
   {
      DLNode ROOT = null;
      DLNode LAST = null;
      DLNode[] results = new DLNode[2];

      String[] items =
          new String[]{"Jane","Dave","Stan","Alex","George","Sara"};

      for(String item : items) {
         results = append_node(ROOT, LAST, item);
         ROOT = results[0];
         LAST = results[1];
      }

      return ROOT;
   }

   public static DLNode[] append_node(DLNode ROOT, DLNode LAST, String
item)
```

```
    {
      if(ROOT == null) {
        ROOT = new DLNode(item);
        ROOT.next = ROOT;
        ROOT.prev = ROOT;
        LAST = ROOT;
        //System.out.println("1DLNode:", ROOT.data);
      } else {
        if(ROOT.next == null) {
          DLNode NEWNODE = new DLNode(item);
          LAST.next = NEWNODE;
          NEWNODE.prev = LAST;
          LAST = NEWNODE;
          //System.out.println("2DLNode:", NEWNODE.data);
        } else {
          DLNode NEWNODE = new DLNode(item);
          LAST.next = NEWNODE;
          NEWNODE.prev = LAST;
          NEWNODE.next = null;
          LAST = NEWNODE;
          //System.out.println("3DLNode:", NEWNODE.data);
        }
      }

      DLNode[] results = new DLNode[2];
      results[0] = ROOT;
      results= LAST;
      return results;
    }

    public static void display_list(DLNode ROOT)
    {
      //System.out.println("Doubly Linked List:");
      DLNode CURR = ROOT;
      while (CURR != null) {
        System.out.print(CURR.data+" ");
        CURR = CURR.next;
      }
      System.out.println("\n");
    }

/*
The code follows these cases for deleting a node:
    NULL   (empty list)
    x      (one node)
    x x    (two nodes)
    x x x  (multiple nodes)
*/
    public static DLNode deleteNode(DLNode ROOT, String item)
    {
      Boolean found = false;
      System.out.println("Searching for "+item+":");

      if(ROOT == null) {
        System.out.println("* empty list *");
        return ROOT;
      }
```

```java
      DLNode CURR = ROOT;
      DLNode PREV = ROOT;

      while (CURR != null) {
        if(CURR.data == item) {
          // three cases for the matched node:
          // root node, middle node, or last node:
          found = true;
          System.out.println("Deleting node with "+item);

          if(CURR == ROOT) {
            // is the list a single node?
            if(ROOT.next == null) {
              ROOT = null;
            } else {
              ROOT = ROOT.next;
              ROOT.prev = null;
            }
            //System.out.println("new root: "+ROOT.data);
          } else {
            DLNode NEXT = CURR.next;
            if(NEXT == null) {
              //System.out.println("final node: "+CURR.data);
              PREV.next = null;
            } else {
              //System.out.println("middle node: "+CURR.data);
              PREV.next = NEXT;
              NEXT.prev = PREV;
            }
          }
          break;
        }
        PREV = CURR;
        CURR = CURR.next;
      }

      if(found == false) {
        System.out.println(item+" not found in linked list");
      }
      return ROOT;
    }

  public static void main( String[] args)
  {
    DLNode ROOT = null;
    ROOT = construct_list();

    System.out.println("Initial list:");
    display_list(ROOT);

    String[] remove_names = new String[]{"Jane", "Stan", "Isaac",
"Sara"};
    for(String name : remove_names) {
      ROOT = deleteNode(ROOT, name);
      System.out.println("Updated list:");
      display_list(ROOT);
    }
  }
}
```

Listing 5.14 defines a `Node` class as before, followed by the `Java` method `append_node()` that contains the logic for initializing a doubly linked list and also for appending nodes to that list.

Launch the code in Listing 5.14 from the command line and you will see the following output:

```
Initial list:
Jane Dave Stan Alex George Sara

Searching for Jane:
Deleting node with Jane
Updated list:
Dave Stan Alex George Sara

Searching for Stan:
Deleting node with Stan
Updated list:
Dave Alex George Sara

Searching for Isaac:
Isaac not found in linked list
Updated list:
Dave Alex George Sara

Searching for Sara:
Deleting node with Sara
Updated list:
Dave Alex George
```

SUMMARY

This chapter started with a description of linked lists, along with their advantages and disadvantages. Then you learned how to perform several operations on singly linked lists, such as append, insert, delete, and update.

Next, you learned about doubly linked lists, and how to perform the same operations on doubly linked lists that you performed on singly linked lists. You also saw how to work with circular lists in which the last element "points" to the first element in a list.

CHAPTER 6

LINKED LISTS (2)

The previous chapter introduced you to singly linked lists, doubly linked lists, and circular lists, and how to perform basic operations on those data structures. This chapter shows you how to perform a variety of tasks that involve more than the basic operations in the previous chapter.

The first part of this chapter contains code samples that add the numbers in a linked list in several different ways, followed by code samples that display the first k and the last k elements in a linked list.

The code samples in the second portion of this chapter reverse a singly linked list and remove duplicates. You will also see how to concatenate two lists and how to merge two ordered lists. In addition, you will learn how to find the middle element of a linked list.

The final portion of this chapter shows you how to reverse a list and how to check if a linked list contains a palindrome.

TASK: ADDING NUMBERS IN A LINKED LIST (1)

Listing 6.1 displays the contents of SumSLNodes.java that illustrates how to add the numbers in a linked list.

LISTING 6.1: SumSLNodes.java

```java
public class SumSLNodes
{
    static class Node {
        int data;
        Node next = null;
        public Node(int data) {
            this.data = data;
            this.next = null;
        }
    }

    public static Node[] append_node(Node ROOT, Node LAST, int item)
```

```
    {
      Node[] results = new Node[2];

      if(ROOT == null) {
        ROOT = new Node(item);
        //System.out.println("1Node: "+ROOT.data);
      } else {
        if(ROOT.next == null) {
          Node NEWNODE = new Node(item);
          LAST = NEWNODE;
          ROOT.next = LAST;
          //System.out.println("2Node: "+NEWNODE.data);
        } else {
          Node NEWNODE = new Node(item);
          LAST.next = NEWNODE;
          LAST = NEWNODE;
          //System.out.println("3Node: "+NEWNODE.data);
        }
      }

      //return ROOT, LAST
      results[0] = ROOT;
      results[1] = LAST;
      return results;
    }

    public static void main(String[] args)
    {
      Node ROOT  = null;
      Node LAST  = null;
      Node[] results = new Node[2];
      int[] items = new int[]{1,2,3,4};

      //append items to list:
      for(int item : items) {
        //ROOT, LAST = append_node(ROOT, LAST, item);
        results = append_node(ROOT, LAST, item);
        ROOT = results[0];
        LAST = results[1];
      }

      System.out.println("Compute the sum of the nodes:");
      System.out.println("=> list items:");

      int sum = 0;
      Node CURR = ROOT;
      while(CURR != null) {
        System.out.println("Node: "+CURR.data);
        sum += CURR.data;
        CURR = CURR.next;
      }

      System.out.println("Sum of nodes: "+sum);
    }
}
```

Listing 6.1 defines a Node class as before, followed by the Java method append_ node() that contains the logic for initializing a singly linked list and also for appending nodes to that list.

Launch the code in Listing 6.1 from the command line and you will see the following output:

```
list of numbers: [1 2 3 4]
=> list items:
Node: 1
Node: 2
Node: 3
Node: 4
Sum of nodes: 10
```

TASK: ADDING NUMBERS IN A LINKED LIST (2)

Listing 6.2 displays the contents of SumSLNodes.java that illustrates how to add the numbers in a linked list.

LISTING 6.2: SumSLNodes2.java

```java
public class SumSLNodes2
{
    static class Node {
      int data;
      Node next = null;
      public Node(int data) {
        this.data = data;
        this.next = null;
      }
    }

    public static Node[] append_node(Node ROOT, Node LAST, int item)
    {
      Node[] results = new Node[2];

      if(ROOT == null) {
        ROOT = new Node(item);
        //System.out.println("1Node: "+ROOT.data);
      } else {
        if(ROOT.next == null) {
          Node NEWNODE = new Node(item);
          LAST = NEWNODE;
          ROOT.next = LAST;
          //System.out.println("2Node: "+NEWNODE.data);
        } else {
          Node NEWNODE = new Node(item);
          LAST.next = NEWNODE;
          LAST = NEWNODE;
          //System.out.println("3Node: "+NEWNODE.data);
        }
      }
```

```
      //return ROOT, LAST
      results[0] = ROOT;
      results[1] = LAST;
      return results;
    }

  public static void main(String[] args)
  {
     Node ROOT  = null;
     Node LAST  = null;
     Node[] results = new Node[2];
     int[] items = new int[]{1,2,3,4};

     System.out.println("=> list items:");
     for(int num : items) {
       System.out.print(num+" ");
     }
     System.out.println("\n");

     //append items to list:
     for(int item : items) {
         results = append_node(ROOT, LAST, item);
         ROOT = results[0];
         LAST = results[1];
     }

     // reconstruct the original number:
     // NB: [1,2,3,4] => 4,321

     int sum = 0, pow = 0, base = 10, term = 0;

     Node CURR = ROOT;
     while(CURR != null) {
       term = (int)java.lang.Math.pow(base,pow);
       term *= CURR.data;
       sum += term;
       pow += 1;
       CURR = CURR.next;
     }
     System.out.println("Reconstructed number: "+sum);
   }
}
```

Listing 6.2 defines a Node class as before, followed by the function append_node() that contains the logic for initializing a singly linked list and also for appending nodes to that list.

Launch the code in Listing 6.2 from the command line and you will see the following output:

```
list of digits:   [1 2 3 4]
Original number:   4321
```

TASK: ADDING NUMBERS IN A LINKED LIST (3)

Listing 6.3 displays the contents of the Java file SumSLNodes3.java that illustrates how to add the numbers in a linked list.

LISTING 6.3: SumSLNodes3.java

```java
public class SumSLNodes3
{
    static class Node {
      int data;
      Node next = null;
      public Node(int data) {
        this.data = data;
        this.next = null;
      }
    }

    public static Node[] append_node(Node ROOT, Node LAST, int item)
    {
      Node[] results = new Node[2];

      if(ROOT == null) {
        ROOT = new Node(item);
        //System.out.println("1Node: "+ROOT.data);
      } else {
        if(ROOT.next == null) {
          Node NEWNODE = new Node(item);
          LAST = NEWNODE;
          ROOT.next = LAST;
          //System.out.println("2Node: "+NEWNODE.data);
        } else {
          Node NEWNODE = new Node(item);
          LAST.next = NEWNODE;
          LAST = NEWNODE;
          //System.out.println("3Node: "+NEWNODE.data);
        }
      }

      //return ROOT, LAST
      results[0] = ROOT;
      results[1] = LAST;
      return results;
    }

    public static void main(String[] args)
    {
      Node ROOT  = null;
      Node LAST  = null;
      Node[] results = new Node[2];
      int[] items = new int[]{1,2,3,4};

      System.out.println("=> list items:");
      for(int num : items) {
        System.out.print(num+" ");
      }
      System.out.println("\n");

      //append items to list:
```

```java
    for(int item : items) {
        results = append_node(ROOT, LAST, item);
        ROOT = results[0];
        LAST = results[1];
    }

    // reconstruct the reversed number:
    // NB: [1,2,3,4] => 1,234

    int sum = 0, pow = 0, base = 10;

    Node CURR = ROOT;
    while(CURR != null) {
        System.out.println("item: "+CURR.data+" sum: "+sum);
        sum = sum*base+ CURR.data;
        pow += 1;
        CURR = CURR.next;
    }
    System.out.println("Reconstructed number: "+sum);
  }
}
```

Listing 6.3 defines a `Node` class as before, followed by the function `append_node()` that contains the logic for initializing a singly linked list and also for appending nodes to that list. Launch the code in Listing 6.3 from the command line and you will see the following output:

```
=> list items:
1 2 3 4

item: 1 sum: 0
item: 2 sum: 1
item: 3 sum: 12
item: 4 sum: 123
Reconstructed number: 1234
```

TASK: DISPLAY THE FIRST K NODES

Listing 6.4 displays the contents of `FirstKNodes.java` that illustrates how to display the first k nodes in a linked list.

LISTING 6.4: FirstKNodes.java

```java
public class FirstKNodes
{
    static class Node {
        String data = "";
        Node next = null;
        public Node(String data) {
            this.data = data;
            this.next = null;
        }
    }
}
```

```java
public static Node[] append_node(Node ROOT, Node LAST, String item)
{
  Node[] results = new Node[2];

  if(ROOT == null) {
    ROOT = new Node(item);
    //System.out.println("1Node: "+ROOT.data);
  } else {
    if(ROOT.next == null) {
      Node NEWNODE = new Node(item);
      LAST = NEWNODE;
      ROOT.next = LAST;
      //System.out.println("2Node: "+NEWNODE.data);
    } else {
      Node NEWNODE = new Node(item);
      LAST.next = NEWNODE;
      LAST = NEWNODE;
      //System.out.println("3Node: "+NEWNODE.data);
    }
  }

  //return ROOT, LAST
  results[0] = ROOT;
  results[1] = LAST;
  return results;
}

public static void first_k_nodes(Node ROOT, int num)
{
  int count = 0;
  Node CURR = ROOT;
  System.out.println("=> Display first "+num+" nodes");

  while (CURR != null) {
    count += 1;
    System.out.println("Node "+count+" data: "+CURR.data);
    CURR = CURR.next;

    if(count >= num)
      break;
  }
}

public static void main(String[] args)
{
  Node[] results = new Node[2];
  Node ROOT  = null;
  Node LAST  = null;

  //append items to list:
  String[] items = new String[]
    {"Stan", "Steve", "Sally", "Alex","George","Fred","Bob"};

  for(String item : items) {
    //ROOT, LAST = append_node(ROOT, LAST, item);
```

```
                  results = append_node(ROOT, LAST, item);
                  ROOT = results[0];
                  LAST = results[1];
            }

            System.out.println("=> Initial list:");
            for(String item : items) {
               System.out.println(item);
            }

            System.out.println();
            int node_count = 3;
            System.out.println("First "+node_count+" nodes:");
            first_k_nodes(ROOT, node_count);
      }
}
```

Listing 6.4 defines a Node class as before, followed by the function append_node() that contains the logic for initializing a singly linked list and also for appending nodes to that list.

Launch the code in Listing 6.4 from the command line and you will see the following output:

```
initial list:
=> Initial list:
Stan
Steve
Sally
Alex
George
Fred
Bob

First 3 nodes:
=> Display first 3 nodes
Node 1 data: Stan
Node 2 data: Steve
Node 3 data: Sally
```

TASK: DISPLAY THE LAST K NODES

Listing 6.5 displays the contents of LastKNodes.java that illustrates how to display the last k nodes of a linked list.

LISTING 6.5: LastKNodes.java

```
public class FirstKNodes
{
    static class Node {
      String data = "";
      Node next = null;
      public Node(String data) {
        this.data = data;
        this.next = null;
      }
```

```
}

public static Node[] append_node(Node ROOT, Node LAST, String item)
{
  Node[] results = new Node[2];

  if(ROOT == null) {
    ROOT = new Node(item);
    //System.out.println("1Node: "+ROOT.data);
  } else {
    if(ROOT.next == null) {
      Node NEWNODE = new Node(item);
      LAST = NEWNODE;
      ROOT.next = LAST;
      //System.out.println("2Node: "+NEWNODE.data);
    } else {
      Node NEWNODE = new Node(item);
      LAST.next = NEWNODE;
      LAST = NEWNODE;
      //System.out.println("3Node: "+NEWNODE.data);
    }
  }

  //return ROOT, LAST
  results[0] = ROOT;
  results[1] = LAST;
  return results;
}

public static int count_nodes(Node ROOT)
{
  int count = 0;
  Node CURR = ROOT;
  while (CURR != null) {
    count += 1;
    CURR = CURR.next;
  }
  return count;
}

public static Node skip_nodes(Node ROOT, int skip_count) {
  int count = 0;
  Node CURR = ROOT;
  while (CURR != null) {
    count += 1;
    CURR = CURR.next;
    if(count >= skip_count)
      break;
  }
  return CURR;
}

public static void last_k_nodes(Node ROOT, int node_count, int num)
{
  int count = 0;
```

```
      node_count = count_nodes(ROOT);
      Node START_NODE = skip_nodes(ROOT,node_count-num);

      Node CURR = START_NODE;
      while (CURR != null) {
        count += 1;
        System.out.println("Node "+count+" data: "+CURR.data);
        CURR = CURR.next;

        if(count >= num)
          break;
      }
    }

    public static void main(String[] args)
    {
      Node[] results = new Node[2];
      Node ROOT  = null;
      Node LAST  = null;

      //append items to list:
      String[] items = new String[]
        {"Stan", "Steve", "Sally", "Alex","George","Fred","Bob"};

      for(String item : items) {
        //ROOT, LAST = append_node(ROOT, LAST, item);
        results = append_node(ROOT, LAST, item);
        ROOT = results[0];
        LAST = results[1];
      }

      System.out.println("=> Initial list:");
      for(String item : items) {
        System.out.println(item);
      }

      System.out.println();

      int list_length = count_nodes(ROOT);
      int node_count = 3;
      System.out.println("Last "+node_count+" nodes:");
      last_k_nodes(ROOT, list_length,node_count);
    }
}
```

Listing 6.5 defines a Node class as before, followed by the function `append_node()` that contains the logic for initializing a singly linked list and also for appending nodes to that list.

Launch the code in Listing 6.5 from the command line and you will see the following output:

```
=> Initial list:
Stan
Steve
Sally
Alex
```

```
George
Fred
Bob

Last 3 nodes:
Node 1 data: George
Node 2 data: Fred
Node 3 data: Bob
```

REVERSE A SINGLY LINKED LIST VIA RECURSION

Listing 6.6 displays ReverseSLList.java that illustrates how to update a node in a linked list.

LISTING 6.6: ReverseSLList.java

```java
public class ReverseSLList
{
    static class Node {
        String data = "";
        Node next = null;
        public Node(String data) {
            this.data = data;
            this.next = null;
        }
    }

    public static Node[] append_node(Node ROOT, Node LAST, String item)
    {
        Node[] results = new Node[2];

        if(ROOT == null) {
            ROOT = new Node(item);
            //System.out.println("1Node: "+ROOT.data);
        } else {
            if(ROOT.next == null) {
                Node NEWNODE = new Node(item);
                LAST = NEWNODE;
                ROOT.next = LAST;
                //System.out.println("2Node: "+NEWNODE.data);
            } else {
                Node NEWNODE = new Node(item);
                LAST.next = NEWNODE;
                LAST = NEWNODE;
                //System.out.println("3Node: "+NEWNODE.data);
            }
        }

        //return ROOT, LAST
        results[0] = ROOT;
        results[1] = LAST;
        return results;
    }
```

```java
public static String reverse_list(Node node, String reversed_list)
{
  if(node == null) {
    return reversed_list;
  } else {
    reversed_list = node.data + " "+ reversed_list;
    return reverse_list(node.next, reversed_list);
  }
}

public static void main(String[] args)
{
    Node ROOT = null;
    Node LAST = null;
    Node[] results = new Node[2];

    //append items to list:
    String[] items = new String[]
       {"Stan", "Steve", "Sally", "Alex","George","Fred","Bob"};

    for(String item : items) {
       results = append_node(ROOT, LAST, item);
       ROOT = results[0];
       LAST = results[1];
    }

    System.out.println("=> Initial list:");
    for(String item : items) {
      System.out.print(item+" ");
    }
    System.out.println("\n");

    System.out.println("Reversed list:");
    String rev_list = "";
    String reversed = reverse_list(ROOT, rev_list);
    System.out.println(reversed);
  }
}
```

Listing 6.6 defines a Node class as before, followed by the Java method append_node() that contains the logic for initializing a singly linked list and also for appending nodes to that list. Launch the code in Listing 6.6 from the command line and you will see the following output:

```
=> Initial list:
Stan Steve Sally Alex George Fred Bob

Reversed list:
Bob Fred George Alex Sally Steve Stan
```

TASK: REMOVE DUPLICATES

Listing 6.7 displays the contents of RemoveDuplicates.java that illustrates how to remove duplicate nodes in a linked list.

LISTING 6.7: RemoveDuplicates.java: FIXME duplicate output?

```java
public class RemoveDuplicates
{
   static class Node {
     String data = "";
     Node next = null;
     public Node(String data) {
       this.data = data;
       this.next = null;
     }
   }

   public static Node[] append_node(Node ROOT, Node LAST, String item)
   {
     if(ROOT == null) {
       ROOT = new Node(item);
       //System.out.println("1Node:", ROOT.data)
     } else {
       if(ROOT.next == null) {
         Node NEWNODE = new Node(item);
         LAST = NEWNODE;
         ROOT.next = LAST;
         //System.out.println("2Node: "+NEWNODE.data)
       } else {
         Node NEWNODE = new Node(item);
         LAST.next = NEWNODE;
         LAST = NEWNODE;
         //System.out.println("3Node: "+NEWNODE.data);
       }
     }

     Node[] results = new Node[2];
     results[0] = ROOT;
     results[1] = LAST;
     return results;
   }

   public static Node delete_duplicates(Node ROOT)
   {
     Node PREV = ROOT;
     Node CURR = ROOT;
     Boolean Found = false;

     System.out.println("=> searching for duplicates");
     int duplicate = 0;
     while (CURR != null) {
       Node SEEK = CURR;
       while (SEEK.next != null) {
         if(SEEK.next.data == CURR.data) {
           duplicate += 1;
           System.out.println("=> Duplicate node #"+
                   duplicate+" with value: "+CURR.data);
           SEEK.next = SEEK.next.next;
```

```
        } else {
          SEEK = SEEK.next;
        }
      }
      CURR = CURR.next;
    }
    return ROOT;
  }

  public static void display_items(Node ROOT)
  {
    System.out.println("=> list items:");
    Node CURR = ROOT;
    while(CURR != null) {
      System.out.println("Node: "+CURR.data);
      CURR = CURR.next;
    }
    System.out.println();
  }

  public static void main(String[] args)
  {
    Node[] results = new Node[2];
    Node ROOT  = null;
    Node LAST  = null;

    // append items to list:
    String[] items = new String[]
        {"Stan", "Steve", "Stan", "George","Stan"};
    for(String item : items) {
      results = append_node(ROOT, LAST, item);
      ROOT = results[0];
      LAST = results[1];
    }

    display_items(ROOT);

    String[] items2 = new String[]
      {"Stan", "Alex", "Sally", "Steve", "George"};
    for(String item2 : items2) {
      ROOT = delete_duplicates(ROOT);
      display_items(ROOT);
    }

    String[] items3 = new String[]
        {"Stan", "Steve", "Stan", "George","Stan"};
    System.out.println("original:");
    System.out.println(items3);

    System.out.println("unique:");
    display_items(ROOT);
    //System.out.println(display_items(ROOT));
  }
}
```

Listing 6.7 defines a `Node` class, which is the same as earlier code samples in this chapter, followed by the function `append_node()` that contains the logic for initializing a singly linked list and also for appending nodes to that list.

Launch the code in Listing 6.7 from the command line and you will see the following output:

```
=> list items:
Node: Stan
Node: Steve
Node: Stan
Node: George
Node: Stan

=> searching for duplicates
=> Duplicate node #1 with value: Stan
=> Duplicate node #2 with value: Stan
=> list items:
Node: Stan
Node: Steve
Node: George

=> searching for duplicates
=> list items:
Node: Stan
Node: Steve
Node: George

=> searching for duplicates
=> list items:
Node: Stan
Node: Steve
Node: George

=> searching for duplicates
=> list items:
Node: Stan
Node: Steve
Node: George

=> searching for duplicates
=> list items:
Node: Stan
Node: Steve
Node: George

original:
[Ljava.lang.String;@6d06d69c
unique:
=> list items:
Node: Stan
Node: Steve
Node: George
```

TASK: CONCATENATE TWO LISTS

Listing 6.8 displays the contents of AppendSLLists.java that illustrates how to split a linked list into two lists.

LISTING 6.8: *AppendSLLists.java*

```
public class AppendSLLists
{
    static class Node {
      int data;
      Node next = null;
      public Node(int data) {
        this.data = data;
        this.next = null;
      }
    }

    public static Node[] append_node(Node ROOT, Node LAST, int item)
    {
      Node[] results = new Node[2];

      if(ROOT == null) {
        ROOT = new Node(item);
        //System.out.println("1Node: "+ROOT.data);
      } else {
        if(ROOT.next == null) {
          Node NEWNODE = new Node(item);
          LAST = NEWNODE;
          ROOT.next = LAST;
          //System.out.println("2Node: "+NEWNODE.data);
        } else {
          Node NEWNODE = new Node(item);
          LAST.next = NEWNODE;
          LAST = NEWNODE;
          //System.out.println("3Node: "+NEWNODE.data);
        }
      }

      //return ROOT, LAST
      results[0] = ROOT;
      results[1] = LAST;
      return results;
    }

    public static void display_items(Node ROOT)
    {
      Node CURR = ROOT;
      while(CURR != null) {
        System.out.println("Node: "+CURR.data);
        CURR = CURR.next;
      }
      System.out.println();
    }
```

```java
public static void main(String[] args)
{
  Node[] results = new Node[2];

  //Node ROOT = null;
  //Node LAST = null;
  Node node2 = null;

  int index = 2, count = 0;

  // append items to list1:
  Node ROOT1 = null;
  Node LAST1 = null;
  //items1 = np.array{300, 50, 30, 80, 100, 200}
  int[] items1 = new int[]{300, 50, 30};

  for(int item : items1) {
    //ROOT1, LAST1 = append_node(ROOT1, LAST1, item);
    results = append_node(ROOT1, LAST1, item);
    ROOT1 = results[0];
    LAST1 = results[1];
    if(count == index)
      node2 = LAST1;
    count += 1;
  }

  System.out.println("FIRST LIST:");
  display_items(ROOT1);

  Node ROOT2 = null;
  Node LAST2 = null;
  //append second set of items to list:
  int[] items2 = new int[]{80, 100, 200};
  for(int item : items2) {
    results = append_node(ROOT2, LAST2, item);
    ROOT2 = results[0];
    LAST2 = results[1];
    if(count == index)
      node2 = LAST2;
    count += 1;
  }

  System.out.println("SECOND LIST:");
  display_items(ROOT2);

  // concatenate the two lists:
  System.out.println("COMBINED LIST:");
  LAST1.next = ROOT2;
  display_items(ROOT1);
}
}
```

Listing 6.8 starts by defining the class Node whose contents you have seen in previous examples in this chapter. The remaining code consists of four static methods: append_node(), display_items, and main() for appending a node, displaying all items, and the main() method of this Java class, respectively.

The append_node() and display_items() methods also contain the same code that you have seen in previous code samples in this chapter. The main() method consists of two blocks of code. The first block of code constructs (and then displays) the first linked list based on the elements in the integer array items1, and the second block of code constructs (and then displays) the second linked list based on the elements in the integer array items2. Notice that both blocks of code invoke the append_node() method in order to construct the two lists. Launch the code in Listing 6.8 and you will see the following output:

```
FIRST LIST:
Node: 300
Node: 50
Node: 30

SECOND LIST:
Node: 80
Node: 100
Node: 200

COMBINED LIST:
Node: 300
Node: 50
Node: 30
Node: 80
Node: 100
Node: 200
```

TASK: MERGE TWO ORDERED LINKED LISTS

Listing 6.9 displays the contents of MergeSLLists.java that illustrates how to merge two linked lists.

LISTING 6.9: MergeSLLists.java

```java
public class MergeSLLists
{
    static class Node {
      int data;
      Node next = null;
      public Node(int data) {
        this.data = data;
        this.next = null;
      }
    }

    public static Node[] append_node(Node ROOT, Node LAST, int item)
    {
      Node[] results = new Node[2];
```

```java
    if(ROOT == null) {
      ROOT = new Node(item);
      //System.out.println("1Node: "+ROOT.data);
    } else {
      if(ROOT.next == null) {
        Node NEWNODE = new Node(item);
        LAST = NEWNODE;
        ROOT.next = LAST;
        //System.out.println("2Node: "+NEWNODE.data);
      } else {
        Node NEWNODE = new Node(item);
        LAST.next = NEWNODE;
        LAST = NEWNODE;
        //System.out.println("3Node: "+NEWNODE.data);
      }
    }

    //return ROOT, LAST
    results[0] = ROOT;
    results[1] = LAST;
    return results;
}

public static void display_items(Node ROOT)
{
  Node CURR = ROOT;
  while(CURR != null) {
    System.out.println("Node: "+CURR.data);
    CURR = CURR.next;
  }
  System.out.println();
}

public static void main(String[] args)
{
   Node[] results = new Node[2];
   Node node2 = null;

   int index = 2, count = 0;

   // create the first list:
   Node ROOT1 = null;
   Node LAST1 = null;
   int[] items1 = new int[]{30, 50, 300};

   for(int item : items1) {
     results = append_node(ROOT1, LAST1, item);
     ROOT1 = results[0];
     LAST1 = results[1];
     if(count == index)
       node2 = LAST1;
     count += 1;
   }
```

```
System.out.println("FIRST LIST:");
display_items(ROOT1);

Node ROOT2 = null;
Node LAST2 = null;

// create a second list:
int[] items2 = new int[]{80, 100, 200};
for(int item : items2) {
  results = append_node(ROOT2, LAST2, item);
  ROOT2 = results[0];
  LAST2 = results[1];
  if(count == index)
    node2 = LAST2;
  count += 1;
}

System.out.println("SECOND LIST:");
display_items(ROOT2);

Node CURR1 = ROOT1;
LAST1 = ROOT1;
Node CURR2 = ROOT2;
LAST2 = ROOT2;
Node ROOT3 = null;
Node LAST3 = null;

while(CURR1 != null && CURR2 != null) {
  //System.out.println("curr1.data: "+CURR1.data);
  //System.out.println("curr2.data: "+CURR2.data);

  if(CURR1.data < CURR2.data) {
    results = append_node(ROOT3, LAST3, CURR1.data);
    ROOT3 = results[0];
    LAST3 = results[1];

    //System.out.println("adding curr1.data: "+CURR1.data);
    CURR1 = CURR1.next;
  } else {
    results = append_node(ROOT3, LAST3, CURR2.data);
    ROOT3 = results[0];
    LAST3 = results[1];

    //System.out.println("adding curr2.data: "+CURR2.data);
    CURR2 = CURR2.next;
  }
}

// append any remaining elements of items1:
if(CURR1 != null) {
  while(CURR1 != null) {
    //System.out.println("MORE curr1.data: "+CURR1.data);
    results = append_node(ROOT3, LAST3, CURR1.data);
    ROOT3 = results[0];
    LAST3 = results[1];
    CURR1 = CURR1.next;
```

```
      }
    }

    // append any remaining elements of items2:
    if(CURR2 != null) {
      while(CURR2 != null) {
        System.out.println("MORE curr2.data: "+CURR2.data);
        results = append_node(ROOT3, LAST3, CURR2.data);
        ROOT3 = results[0];
        LAST3 = results[1];
        CURR2 = CURR2.next;
      }
    }

    System.out.println("MERGED LIST:");
    display_items(ROOT3);
  }
}
```

Listing 6.9 starts by defining the class Node whose contents you have seen in previous examples in this chapter. The remaining code consists of four static methods: append_node(), display_items, and main() for appending a node, displaying all items, and the main() method of this Java class, respectively.

The append_node() and display_items() methods also contain the same code that you have seen in previous code samples in this chapter. The main() method consists of two blocks of code. The first block of code constructs (and then displays) the first linked list based on the elements in the integer array items1, and the second block of code constructs (and then displays) the second linked list based on the elements in the integer array items2. Notice that both blocks of code invoke the append_node() method in order to construct the two lists.

The next portion of the main() method contains a loop that constructs a third list that is based on the contents of the previous pair of lists, and the result is an ordered list of numbers (i.e., from smallest to largest). *This code works correctly because the initial pair of lists are ordered in numerically increasing order*. During each iteration, the following conditional logic is performed, where item1 and item2 are the current elements of list1 and list2, respectively:

If item1 < item2 then append item1 to list3; otherwise append item2 to list3.

The loop finishes executing when the last item of either list is processed. Of course, there might be additional unprocessed elements in either list1 or list2 (but not both), so two additional loops are required: one loop appends the remaining items in list1 (if any) to list3, and another loop appends the remaining items in list2 (if any) to list3. Launch the code in Listing 6.8 and you will see the following output:

```
FIRST LIST:
Node: 30
Node: 50
Node: 300

SECOND LIST:
Node: 80
Node: 100
Node: 200
```

```
MERGED LIST:
Node: 30
Node: 50
Node: 80
Node: 100
Node: 200
Node: 300
```

TASK: SPLIT AN ORDERED LIST INTO TWO LISTS

There are several ways to perform this task. One approach is to iterate through a given list and dynamically create a list of smaller items as well as a list of larger items in the loop. However, the logic is more complex, and therefore more error prone.

A simpler approach involves appending the smaller items to a Java list of Node elements and then appending the remaining items to a larger list, and then return the two lists. At this point you can invoke the append() function to create two linked lists.

Listing 6.10 displays the contents of SplitSLLists.java that illustrates how to split a linked list into two lists.

LISTING 6.10: SplitSLLists.java

```java
import java.util.ArrayList;

public class SplitSLLists
{
   static class Node {
     int data;
     Node next = null;

     public Node(int data) {
       this.data = data;
       this.next = null;
     }
   }

   public static Node[] append_node(Node ROOT, Node LAST, int item)
   {
     Node[] results = new Node[2];

     if(ROOT == null) {
       ROOT = new Node(item);
       //System.out.println("1Node: "+ROOT.data);
     } else {
       if(ROOT.next == null) {
         Node NEWNODE = new Node(item);
         LAST = NEWNODE;
         ROOT.next = LAST;
         //System.out.println("2Node: "+NEWNODE.data);
       } else {
         Node NEWNODE = new Node(item);
         LAST.next = NEWNODE;
         LAST = NEWNODE;
```

```
        //System.out.println("3Node: "+NEWNODE.data);
      }
    }

    //return ROOT, LAST
    results[0] = ROOT;
    results[1] = LAST;
    return results;
}

public static void delete_node(Node node)
{
  Boolean Found = false;

  if(node != null) {
    if(node.next != null) {
      Found = true;
      System.out.println("curr node: "+node.data);
      node.data = node.next.data;
      node.next = node.next.next;
      System.out.println("new  node: "+node.data);
    }
  }

  if(Found == false)
    System.out.println("* Item "+node.data+" not in list *");
}

public static ArrayList[] split_list(Node ROOT, int value)
{
  ArrayList[] results = new ArrayList[2];

  Node node = ROOT;
  ArrayList smaller = new ArrayList();
  ArrayList larger  = new ArrayList();

  System.out.println("Comparison value: "+value);
  while(node != null) {
    if(node.data < value) {
      //System.out.println("LESS curr node: "+node.data);
      smaller.add(node.data);
    } else {
      //System.out.println("GREATER curr node: "+node.data);
      larger.add(node.data);
    }
    node = node.next;
  }
  results[0] = smaller;
  results[1] = larger;

  return results;
}

public static void display_items(Node ROOT)
{
```

```
      Node CURR = ROOT;
      while(CURR != null) {
        System.out.println("Node: "+CURR.data);
        CURR = CURR.next;
      }
      System.out.println();
   }

   public static void main(String[] args)
   {
      Node[] results1 = new Node[2];
      ArrayList[] results2 = new ArrayList[2];
      Node node2 = null;

      int index = 2, count = 0;

      // append items to list1:
      Node ROOT  = null;
      Node LAST  = null;
      int[] items1 = new int[]{300, 50, 30};

      for(int item : items1) {
        results1 = append_node(ROOT, LAST, item);
        ROOT = results1[0];
        LAST = results1[1];

        if(count == index)
          node2 = LAST;
        count += 1;
      }

      System.out.println("=> FIRST LIST:");
      display_items(ROOT);

      int value = 70; //  node2.data;
      results2 = split_list(ROOT, value);
      ArrayList smaller = results2[0];
      ArrayList larger  = results2[1];

      System.out.println("smaller list: "+smaller);
      System.out.println("larger  list: "+larger);
   }
}
```

Listing 6.10 starts by defining the class Node whose contents you have seen in previous examples in this chapter. The remaining code consists of four static methods: append_node(), split_list(), display_items(), and main() for appending a node, splitting a list into two lists, displaying all items, and the main() method of this Java class, respectively.

The append_node() and display_items() methods also contain the same code that you have seen in previous code samples in this chapter. The split_list() splits a given list into two distinct lists. Specifically, the first list consists of the numbers that are less than a comparison value, and the second list consists of the remaining elements. Since the initial list is ordered, the code for this method involves a loop that that performs a comparison of each list element with the comparison value.

The main() method starts by constructing (and then displays) the initial linked list from the elements in the integer array items1. The next portion of the main() method invokes the split_list() method that constricts two sublists (one of which can be empty) and returns the resulting lists. The final portion of the main() method displays the contents of the two sublists. Launch the code in Listing 6.10 and you will see the following output:

```
=> list items:
Node: 300
Node: 50
Node: 30

GREATER curr node: 300
GREATER curr node: 50
GREATER curr node: 30
smaller list: []
larger  list: [300, 50, 30]
```

TASK: REMOVE A GIVEN NODE FROM A LIST

This task starts by constructing a linked list of items, after which an intermediate node is removed from the list.

Listing 6.11 displays the contents of DeleteSLNode2.java that illustrates how to delete a node in a singly linked list.

LISTING 6.11: DeleteSLNode2.java

```java
public class DeleteSLNode2
{
   static class Node {
     String data = "";
     Node next = null;
     public Node(String data) {
       this.data = data;
       this.next = null;
     }
   }

   public static Node[] append_node(Node ROOT, Node LAST, String item)
   {
     Node[] results = new Node[2];

     if(ROOT == null) {
       ROOT = new Node(item);
       //System.out.println("1Node: "+ROOT.data);
     } else {
       if(ROOT.next == null) {
         Node NEWNODE = new Node(item);
         LAST = NEWNODE;
         ROOT.next = LAST;
         //System.out.println("2Node: "+NEWNODE.data);
       } else {
         Node NEWNODE = new Node(item);
```

```
        LAST.next = NEWNODE;
        LAST = NEWNODE;
        //System.out.println("3Node: "+NEWNODE.data);
      }
    }

    results[0] = ROOT;
    results[1] = LAST;
    return results;
  }

  public static void delete_node(Node node)
  {
    Boolean Found = false;

    System.out.println("Delete node: "+node.data);
    if(node != null) {
      if(node.next != null) {
        Found = true;
        //System.out.println("curr node: "+node.data);
        node.data = node.next.data;
        node.next = node.next.next;
        //System.out.println("new  node: "+node.data);
      }
    }

    if(Found == false)
      System.out.println("* Item "+node.data+" not in list *");
  }

  public static void display_items(Node ROOT)
  {
    System.out.println("=> list items:");
    Node CURR = ROOT;
    while(CURR != null) {
      System.out.println("Node: "+CURR.data);
      CURR = CURR.next;
    }
    System.out.println();
  }

  public static void main(String[] args)
  {
    Node[] results = new Node[2];
    Node ROOT  = null;
    Node LAST  = null;
    Node node2 = null;

    int index=2, count = 0;
    String[] items = new String[]
        {"Stan", "Steve", "Sally", "George","Alex"};

    for(String item : items) {
      results = append_node(ROOT, LAST, item);
      ROOT = results[0];
      LAST = results[1];
```

```
        if(count == index)
            node2 = LAST;
        count += 1;
    }

    display_items(ROOT);
    delete_node(node2);
    display_items(ROOT);
  }
}
```

Listing 6.11 starts by defining the class Node whose contents you have seen in previous examples in this chapter. The remaining code consists of the static methods append_node(), delete_node(), display_items(), and main() for appending a node, deleting a node, displaying all items, and the main() method of this Java class, respectively.

The append_node() and display_items() methods also contain the same code that you have seen in previous code samples in this chapter. The delete() method deletes a given node by iterating through the given list. If the node is found in the list, then the "next" pointer of its predecessor is updated so that it points to the successor of the node that will be deleted.

The main() method starts by constructing (and then displaying) the initial linked list from the elements in the items array. The next portion of the main() method invokes the display_items() method, the delete_node() method, and the display_items() method. Launch the code in Listing 6.10 and you will see the following output:

```
=> list items:
Node: Stan
Node: Steve
Node: Sally
Node: George
Node: Alex

Delete node: Sally
=> list items:
Node: Stan
Node: Steve
Node: George
Node: Alex
```

TASK: FIND THE MIDDLE ELEMENT IN A LIST

One solution involves counting the number of elements in the list and then finding the middle element. However, this task has the following constraints:

```
Counting the number of elements is not allowed
No additional data structure can be used
No element in the list can be modified or marked
Lists of even length can have two middle elements
```

This task belongs to a set of tasks that use the same technique: one variable iterates sequentially through a list and a second variable iterates twice as quickly through the same list. In fact, this technique is used to determine whether or not a linked list contains a loop.

Listing 6.12 displays the contents of `MiddleSLNode.py` that illustrates how to determine the middle element in a singly linked list.

LISTING 6.12: MiddleSLNode.java

```java
public class MiddleSLNode
{
    static class Node {
      String data = "";
      Node next = null;

      public Node(String data) {
        this.data = data;
        this.next = null;
      }
    }

    public static Node[] append_node(Node ROOT, Node LAST, String item)
    {
      Node[] results = new Node[2];

      if(ROOT == null) {
        ROOT = new Node(item);
        //System.out.println("1Node: "+ROOT.data);
      } else {
        if(ROOT.next == null) {
          Node NEWNODE = new Node(item);
          LAST = NEWNODE;
          ROOT.next = LAST;
          //System.out.println("2Node: "+NEWNODE.data);
        } else {
          Node NEWNODE = new Node(item);
          LAST.next = NEWNODE;
          LAST = NEWNODE;
          //System.out.println("3Node: "+NEWNODE.data);
        }
      }

      results[0] = ROOT;
      results[1] = LAST;
      return results;
    }

    public static Node[] find_middle(Node ROOT)
    {
      Node[] results = new Node[2];
      Node empty  = new Node("empty");
      Node even   = new Node("even");
      Node odd    = new Node("odd");
      Node result = new Node("");
      Node CURR   = ROOT;
      Node SEEK   = ROOT;
      int count = 0;
```

```
      if(ROOT == null) {
        results[0] = empty;
        results= even;
        return results;
      } else if (ROOT.next == null) {
        count += 1;
        results[0] = ROOT;
        results= odd;
        return results;
      }
      count += 1;

      while (SEEK != null) {
        //System.out.println("=> SEEK: "+SEEK.data);
        //System.out.println("=> CURR: "+CURR.data);
        //System.out.println("count:    "+count);

        if(SEEK.next == null) {
          //System.out.println("1break: null node");
          break;
        } else if(SEEK.next.next == null) {
          //System.out.println("2break: null node");
          count += 1;
          break;
        } else {
          SEEK = SEEK.next.next;
          CURR = CURR.next;
        }
        //count += 1;
      }

    if(count % 2 == 0) {
      result = even;
      System.out.println("=> setting even node");
    } else {
      System.out.println("=> setting odd node");
      result = odd;
    }

    results[0] = CURR;
    results= result;
    return results;
  }

public static void main(String[] args)
{
    Node[] results = new Node[2];
    Node ROOT  = null;
    Node LAST  = null;

    //lists of even length and odd length:
    String[] items = new String[]
            {"Stan", "Steve", "Sally", "Alex"};
```

```
    for(String item : items) {
       //ROOT, LAST = append_node(ROOT, LAST, item);
       results = append_node(ROOT, LAST, item);
       ROOT = results[0];
       LAST = results[1];
    }

    System.out.println();
    System.out.println("=> list items:");

    Node CURR = ROOT;
    while(CURR != null) {
      System.out.println("Node: "+CURR.data);
      CURR = CURR.next;
    }

    results = find_middle(ROOT);
    if(results[1].data == "even")
      System.out.println("list has an even number of items");
    else
      System.out.println("list has an odd number of items");
  }
}
```

Listing 6.12 starts by defining the class Node whose contents you have seen in previous examples in this chapter. The remaining code consists of the static methods append_node(), find_middle(), and main() for appending a node, finding the middle node, and the main() method of this Java class, respectively.

The append_node() and display_items() methods also contain the same code that you have seen in previous code samples in this chapter. The find_middle() method iterates through a given list to find the middle element: if the list has odd length, then there is a single element, otherwise there are two elements that are "tied" for the middle position. Notice that the loop iterates through the given list with the variables CURR ("current" node) and SEEK ("node to search for", both of which are node elements. Moreover, the CURR element iterates linearly, whereas the SEEK node uses a "double time" technique whereby the SEEK node advances twice as fast as CURR through the given list. Hence, when the SEEK node reaches the end of the list, the CURR node is positioned at the midpoint of the given list.

The main() method starts by constructing (and then displaying) the initial linked list from the elements in the items array. The next portion of the main() method invokes the find_middle() method to determine the midpoint of the list. Note that the find_middle() method returns the string "even" if the list has even length; otherwise, the list has odd length and in both cases an appropriate message is printed. Launch the code in Listing 6.12 and you will see the following output:

```
=> list items:
Node: Stan
Node: Steve
Node: Sally
Node: Alex
Node: Dave
=> setting odd node
list has an odd number of items
```

TASK: REVERSE A LINKED LIST

Listing 6.13 displays the contents of `ReverseSLList.javap` that illustrates how to reverse the elements in a linked list.

LISTING 6.13: ReverseSLList.java

```java
public class ReverseSLList
{
    static class Node {
      String data = "";
      Node next = null;
      public Node(String data) {
        this.data = data;
        this.next = null;
      }
    }

    public static Node[] append_node(Node ROOT, Node LAST, String item)
    {
      Node[] results = new Node[2];

      if(ROOT == null) {
        ROOT = new Node(item);
        //System.out.println("1Node: "+ROOT.data);
      } else {
        if(ROOT.next == null) {
          Node NEWNODE = new Node(item);
          LAST = NEWNODE;
          ROOT.next = LAST;
          //System.out.println("2Node: "+NEWNODE.data);
        } else {
          Node NEWNODE = new Node(item);
          LAST.next = NEWNODE;
          LAST = NEWNODE;
          //System.out.println("3Node: "+NEWNODE.data);
        }
      }

      //return ROOT, LAST
      results[0] = ROOT;
      results[1] = LAST;
      return results;
    }

    public static String reverse_list(Node node, String reversed_list)
    {
      if(node == null) {
        return reversed_list;
      } else {
        reversed_list = node.data + " "+ reversed_list;
        return reverse_list(node.next, reversed_list);
      }
```

```
    }

    public static void main(String[] args)
    {
        Node ROOT = null;
        Node LAST = null;
        Node[] results = new Node[2];

        //append items to list:
        String[] items = new String[]
          {"Stan", "Steve", "Sally", "Alex","George","Fred","Bob"};

        for(String item : items) {
            results = append_node(ROOT, LAST, item);
            ROOT = results[0];
            LAST = results[1];
        }

        System.out.println("=> Initial list:");
        for(String item : items) {
          System.out.print(item+" ");
        }
        System.out.println("\n");

        System.out.println("Reversed list:");
        String rev_list = "";
        String reversed = reverse_list(ROOT, rev_list);
        System.out.println(reversed);
    }
}
```

Listing 6.13 starts by defining the class Node whose contents you have seen in previous examples in this chapter. The remaining code consists of the static methods append_node(), reverse_list(), and main() for appending a node, reversing the list, and the main() method of this Java class, respectively.

The append_node() method contains the same code that you have seen in previous code samples in this chapter. The reverse_list() method iterates through a given list to reverse its contents.

The main() method starts by constructing (and then displaying) the initial linked list from the elements in the items array. The next portion of the main() method invokes the reverse_list() method and then displays the contents of the reversed list. Launch the code in Listing 6.12 and you will see the following output:

```
=> Initial list:
Stan Steve Sally Alex George Fred Bob

Reversed list:
Bob Fred George Alex Sally Steve Stan
```

TASK: CHECK FOR PALINDROME IN A LINKED LIST

Listing 6.14 displays the contents of PalindromeSLList.java that illustrates how to determine whether or not a list contains a palindrome.

LISTING 6.14: PalindromeSLList.java

```java
public class PalindromeSLList
{
   static class Node {
     String data = "";
     Node next = null;
     public Node(String data) {
       this.data = data;
       this.next = null;
     }
   }

public static Node[] append_node(Node ROOT, Node LAST, String item)
{
  Node[] results = new Node[2];

  if(ROOT == null) {
    ROOT = new Node(item);
    ROOT.next = null;
    LAST = ROOT;
    System.out.println("1Node: "+ROOT.data);
  } else {
    Node NEWNODE = new Node(item);
    LAST.next = NEWNODE;
    LAST = NEWNODE;
    LAST.next = null;
    if(ROOT.next == null) {
       System.out.println("3Node: point root to last");
       ROOT.next = LAST;
    }
    System.out.println("2Node: "+LAST.data);
  }

  results[0] = ROOT;
  results[1] = LAST;
  return results;
}

   public static String reverse_list(Node node, String reversed_list)
   {
     if(node == null) {
       return reversed_list;
     } else {
       reversed_list = node.data + " "+ reversed_list;
       return reverse_list(node.next, reversed_list);
     }
   }
   public static void main(String[] args)
   {
       String[] items = new String[]{"a", "b", "c", "b", "d"};

       Node[] results = new Node[2];
       Node ROOT = null;
       Node LAST = null;
```

```
    for(String item : items) {
        results = append_node(ROOT, LAST, item);
        ROOT = results[0];
        LAST = results[1];
    }

    String original = "";
    System.out.println("=> Original items:");
    Node CURR1 = ROOT;
    while(CURR1 != null) {
        original = CURR1.data+" ";
        CURR1 = CURR1.next;
    }
    System.out.println(original);

    String rev_list = "";
    String reversed = reverse_list(ROOT, rev_list);
    System.out.println("=> Reversed items:");
    System.out.println(reversed);

    if(original.equals(rev_list))
        System.out.println("found a palindrome");
    else
        System.out.println("not a palindrome");
    }
}
```

Listing 6.14 defines a `Node` class as before, followed by the function `append_node()` that contains the logic for initializing a singly linked list and also for appending nodes to that list.

Launch the code in Listing 6.14 from the command line and you will see the following output:

```
=> list of items:
a b c b a

=> New list of items:
a b c b a

found a palindrome
```

SUMMARY

This chapter started with code samples for displaying the first k nodes in a list as well as the last k nodes of a list. Then you learned how to display the contents of a list in reverse order and how to remove duplicates.

In addition, you saw how to concatenate and merge two linked lists, and how to split a single linked list. Then you learned how to remove the middle element in a list and how to determine whether or not a linked list contains a loop.

Finally, you learned how to calculate the sum of the elements in a linked list and how to check for palindromes in a linked list.

CHAPTER 7

QUEUES AND STACKS

This chapter introduces you to queues and stacks that were briefly introduced in Chapter 4 in the section pertaining to linear data structures.

The first part of this chapter explains the concept of a queue, along with Java code samples that show you how to perform various operations on a queue. Some of the code samples also contain built-in functions for queues, such as `isEmpty()`, `isFull()`, `push()`, and `dequeue()`.

The second part of this chapter explains the concept of a stack, along with Java code samples that show you how to perform various operations on a stack. In addition, you will see code samples for finding the largest and smallest elements in a stack and reversing the contents of a stack.

The final section contains three interesting tasks that illustrate the usefulness of a stack data structure. The first task determines whether or not a string consists of well-balanced round parentheses, square brackets, and curly braces. The second task parses an arithmetic expression that can perform addition, subtraction, multiplication, or division, as well as any combination of these four arithmetic operations. The third task converts infix notation to postfix notation.

WHAT IS A QUEUE?

A queue consists of a collection of objects that uses the FIFO (first-in-first-out) rule for inserting and removing items. By way of analogy, consider a toll booth: the first vehicle that arrives is the first vehicle to pay the necessary toll and also the first vehicle to exit the tool booth. As another analogy, consider customers standing in a line (which in fact is a queue) in a bank: the person at the front of the queue is the first person to approach an available teller. The "back" of the queue is the person at the end of the line (i.e., the last person).

A queue has a maximum size MAX and a minimum size of 0. In fact, we can define a queue in terms of the following methods:

1. `isEmpty()` returns True if the queue is empty
2. `isFull()` returns True if the queue is full
3. `queueSize()` returns the number of elements in the stack
4. `add(item)` adds an element to the back of the queue if the queue is not full
5. `dequeue()` removes the front element of the queue if the queue is not empty

In order to ensure that there is no overflow (too big) or underflow (too small), we must always invoke `isEmpty()` before "popping" an item from the top of the front of a queue and always invoke `isFull()` before "pushing" (appending) an item as the last element of a queue.

Types of Queues

The following list various types of queues that can be created, most of which are extensions of a generic queue, followed by a brief description:

- queue
- circular queue
- qequeue
- priority queue

A *queue* is a linear list that supports deletion from one end and insertion at the other end. A queue is a FIFO (first-in-first-out), just like a line of people waiting to enter a movie theatre or a restaurant: the first person in line enters first, followed by the second person in line, and so forth. The term enqueue refers to adding an element to a queue, whereas dequeue refers to removing an element from a queue.

A *circular queue* is a linear list with the following constraint: the last element in the queue "points" to the first element in the queue. A circular queue is also called a *ring buffer*. By way of analogy, a conga line is a queue: if the person at the front of the queue is "connected" to the last person in the conga line, that is called a *circular queue*.

A *dequeue* is a linear list that is also a double ended queue which insertions and deletions can be performed at *both* ends of the queue. In addition, there are two types of Dequeues:

- Input restricted means that insertions occur only at one end
- Output restricted means that deletions occur only at one end

A *priority queue* is queue that allows for removing and inserting items in any position of the queue. For example, the scheduler of the operating system of your desktop and laptop uses a priority queue to schedule programs for execution. Consequently, a higher priority task is executed before a lower priority task.

Moreover, after a priority queue is created, it's possible for a higher priority task to arrive: in this scenario, that new and higher priority task is inserted into the appropriate location in the queue for task execution. In fact, Unix has the so-called `nice` command that you can launch from the command line in order to lower the execution priority of tasks. Perform an online search for more information regarding the queues discussed in this section.

Now let's turn our attention to creating a basic queue, which is the topic of the next section.

CREATING A QUEUE USING AN ARRAY LIST

Listing 7.1 displays the contents of `MyQueue.java` that illustrates how to use an `ArrayList` class in order to perform various operations on a queue.

LISTING 7.1: MyQueue.java

```java
import java.util.ArrayList;

public class MyQueue
{
   static int MAX = 4;
   static ArrayList myqueue = new ArrayList();

   public static Boolean isEmpty() {
     return myqueue.size() == 0;
   }

   public static Boolean isFull() {
     return myqueue.size() == MAX;
   }

   public static void dequeue() {
      if(myqueue.size() > 0) {
        int front = (int)myqueue.get(0);
        myqueue.remove(0);
        System.out.println("removed item : "+front);
      } else {
        System.out.println("* myqueue is empty *");
      }
   }

   public static void push(int item) {
      if(isFull() == false) {
        myqueue.add(item);
      } else {
        System.out.println("* myqueue is full *");
      }
   }

   public static void main(String[] args)
   {
      System.out.println("=> pushing values onto myqueue:");
      push(10);
      System.out.println("myqueue: "+myqueue);
      push(20);
      System.out.println("myqueue: "+myqueue);
      push(200);
      System.out.println("myqueue: "+myqueue);
      push(50);
      System.out.println("myqueue: "+myqueue);
      push(-123);
      System.out.println("myqueue: "+myqueue);
      System.out.println();

      System.out.println("=> dequeue values from myqueue: ");
      dequeue();
      System.out.println("myqueue: "+myqueue);
      dequeue();
```

```
        System.out.println("myqueue: "+myqueue);
        dequeue();
        System.out.println("myqueue: "+myqueue);
        dequeue();
        System.out.println("myqueue: "+myqueue);
        dequeue();
        System.out.println("myqueue: "+myqueue);
    }
}
```

Listing 7.1 starts by initializing myqueue as an empty list and assigning the value 4 to the variable MAX, which is the maximum number of elements that the queue can contain (obviously you can change this value).

The next portion of Listing 7.1 defines several functions: the isEmpty function that returns True if the length of myqueue is 0 (and false otherwise), followed by the function isFull() that returns True if the length of myqueue is MAX (and False otherwise).

The next portion of Listing 7.1 defines the function dequeue that invokes the pop() method in order to remove the front element of myqueue, provided that myqueue is not empty. Next, the function push() invokes the append() method in order to add a new element to the end of myqueue, provided that myqueue is not full.

The final portion of Listing 7.1 invokes the push() function to append various numbers to myqueue, followed by multiple invocations of the dequeue() method to remove elements from the front of the queue. Launch the code in Listing 7.1 and you will see the following output:

```
=> pushing values onto myqueue:
myqueue: [10]
myqueue: [10, 20]
myqueue: [10, 20, 200]
myqueue: [10, 20, 200, 50]
* myqueue is full *
myqueue: [10, 20, 200, 50]

=> dequeue values from myqueue:
removed item : 10
myqueue: [20, 200, 50]
removed item : 20
myqueue: [200, 50]
removed item : 200
myqueue: [50]
removed item : 50
myqueue: []
* myqueue is empty *
myqueue: []
```

Listing 7.2 displays the contents of MyQueue2.java that illustrates how to define a queue and perform various operations on the queue.

LISTING 7.2: MyQueue2.java

```
import java.util.ArrayList;

public class MyQueue2
{
```

```
static int MAX = 4;
static ArrayList myqueue = new ArrayList();

public static Boolean isEmpty() {
  return myqueue.size() == 0;
}

public static Boolean isFull() {
  return myqueue.size() == MAX;
}

public static void dequeue() {
    if(myqueue.size() > 0) {
      int front = (int)myqueue.get(0);
      myqueue.remove(0);
      System.out.println("removed item : "+front);
    } else {
      System.out.println("* myqueue is empty *");
    }
}

public static void push(int item) {
    if(isFull() == false) {
      myqueue.add(item);
    } else {
      System.out.println("* myqueue is full *");
    }
}

public static void main(String[] args)
{
    int[] arr1 = new int[]{10,20,200,50,-123};

    System.out.println("=> pushing values onto myqueue:");
    for(int num : arr1) {
      push(num);
      System.out.println("myqueue: "+myqueue);
    }

    System.out.println("=> dequeue values from myqueue: ");
    while(myqueue.size() > 0) {
      dequeue();
      System.out.println("myqueue: "+myqueue);
    }
  }
}
```

Listing 7.2 starts by initialing my queue as an empty list and assigning the value 4 to the variable MAX, which is the maximum number of elements that the queue can contain (obviously you can change this value).

The next portion of Listing 7.2 defines several functions: the isEmpty function that returns True if the length of myqueue is 0 (and False otherwise), followed by the function isFull that returns True if the length of myqueue is MAX (and False otherwise).

The next portion of Listing 7.2 defines the function `dequeue90` that invokes the `pop()` method in order to remove the front element of `myqueue`, provided that `myqueue` is not empty. Next, the function `push()` invokes the `append()` method in order to add a new element to the back of `myqueue`, provided that `myqueue` is not full.

The final portion of Listing 7.2 invokes the push() function to append various numbers to `myqueue`, followed by multiple invocations of the `dequeue()` method to remove elements from the front of the queue. Launch the code in Listing 7.2 and you will see the same output at Listing 7.1.

CREATING A QUEUE USING AN ARRAY LIST

Listing 7.3 displays the contents of `QueueArray.java` that illustrates how to use a `Java List` class in order to define a queue using an array.

LISTING 7.3: QueueArray.java

```java
import java.util.ArrayList;

public class QueueArray
{
   static int MAX = 4;
   static ArrayList myqueue = new ArrayList();

   public static Boolean isEmpty() {
     return myqueue.size() == 0;
   }

   public static Boolean isFull() {
     return myqueue.size() == MAX;
   }

   public static void dequeue() {
      if(myqueue.size() > 0) {
        int front = (int)myqueue.get(0);
        myqueue.remove(0);
        System.out.println("removed item : "+front);
      } else {
        System.out.println("* myqueue is empty *");
      }
   }

   public static void push(int item) {
      if(isFull() == false) {
        myqueue.add(item);
      } else {
        System.out.println("* myqueue is full *");
      }
   }

   public static void main(String[] args)
   {
      int[] arr1 = new int[]{10,20,200,50,-123};
```

```
        System.out.println("=> pushing values onto myqueue:");
        for(int num : arr1) {
          push(num);
          System.out.println("myqueue: "+myqueue);
        }

        System.out.println("=> dequeue values from myqueue: ");
        while(myqueue.size() > 0) {
          dequeue();
          System.out.println("myqueue: "+myqueue);
        }
    }
}
```

Listing 7.3 starts by initializing the variables MAX (for the maximum size of the queue), myqueue (which is an array-based queue), along with the integers lpos and rpos that are the index positions of the first element and the last element, respectively, of the queue.

The next portion of Listing 7.3 defines the familiar functions isEmpty() and isFull() that you have seen in previous code samples. However, the dequeue() function has been modified to handle cases in which elements are popped from myqueue: each time this happens, the variable lpos is incremented by 1. Note that this code block is executed only when lpos is less than rpos: otherwise, the queue is empty.

The function shift_left is invoked when lpos is greater than 0 and rpos equals MAX: this scenario occurs when there are open "slots" at the front of the queue and the right-most element is occupied. This function shifts all the elements toward the front of the queue, thereby freeing up space so that more elements can be appended to myqueue. Keep in mind that every element in the array is occupied when lpos equals 0 and rpos equals MAX, in which the only operation that we can perform is to remove an element from the front of the queue.

The final portion of Listing 7.3 initializes the NumPy array arr1 with a set of integers, followed by a loop that iterates through the elements of arr1 and invokes the push() function in order to append those elements to myqueue. When this loop finishes execution, another loop invokes the dequeue() function to remove elements from the front of the queue.

Change the value of MAX so that its value is less than, equal to, or greater than the number of elements in the array arr1. Doing so will exhibit different execution paths in the code. Note that numerous print() statements are included in Listing 7.3 that generates verbose output, thereby enabling you to see the sequence in which the code is executed (you can "comment out" those statements later). Launch the code in Listing 7.3 and you will see the following output:

```
myqueue: [None, None, None, None, None, None]

manually inserted two values:
myqueue: [None, None, 222, 333, None, None]
=> Ready to push the following values onto myqueue:
[ 1000  2000  8000  5000 -1000]

rpos= 4 pushing item onto myqueue: 1000
appended 1000 to myqueue: [None, None, 222, 333, 1000, None]
rpos= 5 pushing item onto myqueue: 2000
```

```
Call shift_left to shift myqueue
before shift: [None, None, 222, 333, 1000, 2000]
left shift count: 2
Completed myqueue shift: [222, 333, 1000, 2000, None, None]
rpos= 4 pushing item: 8000
rpos= 4 Second try: pushing item onto myqueue: 8000
appended 8000 to myqueue: [222, 333, 1000, 2000, 8000, None]
rpos= 5 pushing item onto myqueue: 5000
*** myqueue is full: cannot push item: -1000

=> Ready to dequeue values from myqueue:
dequeued value: 222
lpos: 1 rpos: 6
popped myqueue: [None, 333, 1000, 2000, 8000, 5000]
dequeued value: 333
lpos: 2 rpos: 6
popped myqueue: [None, None, 1000, 2000, 8000, 5000]
dequeued value: 1000
lpos: 3 rpos: 6
popped myqueue: [None, None, None, 2000, 8000, 5000]
dequeued value: 2000
lpos: 4 rpos: 6
popped myqueue: [None, None, None, None, 8000, 5000]
dequeued value: 8000
lpos: 5 rpos: 6
popped myqueue: [None, None, None, None, None, 5000]
dequeued value: 5000
lpos: 6 rpos: 6
popped myqueue: [None, None, None, None, None, None]
```

OTHER TYPES OF QUEUES

In addition to the queues that you have seen thus far in this chapter, there are several other types of queues as listed below:

- circular queues
- priority queues
- dequeues

A *circular queue* is a queue whose "head" is the same as its "tail." A priority queue is a queue in which elements are assigned a numeric priority. A dequeue is a queue in which elements can be added as well as removed from both ends of the queue. Search online for code samples that implement these types of queues.

This concludes the portion of the chapter pertaining to queues. The remainder of this chapter discusses the stack data structure, which is based on a LIFO structure instead of a FIFO structure of a queue.

WHAT IS A STACK?

In general terms, a stack consists of a collection of objects that follow the LIFO (last-in-first-out) principle. By contrast, a queue follows the FIFO (first-in-first-out) principle.

As a simple example, consider an elevator that has one entrance: the last person who enters the elevator is the first person who exits the elevator. Thus, the order in which people exit an elevator is the reverse of the order in which people enter an elevator.

Another analogy that might help you understand the concept of a stack is the stack of plates in a cafeteria:

1. a plate can be added to the top of the stack if the stack is not full
2. a plate can be removed from the stack if the stack is not empty

Based on the preceding observations, a stack has a maximum size MAX and a minimum size of 0.

Use Cases for Stacks

The following list contains use applications and use cases for stack-based data structures:

- recursion
- leeping track of function calls
- evaluation of expressions
- reversing characters
- servicing hardware interrupts
- solving combinatorial problems using backtracking

Operations With Stacks

Earlier in this chapter you saw Java methods to perform operations on queues; in an analogous fashion, we can define a stack in terms of the following methods:

- isEmpty() returns True if the stack is empty
- isFull() returns True if the stack is full
- stackSize() returns the number of elements in the stack
- push(item) adds an element to the "top" of the stack if the stack is not full
- pop() removes the topmost element of the stack if the stack is not empty

In order to ensure that there is no overflow (too big) or underflow (too small), we must always invoke isEmpty() before popping an item from the stack and always invoke isFull() before "pushing" an item onto the stack. The same methods (with different implementation details) are relevant when working with queues.

WORKING WITH STACKS

Listing 7.4 displays the contents of MyStack.java that illustrates how to use the Java ArrayList class to define a stack and perform various operations on the stack.

LISTING 7.4: MyStack.java

```java
import java.util.ArrayList;

public class MyStack
{
    static int MAX = 4; // 100
    static ArrayList mystack = new ArrayList();
    static int[] arr1 = new int[]{10,20,-123,200,50};

    public static Boolean isEmpty()
    {
        return mystack.size() == 0;
    }

    public static Boolean isFull()
    {
        return mystack.size() == MAX;
    }

    public static void push(int item)
    {
        if(isFull() == false) {
          mystack.add(item);
          System.out.println("appended stack item: "+item);
        } else {
          System.out.println("stack is full: cannot append "+item);
          System.out.println("Current stack size: "+mystack.size());
        }
    }

    public static void main(String[] args)
    {
        System.out.println("MAX: "+MAX);
        System.out.println("empty list: "+isEmpty());
        System.out.println("full  list: "+isFull());
        System.out.println();

        System.out.println("=> pushing values onto mystack:");
        for(int item : arr1) {
            push(item);
        }
        System.out.println();

        System.out.println("=> popping values from mystack:");
        while(mystack.size() > 0) {
            System.out.println("Current stack size: "+mystack.size());
            if(isEmpty() == false) {
              int item = (int)mystack.remove(0);
              System.out.println("removed item: "+item);
            } else {
              System.out.println("stack is empty: cannot pop");
            }
        }
```

```
        }
}
```

Listing 7.4 is very similar to Listing 7.1, except that we are working with a stack instead of a queue. In particular, Listing 7.4 starts by initializing mystack as an empty list and assigning the value 4 to the variable MAX, which is the maximum number of elements that the stack can contain (you can change this number).

The next portion of Listing 7.4 defines several functions: the isEmpty function that returns True if the length of mystack is 0 (and False otherwise), followed by the function isFull that returns True if the length of mystack is MAX (and false otherwise).

The next portion of Listing 7.4 defines the function dequeue that invokes the pop() method in order to remove the front element of mystack, provided that mystack is not empty. Next, the function push() invokes the append() method in order to add a new element to the top of mystack, provided that myqueue is not full.

The final portion of Listing 7.4 invokes the push() function to append various numbers to mystack, followed by multiple invocations of the dequeue() method to remove elements from the top of mystack. Launch the code in Listing 7.4 and you will see the following output:

```
MAX: 4
empty list: true
full  list: false

=> pushing values onto mystack:
appended stack item: 10
appended stack item: 20
appended stack item: -123
appended stack item: 200
stack is full: cannot append 50
Current stack size: 4

=> popping values from mystack:
Current stack size: 4
removed item: 10
Current stack size: 3
removed item: 20
Current stack size: 2
removed item: -123
Current stack size: 1
removed item: 200
```

Listing 7.5 displays the contents of MyStack2.java that illustrates how to define a stack and perform various operations on the stack.

LISTING 7.5: MyStack2.java

```java
import java.util.ArrayList;

public class MyStack
{
```

```java
static int MAX = 3; // 100
static ArrayList mystack = new ArrayList();
static int[] arr1 = new int[]{10,20,-123,200,50};

public static Boolean isEmpty()
{
   return mystack.size() == 0;
}

public static Boolean isFull()
{
   return mystack.size() == MAX;
}

public static int pop()
{
   if(isEmpty() == false) {
     //return mystack.shift();
     return 123; //TODO
   } else {
     System.out.println("stack is empty: cannot pop");
     return -1;
   }
}

public static void push(int item)
{
   if(isFull() == false) {
     mystack.add(item);
   } else {
      System.out.println("stack is full: cannot push");
   }
}

public static void main(String[] args)
{
   System.out.println("MAX: "+MAX);
   System.out.println("empty list: "+isEmpty());
   System.out.println("full  list: "+isFull());

   System.out.println("=> pushing values onto mystack:");
   for(int item : arr1) {
      System.out.println("push item: "+item);
   }

   System.out.println("=> popping values from mystack:");
   for(int item : arr1) {
      //System.out.println("popping item: "+item);
   }
}
}
```

Listing 7.5 is straightforward because it's a direct counterpart to Listing 7.2: the latter involves a queue whereas the former involves a stack. Launch the code in Listing 7.5 and you will see the following output:

```
pushing values onto mystack:
mystack: [0]
mystack: [0, 1]
mystack: [0, 1, 2]
* mystack is full *
mystack: [0, 1, 2]
* mystack is full *
mystack: [0, 1, 2]

=> popping values from mystack:
Current stack size: 4
removed item: 10
Current stack size: 3
removed item: 20
Current stack size: 2
removed item: -123
Current stack size: 1
removed item: 200
```

TASK: REVERSE AND PRINT STACK VALUES

Listing 7.6 displays the contents of ReverseStack.java that illustrates how to define a stack and print its contents in reverse order. This code sample uses a "regular" stack data structure.

LISTING 7.6: ReverseStack.java

```java
import java.util.ArrayList;

public class ReverseStack
{
    static int MAX = 4; // 100
    static ArrayList mystack = new ArrayList();
    static int[] arr1 = new int[]{10,20,-123,200,50};

    public static Boolean isEmpty()
    {
        return mystack.size() == 0;
    }

    public static Boolean isFull()
    {
        return mystack.size() == MAX;
    }

    public static void push(int item)
    {
        if(isFull() == false) {
            mystack.add(item);
            System.out.println("appended stack item: "+item);
        } else {
            System.out.println("stack is full: cannot append "+item);
            System.out.println("Current stack size: "+mystack.size());
        }
    }

    public static void main(String[] args)
```

```
    {
        System.out.println("MAX: "+MAX);
        System.out.println("empty list: "+isEmpty());
        System.out.println("full  list: "+isFull());
        System.out.println();

        System.out.println("=> pushing values onto mystack:");
        for(int item : arr1) {
            push(item);
        }
        System.out.println();

        ArrayList reversed = new ArrayList();
        System.out.println("=> reversing contents of mystack:");
        while(mystack.size() > 0) {
            System.out.println("Current stack size: "+mystack.size());
            if(isEmpty() == false) {
                int item = (int)mystack.remove(0);
                System.out.println("removed item: "+item);
                reversed.add(item);
            } else {
                System.out.println("stack is empty: cannot pop");
            }
        }
        System.out.println("reversed: "+reversed);
    }
}
```

Listing 7.6 contains the code in Listing 7.5, along with a loop that invokes the push() function to insert the elements of the NumPy array arr1 (which contains integers) in the variable mystack.

After the preceding loop finishes execution, another loop iterates through the elements of mystack by invoking the pop() method, and in turn appends each element to the array reversed. As a result, the elements in the array reversed are the reverse order of the elements in mystack. Launch the code in Listing 7.6 and you will see the following output:

```
MAX: 4
empty list: true
full  list: false

=> pushing values onto mystack:
appended stack item: 10
appended stack item: 20
appended stack item: -123
appended stack item: 200
stack is full: cannot append 50
Current stack size: 4

=> reversing contents of mystack:
Current stack size: 4
removed item: 10
Current stack size: 3
removed item: 20
Current stack size: 2
removed item: -123
```

```
Current stack size: 1
removed item: 200
reversed: [10, 20, -123, 200]
```

TASK: DISPLAY THE MIN AND MAX STACK VALUES (1)

Listing 7.7 displays the contents of `StackMinMax.java` that illustrates how to define a stack and perform various operations on the stack. This code sample uses a "regular" stack data structure.

LISTING 7.7: StackMinMax.java

```java
import java.util.ArrayList;

public class MinMaxStack
{
    static int MAX = 8; // 100
    static int min_val = 99999;
    static int max_val = -99999;
    static ArrayList mystack = new ArrayList();
    static int[] arr1 = new int[]{1000,2000,8000,5000,-1000};

    public static Boolean isEmpty()
    {
        return mystack.size() == 0;
    }

    public static Boolean isFull()
    {
        return mystack.size() == MAX;
    }

    public static void push(int item)
    {
        if(isFull() == false) {
          mystack.add(item);
          update_min_max_values(item);
        } else {
          System.out.println("stack is full: cannot push");
        }
    }
    public static void update_min_max_values(int item)
    {
        if(min_val > item)
           min_val = item;

        if(max_val < item)
           max_val = item;
    }

    public static void main(String[] args)
```

```
    {
        System.out.println("MAX: "+MAX);
        System.out.println("empty list: "+isEmpty());
        System.out.println("full  list: "+isFull());

        System.out.println("=> pushing values onto mystack:");
        for(int item : arr1) {
            push(item);
            //System.out.println("push item: "+item);
        }

        System.out.println();
        System.out.println("Maximum value: "+max_val);
        System.out.println("Minimum value: "+min_val);
    }
}
```

Listing 7.7 contains the familiar functions isEmpty(), isFull(), and pop() that have been discussed in previous code samples. Notice that the function pop() invokes the function update_min_max_values() each time that an element is removed from the stack. The latter method updates the variables min_val and max_val to keep track of the smallest and largest elements, respectively, in the stack. Launch the code in Listing 7.7 and you will see the following output:

```
=> Pushing list of values onto mystack:
[ 1000  2000  8000  5000 -1000]

min value: -1000
max value: 8000
```

TASK: REVERSE A STRING USING A STACK

Listing 7.8 displays the contents of ReverseString.java that illustrates how to use a stack in order to reverse a string.

LISTING 7.8: ReverseString.java

```
import java.util.ArrayList;

public class ReverseString
{
    static int MAX = 40; // 100
    static ArrayList mystack = new ArrayList();

    public static Boolean isEmpty()
    {
        return mystack.size() == 0;
    }

    public static Boolean isFull()
    {
        return mystack.size() == MAX;
    }

    public static void push(char item)
```

```
{
    if(isFull() == false) {
      mystack.add(item);
      //System.out.println("appended stack item: "+item);
    } else {
      System.out.println("stack is full: cannot append "+item);
      //System.out.println("Current stack size: "+mystack.size());
    }
  }

  public static void main(String[] args)
  {
    //System.out.println("MAX: "+MAX);
    //System.out.println("empty list: "+isEmpty());
    //System.out.println("full  list: "+isFull());
    //System.out.println();
    String myString = "abcdxyz";

    System.out.println("original: "+myString);
    //System.out.println("=> pushing characters onto mystack:");
    for(int i=0; i<myString.length(); i++) {
      push(myString.charAt(i));
      //System.out.println("current char: "+myString.charAt(i));
    }
}
    // => Append characters to a string:
    //System.out.println("=> reversing contents of mystack:");
    String reversed = "";
    while(mystack.size() > 0) {
      if(isEmpty() == false) {
        //char item = (char)mystack.remove(0);
        char item = (char)mystack.remove(mystack.size()-1);
        //System.out.println("popped last item: "+item);
        reversed = reversed + item;
      } else {
        break;
        //System.out.println("stack is empty: cannot pop");
      }
    }
    System.out.println("reversed: "+reversed);
  }
}
```

Listing 7.8 starts by initializing `mystack` as an empty list, followed by the usual functions `isEmpty()`, `isFull()`, and `pop()` that perform their respective operations. The next portion of Listing 7.8 initializes the variable `my_str` as a string of characters, and then pushes each character onto `mystack`. Next, a for loop removes each element from `mystack` and then appends each element to the string reversed (which initialized as an empty string). Launch the code in Listing 7.8 and you will see the following output:

```
string:   abcdxyz
reversed: zyxdcba
```

TASK: FIND STACK PALINDROMES

Listing 7.9 displays the contents of StackPalindrome.java that illustrates how to define a stack and perform various operations on the stack.

LISTING 7.9: StackPalindrome.java

```java
import java.util.ArrayList;

public class StackPalindrome
{
    static int MAX = 40; // 100
    static ArrayList mystack = new ArrayList();

    public static Boolean isEmpty()
    {
        return mystack.size() == 0;
    }

    public static Boolean isFull()
    {
        return mystack.size() == MAX;
    }

    public static void push(char item)
    {
        if(isFull() == false) {
            mystack.add(item);
            //System.out.println("appended stack item: "+item);
        } else {
            System.out.println("stack is full: cannot append "+item);
            //System.out.println("Current stack size: "+mystack.size());
        }
    }
    public static void main(String[] args)
    {
        Boolean palindrome = true;
        String[] myStrings = new String[]
            {"abc", "bob", "radar", "abcdefdcba"};
        // compare characters from opposite ends of the ArrayList:
        for(String currStr : myStrings)
        {
            palindrome = true;
            char item1, item2;
            for(int idx=0; idx<currStr.length()/2; idx++)
            {
                item1 = currStr.charAt(idx);
                item2 = currStr.charAt(currStr.length()-idx-1);
                if(item1 != item2) {
                    palindrome = false;
```

```
                    break;
                }
            }
            System.out.println("string:      "+currStr);
            System.out.println("palindrome: "+palindrome);
            System.out.println();
        }
    }
}
```

Listing 7.9 starts by defining the variable mystic as an instance of the ArrayList class, which is a structure that represents a stack. In addition, Listing 7.9 contains the methods isEmpty(), isFull(), push(), and main() that check for an empty stack, check for a full stack, place a new item on the stack, and the main() method, respectively.

The isEmpty() method returns a Boolean value based on whether or not the stack has size 0, and isFull() method returns a Boolean value based on whether or not the stack has size MAX, which is the maximum allowable size for the stack. The push() method first checks of the isFull() method returns false; if so, an item is added to the stack. Otherwise a message is printed that indicates the stack is full.

The main() method initializes the variable myStrings as an array of strings, followed by a loop that iterates through the elements of myStrings. During each iteration, elements from opposite ends of a given string are compared: if they differ, then the string is not a palindrome, the variable palindrome is set to false and an early exit from the loop is performed via a break statement. After the loop has finished execution, the current string is displayed and a message indicating whether or not the string is a palindrome. Launch the code in Listing 7.12 and you will see the following output:

```
string:      abc
palindrome: false

string:      bob
palindrome: true
string:      radar
palindrome: true

string:      abcdefdcba
palindrome: false
```

TASK: BALANCED PARENTHESES

Listing 7.10 displays the contents of the file StackBalancedParens.java that illustrates how to use a NumPy array in order to determine whether or not a string contains balanced parentheses.

LISTING 7.10: StackBalancedParens.java

```java
import java.util.ArrayList;

public class StackBalancedParentheses
{
    static int MAX = 100;
```

```java
    static ArrayList mystack = new ArrayList();

    public static Boolean isEmpty()
    {
        return mystack.size() == 0;
    }

    public static Boolean isFull()
    {
        return mystack.size() == MAX;
    }

    public static void push(char item)
    {
        if(isFull() == false) {
          mystack.add(item);
        } else {
            System.out.println("stack is full: cannot append "+item);
        }
    }

    public static Boolean pair_in_balan_pairs(String[] balan_pairs,
String str)
    {
      for(String elem : balan_pairs) {
        if(elem.contains(str))
          return true;
      }
      return false;
    }

    public static Boolean check_balanced(String my_expr)
    {
      String left_chars  = new String("([{");
      String right_chars = new String(")]}");
      String[] balan_pairs = new String[]{"'()'","'[]'","'{}'"};
      ArrayList my_stack = new ArrayList();

      System.out.println("checking string: "+my_expr);
      for(int idx=0; idx<my_expr.length(); idx++) {
        char char1      = my_expr.charAt(idx);
        String char1Str = String.valueOf(char1);
        //System.out.println("char: "+char1);

        if(left_chars.contains(char1Str)) {
          my_stack.add(char1Str);
          //System.out.println("appended to my_stack: "+my_stack);
        } else if (right_chars.contains(char1Str)) {
          if(my_stack.size() > 0) {
            String top1Str = (String)my_stack.get(my_stack.size()-1);
            String two_chars = top1Str + char1Str;
            //System.out.println("=> two_chars: "+two_chars);

            if(pair_in_balan_pairs(balan_pairs, two_chars) == true) {
              my_stack.remove(my_stack.size()-1);
              if(my_stack.size() == 0)
                my_stack = new ArrayList();
                //System.out.println("new stack: "+my_stack);
              continue;
            } else {
```

```
        //System.out.println("non-match: "+char1);
        break;
      }
    } else {
      System.out.println("empty stack: invalid string "+my_expr);
      return false;
    }
  } else {
    System.out.println("invalid character: "+char1);
    return false;
  }
}

return (my_stack.size() == 0);
}

public static void main(String[] args)
{
  String[] exprs = new String[]{"[()]{}{[()()]()}",
                                "[()]{}{[()()]()]",
                                "(()]{}{[()()]()]",
                                "(())(()()()()()]"};

  for(String expr : exprs) {
    if( check_balanced(expr) == true)
      System.out.println("=> balanced:     "+expr);
    else
      System.out.println("=> unbalanced:   "+expr);
    System.out.println();
  }
}
}
```

Listing 7.10 is the longest code sample in this chapter that also reveals the usefulness of combining a stack with recursion in order to solve the task at hand, which is to determine which strings comprise balanced parentheses.

Listing 7.10 starts with the function check_balanced that takes a string called my_expr as its lone parameter. Notice the way that the following variables are initialized:

```
left_chars = "([{"
right_chars = ")]}"
String[] balan_pairs = new String[]{"'()'","'[]'","'{}'"};
```

The variables left_chars and right_chars contain the left-side parentheses and right-side parentheses, respectively, that are permissible in a well-balanced string. Next, the variable balan_pairs is an array of three strings that represent a balanced pair of round parentheses, square parentheses, and curly parentheses, respectively.

The key idea for this code sample involves two actions and a logical comparison, as follows:

1. Whenever a *left* parenthesis is encountered in the current string, this parentheses is pushed onto a stack.

2. Whenever a *right* parenthesis is encountered in the current string, we check the top of the stack to see if it equals the corresponding left parenthesis.

3. If the comparison in item 2 is true, we pop the top element of the stack.

4. If the comparison in item 2 is false, the string is unbalanced.

Repeat the preceding sequence of steps until we reach the end of the string: if the stack is empty, the expression is balanced, otherwise the expression is unbalanced.

For example, suppose we the string `my_expr` is initialized as "()". The first character is "(", which is a left parentheses: step #1 above tells us to push "(" onto our (initially empty) stack called `mystack`. The next character in `my_expr` is ")", which is a right parenthesis: step #2 tells us to compare ")" with the element in the top of the stack, which is "(". Since "(" and ")" constitute a balanced pair of parentheses, we pop the element "(" from the stack. We have also reached the end of `my_expr`, and since the stack is empty, we conclude that "()" is a balanced expression (which we knew already).

Now suppose that we the string `my_expr` is initialized as "((". The first character is "(", which is a left parentheses, and step #1 above tells us to push "(" onto our (initially empty) stack called `mystack`. The next character in `my_expr` is "(", which is a left parenthesis: step #1 above tells us to push "(" onto the stack. We have reached the end of `my_expr` and since the stack is nonempty, we have determined that `my_expr` is unbalanced.

As a third example, suppose that we the string `my_expr` is initialized as "(()". The first character is "(", which is a left parentheses: step #1 above tells us to push "(" onto our (initially empty) stack called `mystack`. The next character in `my_expr` is "(", which is a left parenthesis: step #1 above tells us push another "(" onto the stack. The next character in `my_expr` is ")", and step #2 tells us to compare ")" with the element in the top of the stack, which is "(". Since "(" and ")" constitute a balanced pair of parentheses, we pop the topmost element of the stack. At this point, we have reached the end of `my_expr`, and since the stack is nonempty, we know that `my_expr` is unbalanced.

Try tracing through the code with additional strings consisting of a sequence of parentheses. After doing so, the code details in Listing 7.13 will become much simpler to understand.

The next code block in Listing 7.13 initializes the variable `my_expr` as an array of strings, each of which consists of various parentheses (round, square, and curly). The next portion is a loop that iterates through the elements of `my_expr` and in turn invokes the function `check_balanced` to determine which ones (if any) comprise balanced parentheses. Launch the code in Listing 7.13 and you will see the following output:

```
checking string:  [()]{}{[()()]()}
=> balanced:       [()]{}{[()()]()}

checking string:  [()]{}{[()()]()]
=> unbalanced:     [()]{}{[()()]()]
checking string:  (()]{}{[()()]()]
=> unbalanced:     (()]{}{[()()]()]

checking string:  (())(()()()()()]
=> unbalanced:     (())(()()()()()]
```

Consider enhancing Listing 7.13 so that the invalid character is displayed for strings that consists of unbalanced parentheses.

TASK: TOKENIZE ARITHMETIC EXPRESSIONS

The code sample in this section is a prelude to the task in the next section that involves parsing arithmetic expressions: in fact, the code in Listing 7.11 is included in the code in Listing 7.11. The rationale for the inclusion of a separate code sample is to enable you to tokenize expressions that might not be arithmetic expressions.

You need to download the zip file `apache-commons-lang.jar.zip`, uncompress the contents of the zip file, and update the environment variable `CLASSPATH` as follows:

- *http://www.java2s.com/Code/Jar/a/Downloadapachecommonslangjar.htm*
- `export CLASSPATH=$CLASSPATH:apache-commons-lang.jar`

Listing 7.11 displays the contents of `TokenizeExpr.java` that illustrates how to tokenize an arithmetic expression and also remove white spaces and tab characters.

LISTING 7.11: TokenizeExpr.java

```
import org.apache.commons.lang.text.StrTokenizer;

public class TokenizeExpr
{
    public static void main(String[] args)
    {
        String[] exprs = new String[]{"        2789   *   3+7-8-   9",
                                "4 /2   +   1",
                                "2   -   3   +   4      "};

        for(String expr : exprs) {
            String parsed = "";
            System.out.println("String: "+expr);
            StrTokenizer tokenizer = new StrTokenizer(expr, " ");
            while (tokenizer.hasNext()) {
                String token = tokenizer.nextToken().trim();
                //System.out.println("token: "+token);
                parsed = parsed + " " + token;
            }
            System.out.println("Parsed: "+parsed);
            System.out.println();
        }
    }
}
```

Listing 7.11 contains a main() method that initializes the variable exprs as an array of strings, each of which is an arithmetic expression. Next, a loop iterates through the elements of exprs. During each iteration, the variable tokenizer is instantiated as an instance of the Java StrTokenizer class hasNext() method of the variable tokenizer in order to iterate through the tokens of the current string in the exprs variable. During each iteration, the current token is prepended to the string variable parse and then its contents are displayed. Launch the code in Listing 7.11 and you will see the following output that has removed the extra white spaces from each string in the exprs variable:

```
String:          2789  *  3+7-8-  9
Parsed:  2789 * 3+7-8- 9

String: 4 /2  +  1
Parsed:  4 /2 + 1

String: 2  -  3  +  4
Parsed:  2 - 3 + 4
```

TASK: CLASSIFY TOKENS IN ARITHMETIC EXPRESSIONS

Evaluating arithmetic expressions is an interesting task because there are various ways to approach this problem. First, some people would argue that the "real" way to solve this task involves levers and parsers. However, the purpose of this task is to familiarize you with parsing strings, after which you will be better equipped to do so with nonarithmetic expressions.

Listing 7.12 displays the contents of the file parse_expr.py that illustrates how to parse and evaluate an arithmetic expression using a stack.

LISTING 7.12: ClassifyTokens.java

```java
import java.util.ArrayList;
import org.apache.commons.lang.text.StrTokenizer;

public class ClassifyTokens
{
   //parse a string into tokens and classify them
   public static void tokenize(String my_expr)
   {
      ArrayList tokens_types = new ArrayList();
      String[] math_symbols = new String[] {"*","/","+","-"};
      String all_digits = new String("0123456789");
      String oper = "";
      String int_str1 = "";

      my_expr = parseString(my_expr);
      System.out.println("STRING: "+my_expr);

      int idx=0;
      while(idx<my_expr.length()) {
        // 1) extract integer:
        int_str1 = "";
        char token = my_expr.charAt(idx);
        String tokenStr = String.valueOf(token);

        System.out.println("extract number:");
        while(idx<my_expr.length())
```

```
      {
         System.out.println("tokenStr: "+tokenStr+ " idx: "+idx);
         if(all_digits.contains(tokenStr)) {
            int_str1 += tokenStr;
            idx += 1;
         } else {
           break;
         }

         if( idx == my_expr.length()) {
            System.out.println("Reached end of string");
            break;
         }

         token = my_expr.charAt(idx);
         tokenStr = String.valueOf(token);
      }
      tokens_types.add("token: "+int_str1 + " type: NUMERIC");
      System.out.println("=> int_str1: "+int_str1);
      System.out.println();

      // 2) check for an arithmetic symbol: *, /, +, or -
      if(substr_in_array_strings(math_symbols, tokenStr) == true) {
        oper = tokenStr;
        System.out.println("=> found operator: "+oper);
        System.out.println();
        tokens_types.add("token: "+oper + " type: SYMBOL");
      }
      idx += 1;
   }
   System.out.println("SUMMARY:");
   for(int i=0; i<tokens_types.size(); i++)
   {
       System.out.println("string/type: "+tokens_types.get(i));
   }
   System.out.println("-------------------\n");
}
public static Boolean substr_in_array_strings(String[] my_
array,String str)
{
   for(String elem : my_array) {
     if(elem.contains(str))
        return true;
   }
   return false;
}

public static String parseString(String expr)
{
   String parsed = "";
   //System.out.println("String: "+expr);
   StrTokenizer tokenizer = new StrTokenizer(expr, " ");
   while (tokenizer.hasNext()) {
      String token = tokenizer.nextToken().trim();
      //System.out.println("token: "+token);
      parsed = parsed + token;
```

```
        }
        System.out.println();
        return parsed;
    }

    public static void main(String[] args)
    {
        String[] exprs = new String[]{"        2789  *  3+7-8-  9",
                                "4 /2  +  3",
                                "4 /2  +  1",
                                "9  -  3  +  4      "};

        for(String expr : exprs) {
            tokenize(expr);
        }
    }
}
```

Listing 7.12 starts by defining the variable tokens_types as an instance of the Java ArrayList class, followed by the variable math_symbols that contains a 7.12 also defines the methods tokenize(), substr_in_array_string(), and parseString() that tokenizes a string, checks a string for a substring, and parses a string, respectively.

The code for parseString() is the same as the method in the TokenizeExpr class in the previous section. The substr_in_array_string() method checks if a given string is an element of an array of strings. The parseString() method is also the same as the method in the TokenizeExpr class in the previous section.

The main() method that initializes the variable exprs as an array of strings, each of which is an arithmetic expression. Next, a loop iterates through the elements of exprs. During each iteration, the method tokenize() is invoked with the current element in the exprs array. Launch the code in Listing 7.12 and you will see the following output:

```
STRING: 2789*3+7-8-9
extract number:
tokenStr: 2 idx: 0
tokenStr: 7 idx: 1
tokenStr: 8 idx: 2
tokenStr: 9 idx: 3
tokenStr: * idx: 4
=> int_str1: 2789

=> found operator: *

extract number:
tokenStr: 3 idx: 5
tokenStr: + idx: 6
=> int_str1: 3
=> found operator: +

EXTRACT NUMBER:
TOKENSTR: 7 IDX: 7
TOKENSTR: - IDX: 8
=> INT_STR1: 7
```

```
=> FOUND OPERATOR: -

EXTRACT NUMBER:
TOKENSTR: 8 IDX: 9
TOKENSTR: - IDX: 10
=> INT_STR1: 8

=> FOUND OPERATOR: -

EXTRACT NUMBER:
TOKENSTR: 9 IDX: 11
REACHED END OF STRING
=> INT_STR1: 9

SUMMARY:
STRING/TYPE: TOKEN: 2789 TYPE: NUMERIC
STRING/TYPE: TOKEN: * TYPE: SYMBOL
STRING/TYPE: TOKEN: 3 TYPE: NUMERIC
STRING/TYPE: TOKEN: + TYPE: SYMBOL
STRING/TYPE: TOKEN: 7 TYPE: NUMERIC
STRING/TYPE: TOKEN: - TYPE: SYMBOL
STRING/TYPE: TOKEN: 8 TYPE: NUMERIC
STRING/TYPE: TOKEN: - TYPE: SYMBOL
STRING/TYPE: TOKEN: 9 TYPE: NUMERIC
--------------------


STRING: 4/2+3
EXTRACT NUMBER:
TOKENSTR: 4 IDX: 0
TOKENSTR: / IDX: 1
=> INT_STR1: 4

=> FOUND OPERATOR: /

EXTRACT NUMBER:
TOKENSTR: 2 IDX: 2
TOKENSTR: + IDX: 3
=> INT_STR1: 2

=> FOUND OPERATOR: +

EXTRACT NUMBER:
TOKENSTR: 3 IDX: 4
REACHED END OF STRING
=> INT_STR1: 3

SUMMARY:
STRING/TYPE: TOKEN: 4 TYPE: NUMERIC
STRING/TYPE: TOKEN: / TYPE: SYMBOL
STRING/TYPE: TOKEN: 2 TYPE: NUMERIC
STRING/TYPE: TOKEN: + TYPE: SYMBOL
STRING/TYPE: TOKEN: 3 TYPE: NUMERIC
--------------------
```

```
STRING: 4/2+1
EXTRACT NUMBER:
TOKENSTR: 4 IDX: 0
TOKENSTR: / IDX: 1
=> INT_STR1: 4

=> FOUND OPERATOR: /

EXTRACT NUMBER:
TOKENSTR: 2 IDX: 2
TOKENSTR: + IDX: 3
=> INT_STR1: 2

=> FOUND OPERATOR: +

EXTRACT NUMBER:
TOKENSTR: 1 IDX: 4
REACHED END OF STRING
=> INT_STR1: 1

SUMMARY:
STRING/TYPE: TOKEN: 4 TYPE: NUMERIC
STRING/TYPE: TOKEN: / TYPE: SYMBOL
STRING/TYPE: TOKEN: 2 TYPE: NUMERIC
STRING/TYPE: TOKEN: + TYPE: SYMBOL
STRING/TYPE: TOKEN: 1 TYPE: NUMERIC
-------------------


STRING: 9-3+4
extract number:
tokenStr: 9 idx: 0
tokenStr: - idx: 1
=> int_str1: 9

=> found operator: -

extract number:
tokenStr: 3 idx: 2
tokenStr: + idx: 3
=> int_str1: 3

=> found operator: +

extract number:
tokenStr: 4 idx: 4
Reached end of string
=> int_str1: 4
SUMMARY:
string/type: token: 9 type: NUMERIC
string/type: token: - type: SYMBOL
string/type: token: 3 type: NUMERIC
string/type: token: + type: SYMBOL
string/type: token: 4 type: NUMERIC
--------------------
```

INFIX, PREFIX, AND POSTFIX NOTATIONS

There are three well-known and useful techniques for representing arithmetic expressions: infix notation, prefix notation, and postfix notation.

Infix notation involves specifying operators *between* their operands, which is the typical way that we write arithmetic expressions (example: 3+4*5).

Prefix notation (also called Polish notation) involves specifying operators *before* their operands. For example, the infix expression 3+4 has the sequence + 3 4 as its equivalent prefix expression.

Postfix notation (also called reverse Polish notation) involves specifying operators *after* their operands, examples of which are here:

4*5 becomes 4 5 *
a*b + c*d becomes a b * c d * +
a * b − (c + d) becomes a b * c d + −
3+4*5 becomes 3 4 5 * +

You can use a stack to perform operations on postfix operations that involve pushing numeric (or variable) values onto a stack, and when a binary operator is found in the postfix expression, apply that operator to the top two elements from the stack and replace them with the resulting operation. As an example, let's look at the contents of a stack that calculate the expression 3+4*5 whose postfix expression is 3 4 5 * +:

Step 1: push 3
3
Step 2: push 4
4
3
Step 3: push 5
5
4
3
Step 4: apply * to the two top elements of the stack
20
3
Step 5: apply + to the two top elements of the stack
23

Since we have reached the end of the postfix expression, we see that there is one element in the stack, which is the result of evaluating the postfix expression.

The following table contains additional examples of expressions using infix, prefix, and postfix notation.

Infix	Prefix	Postfix
x+y	+xy	xy+
x-y	-xy	xy-
x/y	/xy	xy/

```
x*y          *xy          xy*
x^y          ^yx          yx^


(x+y)*z      *(x+y)z      (x+y)z*
(x+y)*z      *(+xy)z      (xy+)z*
```

Let's look at the following slightly more complex infix expression (note the "/" that is shown in bold):

```
[[x+(y/z)-d]^2]/(x+y)
```

We will perform an iterative sequence of steps to convert this infix expression to a prefix expression by applying the definition of infix notation to the top-level operator. In this example, the top-level operator is the "/" symbol that is shown in bold. We need to place this "/" symbol in the left-most position, as shown here (and notice the "^" symbol shown in bold):

```
/[[x+y/z-d]^2](x+y)
```

Now we need to place this "^" symbol immediately to the left of the second left square bracket, as shown here (and notice the "/" shown in bold):

```
/[^[x+(y/z)-d]2](+xy)
```

Now we need to place this "/" symbol immediately to the left of the variable y, as shown here (and notice the "+" shown in bold):

```
/[^[x+(/yz)-d]2](+xy)
```

Now we need to place this "+" symbol immediately to the left of the variable x, as shown here (and notice the "/" shown in bold):

```
/[^[+x(/yz)-d]2](+xy)
```

Now we need to place this "/" symbol immediately to the left of the variable x, as shown here, which is now an infix expression:

```
/[^[-(+(/yz))d]2](+xy)
```

Perform non online search for more examples of prefix and postfix expressions as well as code samples that implement those expressions using a Java data structure.

SUMMARY

This chapter started with an introduction to queues, along with real-world examples of queues. Next, you learned about several functions that are associated with a queue, such as isEmpty(), isFull(), push(), and dequeue().

Next you learned about stacks, which are LIFO data structures, along with some Java code samples that shows you how to perform various operations on stacks. Some examples include reversing the contents of a stack and also determining whether or not the contents of a stack form a palindrome.

In the final portion of this chapter, you learned how to determine whether or not a string consists of well-balanced round parentheses, square brackets, and curly braces; how to parse an arithmetic expression; and also how to convert infix notation to postfix notation.

INDEX